T0329270

CAMBRIDGE CLASSICAL STUDIES

General Editors

F. M. CORNFORD, D. S. ROBERTSON, F. E. ADCOCK

ALBINUS AND THE HISTORY OF MIDDLE PLATONISM

*TRANSACTIONS OF
THE CAMBRIDGE PHILOLOGICAL SOCIETY*

VOLUME VII

1937

ALBINUS AND THE HISTORY
OF
MIDDLE PLATONISM

BY

R. E. WITT, Ph.D.

CAMBRIDGE
AT THE UNIVERSITY PRESS
1937

CAMBRIDGE UNIVERSITY PRESS
Cambridge, New York, Melbourne, Madrid, Cape Town,
Singapore, São Paulo, Delhi, Mexico City

Cambridge University Press
The Edinburgh Building, Cambridge CB2 8RU, UK

Published in the United States of America by Cambridge University Press, New York

www.cambridge.org
Information on this title: www.cambridge.org/9781107674073

First published 1937
First paperback edition 2013

A catalogue record for this publication is available from the British Library

ISBN 978-1-107-67407-3 Paperback

CONTENTS

vii

PREFACE

The following work is an abridgment of a Dissertation written during my tenure of a Research Studentship at Trinity College, Cambridge, and approved in 1934 for the degree of Ph.D. Circumstances then compelled me to turn from ancient philosophy to other studies. The manuscript was put away and forgotten until recently, when its publication was discussed and rendered possible by the very generous assistance of the Cambridge Philological Society.

The main purpose of my Dissertation was to study the *Didaskalikos* of Albinus ("Alkinoos"). Those who had contributed most to the subject were Freudenthal (in *Hellenistische Studien*, III) and Praechter (*Überwegs Grundriss*[12], 541 sqq.). Various passages had also been incidentally elucidated by Hobein, Sinko and Strache in their monographs on Maximus Tyrius, Apuleius and Arius Didymus respectively, and by Theiler (*Die Vorbereitung des Neuplatonismus*). But I claimed to be the first to make an exhaustive examination of the *Didaskalikos* itself.

This epitome of Plato's philosophy may be considered under various aspects. Here it will be studied chiefly in connexion with the relevant philosophies of the pre-Christian Era, with the Platonism of the first two centuries of our Era—conveniently termed "Middle Platonism"—of which it is a typical product, and with the Neoplatonism of Plotinus.

Along with the Dissertation were submitted an emended text of the *Didaskalikos*, information about manuscripts and editions, a critical apparatus which was pressingly required in view of Hermann's misleading preface, and a new translation. Unfortunately the addition of these aids is here precluded by considerations of space.

To Mr F. H. Sandbach I owe much. Without his valued help and constant encouragement this work would never have come to publication. I have also been helped in various ways by Prof. G. F. Forsey, Dr F. W. G. Foat, and my pupils at the Royal Liberty School, Romford. There are many allusions to Plotinus. For my first acquaintance with this philosopher I have to thank Prof. E. R. Dodds, now Regius Professor of Greek at Oxford. Lastly, it is fitting that I should record my debt to Prof. F. M. Cornford, the Senior Editor of this Series.

R. E. W.

31 *August* 1936

ABBREVIATIONS COMMONLY USED

Apul.: *Apuleii.... de philosophia libri*, Thomas.

CD.: Augustine, *De Civitate Dei.*

Cic. *ND.*: Cicero, *De Natura Deorum.*

   A. Po.: *Academica Posteriora.*

   Fin.: *De Finibus.*

   Luc.: *Lucullus* (*Academica Priora*).

Did.: *Didaskalikos*, Hermann, *Plato*, VI, 152.

D. L.: Diogenes Laertius.

Gal. *Hist. Phil.*: *Historia Philosophiae* (in *Doxographi Graeci*).

   H.P.: *De Placitis Hippocratis et Platonis.*

Hermet.: *Corpus Hermeticum* (Scott).

M. A.: Marcus Aurelius.

M. T.: Maximus Tyrius (Dübner).

PE.: Eusebius, *Praeparatio Evangelica.*

Ph. Al.: Philo Alexandrinus (Cohn-Wendland).

Plot. (*Enn.*): Plotinus (*Enneads*) Müller.

Plut.: Plutarch, *Moralia.*

   An. Pr.: *De Animae Procreatione in Timaeo Platonis.*

Prol.: Albinus, *Prologos*, Hermann, *Plato*, VI, 147.

Stob.: Stobaeus (Wachsmuth).

ABA.: *Abhandlungen Berliner Akademie.*

Am. Cor.: *Amicitiae Corolla* (ed. H. G. Wood).

Baeumker: *Das Problem der Materie.*

Brochard: *Les Sceptiques grecs.*

C.P.: *Classical Philology.*

CQ.: *Classical Quarterly.*

DDG.: *Doxographi Graeci*, Diels.

Frl.: *Hellenistische Studien*, III (Freudenthal).

Goed.: *Geschichte des griechischen Skeptizismus* (Goedeckemeyer).

Hirzel: *Untersuchungen zu Cicero's philosophischen Schriften.*

Hobein, *Diss.*: *De Maximo Tyrio quaestiones philologicae selectae.*

Hoyer: *De Antiocho Ascalonita.*

JP.: *Journal of Philology.*

i

INTRODUCTION. THE *DIDASKALIKOS* AND ITS DESIGN

Nearly half a century before the production of the *editio princeps* of the original works of Plato in 1513,[1] there was first printed in a Latin translation an old epitome of the Platonic philosophy, concerning which Petrus Balbus, the translator, in his dedicatory epistle to the learned Cardinal Nicholas of Cusa,[2] wrote as follows: "Cum libellos meos nuper evolverem, Alcinoi opusculum repperi, in quo sub compendiaria miraque brevitate opinio atque singula documenta Platonis attinguntur." Balbus was soon followed by Ficinus, who first made a fresh Latin translation and then edited the Greek text. Before this, however, there had appeared in 1521 the Aldine edition.

During the next two centuries the *Didaskalikos*, as the work is properly entitled, was destined to remain in high repute. It went through several editions. In England it attracted the attention of Doctor Fell and was translated by the poet Thomas Stanley. On the Continent it was published in various forms in Italy, France, Holland and Germany. Allusions to it in Cudworth, Leibnitz and Berkeley imply that it retained a place among the recognized textbooks on the philosophy of Plato.[3]

After the eighteenth century, however, interest in the *Didaskalikos* began to decline. In the nineteenth century there was considerable mistrust of the views which had been held of Plato in later antiquity. Plato's ancient interpreters, it was argued, without conducting a scientific investigation, attributed to him views which cannot be discovered in his works. They paid no attention to the inner form

---

[1] Ficinus had already translated Plato—and edited Plotinus.

[2] Cf. Bett, *Nicholas of Cusa*, 93.

[3] Cudworth, *Intell. Syst.* I, I, xi; Leibnitz, *De Arte Combin.* II, 24; Berkeley, *Siris*, 284.

of Plato's writings. They had no appreciation of the influence of the *Zeitgeist*, and lacked *die genetische Auffassung*.

Now it is quite true that the writer of the work which we are about to study does not pursue the historical method which was so frequently applied in the nineteenth century. Nevertheless, it is obvious that a complete account such as he gives of the Platonic philosophy does not deserve to be completely neglected. For one of the functions of the historian is to judge the effects of events. Here we have a complete picture of the Platonic philosophy as it appeared to a writer who (as we shall subsequently see) was separated from Plato by a period of some five hundred years. There may be considerable distortion, the picture may even to some appear false. But, if only because of its antiquity, it ought not simply to be ignored by serious students of Platonic problems.

Accordingly, in the subsequent investigation the *Didaskalikos* will be exhaustively examined. In the first part of the inquiry the philosophical structure of the work will be considered, and its doctrines will be brought into relation with the Schools of the pre-Christian Era. In the second part the question of the writer's identity will be discussed and an attempt will be made to estimate his achievement and importance in the history of Platonism.

As is to be expected in an elementary textbook, the tone throughout is dogmatic. The *Didaskalikos* is intended to be an exposition and not a criticism of the Platonic philosophy: a λόγος ὑφηγητικός, not a λόγος ζητητικός.[1] Plato is always spoken of with respect.[2] We are distinctly informed at the beginning and again at the end that the views recorded are his, but these statements, and also the occasional use of φησι, καλεῖ, and the like, are not meant to be pressed. It is elsewhere quite evident that by no means all the utterances are intended to pass as the *ipsissima verba* of the Master himself.[3] To some critics there will appear to be a good deal of

[1] Cf. *Did.* 58, 16; *Prol.* 48, 25; D. L. III, 49.

[2] Cf. e.g. 59, 37; also Cic. *ND.* II, 32; "ille heros", Apul. 109, 18; "aequiperabilia diis immortalibus disserens", *ibid.* 9, 14; Plot. II, ix, 6.

[3] ἔοικεν εἶναι, 53, 22; οὔτε τοῖς πλείστοις τῶν ἀπὸ Πλάτωνος ἀρέσκει, 63, 22 (like Plut. *An. Pr.* 1012 B). The substantive ἀναζωγράφησις, 55, 14, is used by Chrysippus and Posidonius but not by Plato (yet ἀποζωγραφεῖν, *Tim.* 71 c).

distortion, and it will be easy for an historian of Logic to find fault with the statement that Plato makes use of the syllogistic method and foreshadows the ten categories of Aristotle.[1] But it is only fair to state that other writers on Plato have arrived at similar conclusions, Plutarch and Themistius in antiquity, and Gercke in modern times.[2] Incidentally this is an excellent illustration of a tendency, which we shall be constantly encountering, to expound the Platonic philosophy in terms of later systems.

It is important to notice the admission that superficially Plato appears often inconclusive and that certain passages in his writings do not encourage too dogmatic an interpretation. Plato finds himself compelled to adopt eristic methods[3] and destructive arguments,[4] and to meet his contemporary sceptics, the eristic sophists such as Euthydemus and Hippias, on their own ground. Whether he believed in the immortality of irrational souls is regarded as one of the questions which can receive no certain answer, although the probability is that he rejected it.[5] The reader, nevertheless, who carefully peruses Plato's writings (ἀκριβῶς ἐντυγχάνειν[6]) will discover that they are coherent and for the most part express Plato's own positive doctrines.[7] Thus we see that the writer does not share the belief ascribed to the Middle Academy, that in Plato "Nihil affirmatur, et in utramque partem multa disseruntur, de omnibus quaeritur, nihil certi dicitur".[8]

In contrast with the treatise on Plato written by Apuleius and for the most part presenting in a Latin version the same account that

---

[1] "Unverschämtheit", Prantl, 610.

[2] *An. Pr.* 1023 E–F. Philoponus in *An. Pr.* 6, 14. Gercke in *Arch. G. Phil.* IV, 424–41. What might be criticized in the *Did.* is the failure to perceive that Plato, while carrying out logical operations, had no system of formal logic (cf. *UPG.* 529).

[3] 58, 26.　　　　　　　　　　[4] 59, 23.

[5] τῶν ἀμφισβητουμένων, πιθανόν, 78, 21.

[6] 59, 32. Cf. also 79, 35.

[7] For δόγματα cf. Apul. 86, 3; D. L. III, 51 sqq.; *Prol.* 50, 24.

[8] *A. Po.* 46. Menodotus and Aenesidemus thought otherwise: Plato, in expressing views on the Ideas, Providence, the life of virtue, εἴτε ὡς ὑπάρχουσι τούτοις συγκατατίθεται, δογματίζει, εἴτε ὡς πιθανωτέροις προστίθεται...ἐκπέφευγε τὸν σκεπτικὸν χαρακτῆρα κτα. S. E. *Hyp.* I, 222.

we have in the *Didaskalikos*, the latter is a well-constructed work.[1] The suggestion is made in the concluding chapter that possibly the reader may find the subject-matter not always nicely digested and the treatment of some topics inadequate. But such apologies were customary in this *genre* of literary composition and the form in which they are made seems stereotyped.[2] When we remember that the writer never claims to give more than an *aperçu*, we may justly consider that to reprove him for failing to adhere to every detail of the ambitious scheme set forth in Chapter IV, or for afterwards altering without any given reason the order of discussion and taking mathematics first,[3] is only hypercritical. Nor need the fact of occasional overlapping[4] be adversely criticized, for the author himself recognizes that in a work of this type (where large use is made of earlier doxographical material) some repetition is inevitable.[5]

The extent to which the various Platonic writings are used may be conveniently indicated here. The most important is unquestionably the *Timaeus*, the ultimate basis on which about a third of the work is founded. Next in importance comes the *Republic*. This along with the *Symposium* and the *Seventh Epistle* supplies the main lines of Plato's theology. The *Parmenides* is regarded as a sort of logical exercise-book. In epistemology reference is indeed made to the *Theaetetus*, to which, however, less space is devoted than later to the *Cratylus*. The Theory of Ideas is derived from the *Timaeus*. The reader is introduced to Plato's psychology by means of the *Republic*, the *Phaedo* and the *Phaedrus*, which dialogues together with the *Laws*, the *Symposium* and the *Theaetetus* are turned to account throughout the later chapters. The *Philebus* inspires Chapter XXXII, and the *Critias* has some influence on the concluding portion of Chapter XXXIV. Appended to the account of genuine philosophy and the real philosopher is a brief sketch of the sophist and of his methods, for which the writer is indebted to the Platonic dialogue which surveys the same subject. References are made during the

---

[1] A fact which the garrulous 1748 editor did not overlook.

[2] Cf. Cic. *Fin.* III, 26. 19. Galen, *Hist. Phil.* fr. 2, *DDG*.

[3] 61, 8. See Frl. 301 and *UPG*. 542.

[4] E.g. IX–XII, XXVIII–XXIX, XXIV–XXXII.

[5] 76, 6. The question whether this has any significance for the study of the sources followed may be deferred till later.

4

course of the work to the *Euthydemus* and the *First* and the *Second Alcibiades*.[1]

Despite the breadth of treatment, some important features of Plato are either lightly touched upon or wholly neglected. The categories which Neoplatonism discovered in the *Philebus*[2] and the *Sophist*[3] are conspicuously absent. No appeal is made during the theological discussion to two passages which the Neoplatonists continually invoke, the one in the *Republic*, where the Good is described as ἐπέκεινα τῆς οὐσίας, and the other in the *Second Epistle*, where the enigmatical statement is made, περὶ τὸν πάντων βασιλέα πάντ' ἐστί, καὶ ἐκείνου ἕνεκα πάντα. δεύτερον δὲ περὶ τὰ δεύτερα, καὶ τρίτον περὶ τὰ τρίτα.[4] The theology and the religious persecution which Plato inculcates in *Laws*, x excite no comment. Nor is the philosopher recommended as by Plato in *Republic*, II to adopt an uncompromising attitude towards popular religion. Plato's treatment of rhetoric in the *Gorgias* and the *Phaedrus*, to which Apuleius devotes considerable space, is much less amply reported in the *Didaskalikos*. Apuleius refers to the final chapter of the *Timaeus* in which Plato explains the facts of sexual physiology.[5] This part of Platonic speculation is entirely unmentioned in the *Didaskalikos*. No detailed examination of Plato's eschatological utterances is attempted, nor is the function of myth explained.[6]

Determinism and the problems of freewill and divine providence certainly occupy the writer's attention, but he neither raises the question which Plotinus seeks to solve, " πόθεν τὰ κακά; " nor provides information about the relation between existing evil and the supremely perfect First God. Plato sometimes speaks as though Ananke or Necessity were a power greater even than God, and in

---

[1] See further the list of Loci Platonici *infra*.

[2] For διάκρισις (23 B–D) as the πέμπτον γένος (cf. *ad fin.*), see Plut. 391 B and Robin (*Cinqu. Genre de l'Etre dans Phil.*). The five are then: ἄπειρον, πέρας, μικτόν, αἰτία, διάκρισις. Yet in the *Did.* Matter is ἄμετρος (63, 31), the Idea μέτρον (63, 14), the Sensible World ἄθροισμα (56, 10) and God the First Cause (64, 18).

[3] The μέθεξις of the γένη in *Soph.* enables them to become for Plotinus categories of the Intelligible World.

[4] Important in Christian Platonism. Cf. Witt, *CQ*. xxv, 198.

[5] Apul. 101, 6.

[6] Cf. e.g. Plut. *Ser. Vind. DDG.* 568, 16.

the *Timaeus* conceives it as being ruled by the latter only by means of persuasion.[1] But in the work before us this mysterious Demogorgonic principle is not brought into prominence, and does not disturb the theology of Chapter x.

Another writer might possibly have left himself room for a discussion of Plato's educational projects which are brought forward in the *Republic* and the *Laws*: the fundamental principle, however, that μουσική and γυμναστική are equally indispensable is by no means overlooked.[2] The communistic system under which Plato proposes that the Guardians of the *Republic* should live is passed over in silence. But, as though to answer criticism and to prove that (whatever view Plato may have entertained in the *Republic*) he was at any rate orthodox in the *Laws*, the fact is emphasized that, in the State which is there envisaged, he does *not* advocate that women should be possessed in common.[3] Another notorious point of criticism in the *Republic* has always been that Plato in his Ideal State will not grant a place to the artist and the poet, excluding them on the ground that, by making an image of an image and not looking towards the original archetype, each is but τρίτος ἀπὸ τῆς ἀληθείας.[4] In the *Didaskalikos* nothing is said on the subject either in Chapter xxxiv or elsewhere.

Most of the above omissions are doubtless due to the exigencies of compression,[5] and need have no particular significance. But it can hardly be by accident that Aristotle's categories are read into the *Parmenides* and other dialogues, whereas the *Philebus* and the *Sophist* remain unmentioned in that connexion.[6] Again, the absence of the text on Ananke and Persuasion is probably due to the desire, whether of the writer himself or of the authority whose *Timaeus*

[1] Cf. *Laws* 741 A: "Ananke cannot be constrained even by divinity" (explained in 818 B as referring to mathematics); *Tim.* 48 A (Plot. I, viii, 7; Ananke belongs to Nous, persuasion to Soul, v, iii, 6).

[2] Cf. *Did.* 61; 82, 5 sqq.; Apul. 103, 2 sqq. (*Tim.* 88).

[3] Epictetus blames the Roman ladies: μετὰ χεῖρας ἔχουσι τὴν Πλάτωνος Πολιτείαν, ὅτι κοινὰς ἀξιοῖ εἶναι τὰς γυναῖκας. τοῖς γὰρ ῥήμασι προσέχουσι τὸν νοῦν, οὐ τῇ διανοίᾳ τἀνδρός κτα., fr. 15.

[4] Plot. v, viii, 1 corrects Plato. Cf. also v, ix, 5 τῆς τέχνης αὐτῆς... τὸν ἀληθῆ ἀνδριάντα καὶ κλίνην ἐχούσης M. T. 10, 7.

[5] The *Did.* about equals the *Euthydemus* in length.

[6] *Did.* 69, 23, is based on *Tim.* 35 sqq.

commentary he may have used, to avoid endangering in this way the doctrine of God's omnipotence. Significant, also, in view of Neoplatonic teaching, is the silence of the writer about the statement that the Good transcends Reality, no less than his neglect of the theological passage from the *Second Epistle*. But, at present, the attitude which the writer whom we are studying adopts towards Plato, as compared or contrasted with that exhibited by Plotinus, need not be further examined.

ii

LYCEUM AND STOA. GENERAL INFLUENCE

Reference has already been made to a fact which no reader of the *Didaskalikos* would be likely to overlook, that many Stoic and Aristotelean doctrines and phrases are attributed to Plato. Indeed, one is reminded of the judgment which Porphyry formed of the *Enneads*: ἐμμέμικται καὶ τὰ Στωικὰ λανθάνοντα δόγματα καὶ τὰ Περιπατητικά.[1] Our writer loses no opportunity of displaying the affinities, and for the most part minimizes or disregards the differences, between the Platonic philosophy and the two later systems.

The more obvious of borrowed ideas and idioms may be at once noticed here. The constant recurrence of θεωρεῖν, of its derivatives, and of θεωρία, is not without significance. It need hardly be said that Plato himself in a famous sentence described philosophy as θεωρία παντὸς μὲν χρόνου πάσης δὲ οὐσίας. But in the *Didaskalikos* it is often clear from the context that the use of these words is inspired not so much by Plato as by Aristotle. Thus the contrast between θεωρία and πρᾶξις is drawn in the Aristotelean manner,[2] and the βίος θεωρητικός is placed before the βίος πρακτικός. Aristotle had divided theoretical philosophy into theology or metaphysics, physics and mathematics.[3] This tripartite scheme is adopted in the *Didaskalikos*.[4]

The definition of the syllogism is taken directly or indirectly from the *Prior Analytics*.[5] The technical terms of Aristotelean logic are readily introduced, as when reference is made to propositions which do not admit of any intermediate term between the subject and the predicate (ἄμεσοι προτάσεις)[6], or to contraries between

[1] *Vit. Plot.* 14.

[2] But the influence of several Platonic passages written in a similar sense is not to be overlooked, e.g. *Tht.* 172 c–176 c; *Polit.* 258; *Gorg.* 500; *Rep.* 540 B.   [3] *Met.* 26 a 19.   [4] 53, 36; 60, 37.

[5] 24 b 18; *Did.* 58, 17 (cf. also Apul. 184, 13–15).

[6] 57, 12. Alex. *in Met.* 130, 15 writes: τὰ ἀξιώματα, φυσικαί τινες οὖσαι ἔννοιαι καὶ προτάσεις ἄμεσοι.

8

which nothing intermediate exists (ἄμεσα ἐναντία).[1] The purpose of the *Euthydemus* is described as being the discovery of the possible kinds of fallacies, of which the two main classes (as by Aristotle) are referred to as fallacies *in dictione* and those *extra dictionem*.[2] The verb ἐπαχθῆναι is used in the sense it sometimes bears in Aristotle, that of making an induction.[3] The laws of contradiction and excluded middle are given prominence as by Aristotle and the Porch,[4] while the discussion of the meaning of possibility is dependent ultimately on the classical treatment of this problem in the *Metaphysics* and *De Interpretatione*.[5] Plato, besides being represented as the discoverer of the ten categories, is made to argue like any Peripatetic or Stoic logician. In his writings (especially it would appear in the *Parmenides* and the *First Alcibiades*[6]) are to be found examples of syllogistic reasoning in each of the three figures recognized by Aristotle.

The influence of Aristotelean physics is apparent when the view is advanced that every body must be a compound of matter and form.[7] In the eleventh chapter Aristotle's aid is sought against the Stoic theory that qualities are corporeal. In particular his conception of place, as that which contains nothing else but the one body occupying it, is emphasized against the Stoic theory of κρᾶσις δι' ὅλου, on which more than one body may occupy the same place at the same time.[8] On the other hand, the belief that up and down are not merely relative to the observer, which Aristotle and Epicurus had both upheld, is rejected as conflicting with what Plato says in the *Timaeus* 62 B.[9]

One-sided causality, which is common to the theology of the *Didaskalikos* and the metaphysics of the *Enneads*, is a principle

[1] 77, 30. Cf. *Phaedo* 71 C, 104 B; Arist. *Cat.* 12 a; *DDG.* 568, 27; M. T. 15, 2; Plot. I, viii, 6 E, VI, iii, 20.

[2] 59, 33. Cf. e.g. *Euth.* 277 B (*An. Post.* 74 b 23), 298 E (*Soph. El.* 179 a 34), 300 (*Soph. El.* 166 a 12).

[3] 64, 7; 78, 2.

[4] *Did.* 77, 1 (cf. Plato, *Ph.* 103; *Rep.* 436; Arist. *Cat.* 14 a 11; *Met.* 18 a 25; *SVF.* II, 956–62).

[5] *Did.* 79, 17; *Met.* 19 b 28–30, etc.; *Int.* 18 b 1 sqq.

[6] Some Platonists found ten in it (*Plato*, Herm. VI, 213).

[7] 66, 3. [8] 66, 24.

[9] 75, 12.

derived from Aristotle.[1] The doctrine that God is purely actual Being who causes motion by being an object of desire is faithfully reproduced, and the First God of the *Didaskalikos*, in imitation of the Aristotelean Prime Mover, is supracelestial and has eternal intellection of Himself: ταὐτὸν νοῦς καὶ νοητόν.[2] This intellection is viewed as His appropriate ἐνέργεια—an Aristotelean term which like θεωρία is elsewhere turned to account.[3]

During the discussion in the last part of the *Didaskalikos* of the subject of Ethics, Aristotle's influence is generally perceptible. His definition of virtue—which, however, is similar to one of the "Platonic" *Definitions*[4]—is introduced as though it were Plato's at the opening of Chapter XXIX, while, as Aristotle and the Old Academy alike taught, virtue in the next chapter is regarded as a mean. A protest is raised against the severe ethical dualism of the Porch and the tripartite division of mankind is adopted in agreement with Aristotle.[5] The distinction which he drew between theoretical and practical virtue appears.[6] The ideal human relation in Chapter XXXIII is declared to be φιλία, into which significantly ἔρως must finally be transformed: τέλος δὲ αὐτοῖς τὸ ἀντὶ ἐραστοῦ καὶ ἐρωμένου γενέσθαι φίλους. Platonic passages could be found in support of such a view,[7] but the eighth book of the *Nikomachean Ethics* exercises considerable influence, both here and throughout the chapter. Probably we ought also to treat as due to ultimate dependence on the *Ethics* the statement that among the requirements needed by the philosopher are ἐλευθερία, παιδεία ὀρθή and διδασκαλία.[8]

Following the example of Xenocrates and the Peripatetics, Stoicism commonly divided philosophy into the three main departments of

---

[1] But the statement in *Parmenides* 139 A that "the One is unmoved" is an interesting anticipation.

[2] *Met.* 72 b 20 sqq. The importance of this for Plotinus is of course very great (cf. V, V).

[3] Cf. ζωὴν ἀεὶ ἐνεργοῦσαν, 78, 18 with *EN.* 98 a 13, and note also ἐνέργεια τοῦ νοῦ νοοῦντος τὰ νοητά, 53, 2.

[4] *Deff.* 411 C–E; Arist. *Pol.* 1323 b 13; *EE.* 1218 b 37.

[5] 83, 29; 56, 35; *EN.* 98 b 12.

[6] 89, 3; *EN.* 40 a 1.

[7] E.g. *Phdr.* 252 E sqq.

[8] 52, 15 and 20 (*EN.* 04 b 13); 77, 13 (*EN.* 03 a 14).

speculation, ethics and logic.[1] This scheme is adopted by our writer,[2] who uses the term διαλεκτική in the sense given it by Stoic philosophers to denote the third branch, which, notwithstanding, subsequently appears first in the order of discussion. The order in which the three branches were treated is said to have varied among the Stoics, but Zeno himself, like our writer, took logic first and ethics last.[3] The phrase ἡ τοῦ λόγου θεωρία, which is synonymous with διαλεκτική, is suggestive of Stoicism rather than of Aristotle.[4]

To this department belongs epistemology, which is elaborately explored in the Stoic manner. But there is one difference, the importance of which will become evident in the sequel, namely that whereas orthodox Stoicism made what it called καταληπτικὴ φαντασία the criterion of truth, the *Didaskalikos*, avoiding a naïve sensationalism which Scepticism had easily attacked and ridiculed,[5] attempts a more adequate explanation. Two criteria are found to be necessary in the act of judging, an agent and an instrument. We may grant with Stoicism that an important part is played by natural discursive reason, which is in fact the instrument operating in conjunction with sensation, and the function of which is to express opinions.[6] But, in order that knowledge may be possible, there is need of the agency of the intuitive intellect (ὁ ἐν ἡμῖν νοῦς),[7] a principle which Stoic philosophy did not recognize, since it denied the existence of transcendental ideas.[8]

Throughout the chapter the attempt to conflate Stoic and Platonic elements can be observed. Thus the φυσικὴ ἔννοια of the Porch is transferred to Plato's theory of innate ideas. But no mention is made of the fundamental dissimilarity between the view that knowledge is acquired by recollection of prenatal ideas, and the Stoic doctrine that the mind at birth is only a *tabula rasa* and derives all its knowledge subsequently from sensation. The φυσικαὶ ἔννοιαι

---

[1] *SVF.* III, 687 (Xen. fr. 1).   [2] 53, 21.   [3] *SVF.* I, 46.

[4] See below (Aristotle has θεωρητικὴ διάνοια, *EN.* 39 a 28).

[5] Cf. e.g. S. E. *AM.* VII, 401 sqq.

[6] See 56, 7–9, 12–13. Here δοξαστικὸς λ. is presumably the same as the φυσικὸν ὄργανον, φυσικὸς λόγος, of 54, 13, 15. But in 55, 30, ἐπιστημονικὸς λ. seems also φυσικὸς λ.

[7] 54, 12. Boethus makes νοῦς one of his criteria (fr. 1). But in Stoicism νοῦς and αἴσθησις are two aspects of the same faculty (*SVF.* II, 849).   [8] *SVF.* I, 65.

are described as the standards to which we refer, when we are testing the data with which sense-perception has supplied us.[1] Stoicism upheld the existence of κοιναὶ ἔννοιαι of what is morally good and bad,[2] and Chrysippus invoked the aid of such ideas in physics.[3]

Our author uses the technical terms of Stoic logic when he is dealing with hypothetical syllogism.[4] When he enters into the questions of divine providence and human freewill, he shows himself like Plotinus opposed to the absolute determinism of the Porch, whose influence, nevertheless, both he and Plotinus by no means completely escape.[5] In the department of Ethics Stoicism supplies him with the definition of φρόνησις as "the knowledge of good and evil and of the morally indifferent".[6] The doctrine that the perfect virtues are inseparable is likewise due primarily to Stoic influence, although the fact of its earlier occurrence in the writings of Plato and Aristotle should not be overlooked.[7] To Stoicism the obvious corollary of this proposition had seemed to be that the bad man must have all the vices. But their concomitance is rejected in the *Didaskalikos*, on the ground that two vices may be in mutual opposition—not to mention the sheer impossibility that a single person should be subjected to all the vices at once. Another important criticism brought against the Stoic treatment of virtue and vice is that there can be no abrupt transition from either of these states to its opposite. The belief in sudden conversion, the achievement of moral perfection *per saltum*, must accordingly be declared mistaken: οὐ γὰρ ῥᾴδιον εὐθέως ἀπὸ κακίας ἐπ' ἀρετὴν μεταβῆναι.[8] For these reasons the "natural abilities" (εὐφυΐαι) are not to be classed as by Stoicism simply among "things preferred" (προηγμένα) and excluded, as being indifferent, from the class of things which are good.[9] They are in fact entitled to the name of virtues.[10]

[1] 56, 19.   [2] *SVF.* III, 218.

[3] *SVF.* 473, "πειρᾶται πιστοῦσθαι διὰ τῶν κοινῶν ἐννοιῶν". So Plotinus remarks that κοινή τις ἔννοιά φησι God's ubiquity not to be incompatible with His oneness and identity (VI, v, 1).

[4] 59, 22, etc.   [5] *Did.* XXVI; *Enn.* III, i, ii, iii, IV, iv, 45, etc.

[6] 82, 23; *SVF.* III, 265, 266.

[7] See *EN.* 44 b 10, with Burnet's note *ad loc.*; *SVF.* III, 295.

[8] 83, 30.

[9] "οὐδὲν τῶν ἀγαθῶν εἶναι προηγμένον", *SVF.* I, 192. But εὐφυΐα is a προηγμένον, *ibid.* III, 127.   [10] 83, 15; 52, 20.

Among the early Stoics Zeno had held that πάθη are the outcome of wrong judgments, while Chrysippus, going further, had declared them actually to *be* judgments. Posidonius, although a member of the School founded by Zeno, was too much a Platonist to follow Zeno on this point, and he openly attacked Chrysippus for identifying πάθη with operations of the rational faculty.[1] In the treatment of πάθη (Chapter XXXII) the writer of the *Didaskalikos* controverts the view of Chrysippus and, as will be subsequently shown, is there writing from the standpoint of Posidonius, as is Plotinus in a passage of similar import.[2]

[1] *SVF.* III, 259, 460, 469.
[2] *Enn.* I, i, 9 (cf. Witt in *CQ.* XXIV, 205).

iij

TRACES OF XENOCRATES

Of the scholarchs who first occupied the chair of Plato, Xenocrates appears to have been the least inclined through specialization to lose sight of the wide range of the Platonic philosophy. He was the first systematizer[1] and by his clear interpretation of certain Platonic passages, which as they stand admit of more than one possible meaning, he begins a dogmatism which is of much consequence. Among Platonizers and Platonists who were in varying ways affected by him are to be counted Posidonius, Antiochus, Plutarch, and the writer of the work before us.[2]

Attention has already been directed to the variable meaning of the term φρόνησις in the *Didaskalikos*.[3] A fragment of Xenocrates (6) affords the best explanation of this twofold use. "Theoretical wisdom (σοφία) is the knowledge of first causes and of intelligible reality,[4] according to Xenocrates in his περὶ φρονήσεως, who holds that understanding is twofold, the one kind being practical and the other speculative. For this cause theoretical wisdom is understanding, whereas not all understanding is theoretical wisdom (ἡ μὲν σοφία φρόνησις, οὐ μὴν πᾶσα φρόνησις σοφία)."[5] Sextus Empiricus ascribes to Xenocrates a theory of knowledge, which seems to play a part in Chapter IV of the *Didaskalikos*.[6] Xenocrates, we are told, adopted a triple scheme, in which knowledge or scientific reason

---

[1] Heinze, p. 2, sees in Xenocrates "Eine Hinneigung zu streng systematischer Gliederung".

[2] Xenocrates's influence here seems to have been little discussed hitherto.

[3] 53, 6; 82, 24.

[4] Cf. *Did.* 53, 37 (where an Aristotelean parallel has been noted) and 81, 1.

[5] φρόνησις and σοφία in Plato, as says Burnet on *EN.* 40 a 24 sqq., are not distinguished as by Aristotle who, unlike Xenocrates, confines φ. to the practical sphere.

[6] *AM.* VII, 147–8.

(ἐπιστήμη, ἐπιστημονικὸς λόγος) apprehends supracelestial or intelligible reality, opinion (δόξα), the heaven itself, and sense-perception (αἴσθησις), the world of sensible reality enclosed within the vault of heaven. While opinion may be either true or false, knowledge and sense-perception are each true, knowledge, however, differing from sense-perception in respect of its certainty: τὸ μὲν διὰ τοῦ ἐπιστημονικοῦ λόγου κριτήριον βέβαιόν τε ὑπάρχειν καὶ ἀληθές, τὸ δὲ διὰ τῆς αἰσθήσεως ἀληθὲς μέν, οὐχ οὕτω δὲ ὡς τὸ διὰ τοῦ ἐπιστημονικοῦ λόγου, τὸ δὲ σύνθετον κοινὸν ἀληθοῦς τε καὶ ψευδοῦς ὑπάρχειν· τῆς γὰρ δόξης τὴν μέν τινα ἀληθῆ εἶναι, τὴν δὲ ψευδῆ. The *Didaskalikos* describes the λόγος which is peculiar to the human mind as being of two kinds: ὁ μὲν περὶ τὰ νοητὰ ἐπιστήμη τέ ἐστι καὶ ἐπιστημονικὸς λόγος, ὁ δὲ περὶ τὰ αἰσθητὰ δοξαστικός τε καὶ δόξα. ὅθεν ὁ μὲν ἐπιστημονικὸς τὸ βέβαιον ἔχει καὶ μόνιμον, ἅτε περὶ τῶν βεβαίων καὶ μονίμων ὑπάρχων, ὁ δὲ πιθανὸς καὶ δοξαστικὸς πολὺ τὸ εἰκὸς διὰ τὸ μὴ περὶ τὰ μόνιμα εἶναι. Without overlooking the possibility that the account of Xenocrates's epistemology given by Sextus may not be altogether reliable,[1] we need have no hesitation in regarding the term ὁ ἐπιστημονικὸς λόγος as a genuine product of the Old Academy[2] (its use is earlier in the same passage attributed by Sextus to Speusippus also), and deciding that, when it is associated in the *Didaskalikos* with τὸ βέβαιον, it is derived (though not of course necessarily at first hand) from Xenocrates.

When the subject of rhetoric is under discussion, the view that the orator studies the art of persuasion, and the definition of this department of philosophy as ἐπιστήμη τοῦ εὖ λέγειν, need be due simply to following Plato himself.[3] The same definition, however, is given by Xenocrates, who is doubtless responsible for its popularization and from whom it is borrowed by the Stoics.[4]

---

[1] So *UPG.* 344: "Es fragt sich, ob Sextos, unsere einzige Quelle, in seiner Wiedergabe im einzelnen zuverlässig ist." Theiler (*VN.* 55 n.) speaks of "the so-called fragments of Speusippus and Xenocrates", but I fail to see how their *Unechtheit* can be proved.

[2] It may be noted that Aristotle (*EN.* 39 a 6 sqq.) refers to τὸ λόγον ἔχον as divisible into τὸ ἐπιστημονικόν and τὸ λογιστικόν (cf. also *An.* 481 b 27; Plut. 443 E).

[3] *Phdr.* 259 E, 268 E, etc.   [4] *SVF.* II, 294; Xen. frs. 13, 14.

15

Another definition which we meet is that of the Idea as παράδειγμα τῶν κατὰ φύσιν αἰώνιον.[1] Our writer does not mention his authority for this statement, but there can be no doubt that it is ultimately inspired by Xenocrates.[2] The Platonic passage, which most nearly approaches the definition which we actually have, is *Timaeus* 28 A. Xenocrates, relying on this (and indeed he might have sought justification elsewhere), propounded the formula reproduced in the *Didaskalikos*. Heinze rightly accepts Proclus's interpretation of the Xenocratean definition, according to which παράδειγμα signifies not the efficient cause but the formal, and adds that, on that view, the Ideas fulfil exactly the same rôle which Plato assigns to them in the *Timaeus*, where the creation of sensible things by God is the result of His looking towards the Eternal Archetypes.[3] Heinze might well have mentioned the fact that in the *Didaskalikos* not only is the Xenocratean definition used, but in the same chapter the distinction is also drawn between the creative and the formal cause. The Universe, we learn, must have been produced not only ἔκ τινος and ὑπό τινος but also πρός τι. The three causes are respectively Matter, the Demiurge, and the Idea.[4] Nor is the use of πρός τι without interest. For this is the name of one of the two categories which alone Xenocrates recognized.[5]

The theological scheme which we meet in the *Didaskalikos* seems to be influenced by that of Xenocrates, who had been more explicit than Plato is in his writings on the position occupied by God, by the subordinate deities, and by the demons. We learn that he personified the Monad as Zeus, whom he also called νοῦς and viewed as πρῶτος θεός.[6] The last two names appear in the *Didaskalikos*.[7] Xenocrates, furthermore, regarded the First God as dwelling transcendent in the sphere of fixed stars, while the Dyad or World Soul

[1] 63, 21.   [2] fr. 30.
[3] Heinze, 50.   [4] 63, 35 sqq.
[5] fr. 12. The contrast appears in Plato, *Phil.* 51 C. The categories of the Platonists will be discussed below.
[6] Plato has nothing to say about a πρῶτος θεός dwelling in the sphere of fixed stars (though made to say "τὸν ἀνωτάτω θεὸν ἐν τῇ πυρώδει οὐσίᾳ εἶναι" in ps.-Justin, *Cohort.* 5, 31 E).
[7] The πρ. θ. in *Did.* 81, 36 is ὑπερουράνιος (yet also fr. 5 of "Xenocrates" contains reference to ἡ ἐκτὸς οὐρανοῦ καὶ νοητὴ οὐσία: and Apuleius makes God "caelestis" and "ultramundanus").

occupied all the infracelestial region and was "mother" of the Olympian deities. These were the five planets, Saturn, Jupiter, Mars, Mercury, Venus, and finally the Sun and the Moon. The region between the Moon and the Earth was inhabited by invisible demons and each of the elements was haunted by divine powers.[1] In Chapters xiv and xv of the *Didaskalikos* a closely similar system is apparent. We observe the World Soul (although not termed the Dyad), the seven divine planets enclosed within the outermost sphere of fixed stars, and the demons dwelling—some visible, others invisible—within each of the elements.

Xenocrates had assumed that the corporeal elements may be constructed from triangular planes (which is of course Plato's view in the *Timaeus*), and that the ultimate element from which the plane itself is derived is the indivisible minimal line[2] (a view which, if we may credit Aristotle, Plato himself sometimes professed[3]). In the *Didaskalikos* we may trace the same doctrine.[4]

The metaphorical meaning of the "generation" both of the visible Universe[5] and of the Ideas[6] is carefully emphasized by Xenocrates. From his day this continued to be the generally accepted interpretation among Platonists. Unlike Plotinus,[7] our writer does not repeat what seems to have been the Xenocratean catchword, διδασκαλίας χάριν.[8] But he insists none the less that there never was a time when either the Cosmos or the Ideas were nonexistent.[9]

In the department of Ethics Xenocrates had prepared the way for the Stoics by declaring that well-being is dependent on the possession of οἰκεία ἀρετή[10] and that, briefly put, the End is φύσις or τὸ κατὰ φύσιν.[11] The Xenocratean conception of virtue as a functioning in accordance with nature (ἐνεργοῦσα οἰκείως)[12] is followed in the *Didaskalikos*, where οἰκεῖος and kindred words are of comparatively

---

[1] fr. 15.   [2] frs. 41 sqq.
[3] *Met.* 992 a 20 sqq. See also Robin, *TPIN.* 229.
[4] 65, 32.   [5] fr. 54.   [6] fr. 33.
[7] δεῖ...τὴν ἐμψύχωσιν διδασκαλίας καὶ τοῦ σαφοῦς χάριν γίνεσθαι νομίζειν (IV, iii, 9). Cf. also δηλώσεως χάριν in III, vii, 6 E.
[8] frs. 33, 54.   [9] 69, 28.
[10] fr. 77.   [11] fr. 78.
[12] *Ibid.*

frequent occurrence.[1] But the influence of Stoicism and Antiochus of Ascalon has to be reckoned with here. We have already observed that our writer agrees with Aristotle on the doctrine that Virtue is a mean. This conception of Virtue is already present in Plato[2] and is adopted by the Lyceum and the Old Academy alike.[3] Crantor, a pupil of Xenocrates, developed the view of metriopathy in his treatise περὶ πένθους, a work which enjoyed great success among students of Plato in later times.[4] The recognition in the *Didaskalikos* of the fact that the affections are good, provided there be neither deficiency nor excess, and that they are naturally indispensable and proper to mankind,[5] is probably due again to the influence of the Platonism which Xenocrates formulated in the Old Academy.[6]

A definition which, while hardly original,[7] is associated especially with the name of Xenocrates is the etymological one: εὐδαίμονα εἶναι τὸν τὴν ψυχὴν ἔχοντα σπουδαίαν· ταύτην γὰρ ἑκάστου εἶναι δαίμονα.[8] From him it passed into Stoicism, and Posidonius could extend the notion by giving as the reason for ὁ κακοδαίμων βίος the failure to follow one's demon: τὸ μὴ κατὰ πᾶν ἕπεσθαι τῷ ἐν αὐτῷ δαίμονι.[9] In the *Didaskalikos* two similar definitions appear: τὴν μὲν κακοδαιμονίαν τοῦ δαίμονος εἶναι κάκωσιν, τὴν δὲ εὐδαιμονίαν τοῦ δαίμονος εὐεξίαν.[10] This passage Strache connects with Arius Didymus, because the latter declares Plato (in agreement with Democritus) to have described τὸ εὔδαιμον in the words (*Timaeus* 90 A) ὡς ἄρ᾿ αὐτὸ δαίμονα ἡμῖν δέδωκεν ὁ θεός.[11] The possibility that our writer is using Arius in this instance is not to be denied. But there is no need on that account to deny here the same kind of

---

[1] Cf. 72, 15; 83, 1; 84, 6; 86, 16, 19; 53, 8; 56, 16; 60, 11; 61, 26. Note also *SVF.* III, 178, 181, etc., the Cyrenaic theory τὸ ᾠκειῶσθαι πρὸς ἡδονήν (D. L. II, 88), and see the discussion below of the Antiochean oikeiosis-doctrine.

[2] *Rep.* 603 E; *Polit.* 283–4; *Laws* 728 E, 792 D.

[3] Cic. *Luc.* 135.   [4] Cic. *ibid.*   [5] p. 86.

[6] Metriopathy is approved by Plutarch 443 (see *UPG.* 539).

[7] See Heraclitus and Xen. Stob. V, 925 W; Burnet, Introduct. to *EN.* I (Plato, *Rep.* 540 C plays on "δαίμοσιν" and "εὐδαίμοσι").

[8] fr. 81.

[9] See *SVF.* III, 460. M. A. 7, 17 has εὐδαιμονία ἐστὶ δαίμων ἀγαθός.

[10] 82 (the "well-being" is of the sort mentioned in M. A. 2, 17).

[11] Strache, *Diss.* 91; Stob. II, 52, 1 sqq.

indirect debt to Xenocrates that we have seen elsewhere. Arius used Posidonius or Antiochus. And Posidonius or Antiochus followed Xenocrates.

The effort made by Xenocrates to establish a coherent system has already been mentioned. This led him sometimes to adopt a Procrustean treatment, and the same may be said of our epitomator. Xenocrates delighted in schematization and especially trichotomy.[1] Our writer shows similar tendencies. Xenocrates tersely called the mathematical sciences λαβαὶ φιλοσοφίας.[2] In the *Didaskalikos* they are described as προτέλεια καὶ προκαθάρσια τοῦ ἐν ἡμῖν δαίμονος[3] and receive treatment before the two other branches of theoretical philosophy, theology and physics.[4]

But although there is much in the Platonism of the writer with whom we are concerned which is reminiscent of Xenocrates, to connect them too closely would be a mistake. Certain doctrines which Xenocrates took over from the Pythagoreans are significantly absent. The First Principle was termed both by Speusippus and by Xenocrates τὸ ἕν, a name which was to reappear in the Platonism of Eudorus and Plotinus,[5] and Speusippus, who is said to have distinguished it, as did Plotinus, from νοῦς,[6] may have anticipated him also in placing it beyond Reality.[7] In the *Didaskalikos*, on the other hand, the highest principle is simply a superior Nous and a refined Essence (οὐσιότης).[8] Its oneness is certainly mentioned, but τὸ ἕν never replaces νοῦς as a technical term.[9]

While Speusippus would allow that only μαθηματικά are transcendent, Xenocrates identified μαθηματικά with the Ideas. Plato, as revealed to us in his own writings and in those of Aristotle, distinguished the two classes of objects and so, apparently, does our

[1] See Diels, *SBA.* 1882, 479.
[2] D. L. IV, 10 (referring to music, geometry and astronomy. The *Did.* adds arithmetic and distinguishes στερεομετρία from γεωμετρία).
[3] 82, 7.
[4] Chapter VII. Plato, Speusippus and Xenocrates agree (cf. also *Epin.* 991 E).
[5] Cf. E. R. Dodds in *CQ.* XXII, 136, 139.
[6] *DDG.* 303 b 3.
[7] Arist. *Met.* Z, 2 (cf. Dodds, *loc. cit.*).   [8] 64, 24, 30.
[9] "Nirgends als Subjectsbegriff Gottes angesehen", Frl. 294.

writer also.[1] Again, Xenocrates defined soul as a self-moving number, an expression which Plutarch truly says is un-Platonic.[2] His definition of time is different from that which is given in the *Timaeus* and followed in the *Didaskalikos*.[3] His view of matter, moreover, seems to be of no importance for our writer.[4]

[1] For the "Secondary Intelligibles" of 55, 35 presumably include μαθ. (after *Rep.* 510–11).

[2] *An. Pr.* 1013 C. Cf. also D. L. III, 67. Plot. V, i, 5 makes Nous, *per se* indeterminate Dyad, determinate number by the agency of the One, adding: ἀριθμὸς δὲ ὡς οὐσία· ἀριθμὸς δὲ καὶ ἡ ψυχή.

[3] fr. 40; *Tim.* 37 D.

[4] Perhaps (as Baeumker thinks, p. 205) Xenocrates regarded matter as evil.

iv

ANTIOCHUS. HIS DOGMATISM AND ITS CONSEQUENCES

The history of Platonism in the Academy is inextricably linked up with the study of the Sceptical philosophy first formulated by Pyrrho and the dogmatic system established in the Porch by Zeno. The rivalry between Arcesilaus and Zeno was notorious in antiquity, and for more than a century the members of the Academy continued to assail the epistemological bulwark of the Porch,[1] using the weapons which Pyrrhonism had put in their hands. The most brilliant opponent whom the Stoics had to face was unquestionably Carneades. He repudiated with no less emphasis than Arcesilaus the Stoic καταληπτικὴ φαντασία as the criterion of truth, but admitted that some things are more evident to us than others: πάντα μὲν εἶναι ἀκατάληπτα, οὐ πάντα δὲ ἄδηλα.[2] Carneades's pupil, Clitomachus, was succeeded by Philo of Larissa, who is said by Numenius[3] to have begun by enlarging the body of doctrine bequeathed to him by Clitomachus and to have pressed forward the attack against the Porch. But later, mainly (we may presume) because of his strong ethical interests, and possibly because of a stoicizing tendency in his psychology,[4] Philo came round to the view that things are in their own nature comprehensible, although he strenuously denied that they can be grasped, as Stoicism had affirmed, by means of a presentation which guarantees its own truth.[5] Clearly by this admission Philo became the most dogmatic teacher in the Academy since the days of Polemo and Crates.[6]

[1] Cf. *SVF.* II, 38.   [2] *PE.* 736 D.   [3] *Ibid.* 739 B.

[4] Schmekel (389) interprets the Numenian phrase ἡ τῶν παθημάτων ἐνάργεια (Euseb. *PE.* 739 B) in a strictly psychological sense: "die Augenscheinlichkeit der Vorstellungen". But παθήματα may mean facts of experience generally.

[5] S. E. *Hyp.* I, 235.

[6] Schmekel (387) argues that he did not himself believe that he had changed his ground.

21

The chief pupil and successor of Philo was Antiochus of Ascalon. Cicero, who had studied under both philosophers and been deeply impressed by Philo's earlier Scepticism,[1] writes of Antiochus: "Haec ipsa, quae a me defenduntur, et didicit apud Philonem tam diu, ut constaret, diutius didicisse neminem, et scripsit de his rebus acutissime, et idem haec non acrius accusavit in senectute, quam antea defensitaverat."[2] More than a single cause may be supposed for this rupture. It is possible that in the judgment of his pupil Philo had surrendered by half-opening the doors of the Academy to dogmatism,[3] and left him no other course than that of deserting. Moreover, Antiochus may have been ambitious and contentious.[4] It is known that Antiochus had studied not only under Philo but also under Mnesarchus the successor of the great Middle Stoic Panaetius, and Mnesarchus may have exercised a decisive influence and have led him to adopt an eclecticism of the type that Panaetius had evolved.[5] Schmekel suggests that it was precisely the final revolt of Antiochus from Academic Scepticism to dogmatism which induced Philo to abandon the standpoint of Clitomachus and to admit the truth of the objections raised by the dogmatists, among whom his pupil had now ranged himself.[6] But the complete lack of evidence for this opinion does not encourage us to adopt it in place of the more obvious view advanced by Hirzel, that Philo began the stoicizing movement which Antiochus completed.[7]

Both Philo and Antiochus paid close attention to the history of their School. Philo claimed that there had been one and only one Academy of which he was the living head.[8] Possibly he may have held the theory, which we meet in the *Lucullus*[9] and in the *Contra*

[1] Cf. *Div.* II, 150; *Brut.* 306.   [2] *Luc.* 69.
[3] See August. *C. Acad.* III, 40 sqq.
[4] Plut. *Cic.* 4. Cf. *Luc.* 69–70.
[5] See Schmekel, 391. Zeller accepts this suggestion of Schmekel, only refusing to grant that Antiochus attached himself to Panaetius. Zeller's modification is justified.
[6] Schmekel, 387.   [7] Hirzel, III, 227, 236–7.
[8] *A. Po.* 13.
[9] 60: "Quae sunt tandem ista mysteria? aut cur celatis, quasi turpe aliquid, sententiam vestram?" Both Reid, *ad loc.* and Brochard, 115 sqq. seek to explain away what seems a clear allusion to esoteric dogmatism. Cf. also S. E. *Hyp.* I, 234 (perhaps meaning Philo).

Academicos of Saint Augustine,[1] of an unbroken tradition, preserved beneath the mask of Scepticism in the form of an esoteric dogmatism.[2] Certainly he likened θεωρήματα to παραγγέλματα, and regarded them as the means whereby the soul's health is secured after false opinions have been purged away—a figure which he would most naturally have borrowed from Plato's *Sophist*.[3] Philo, in fact, by striving to rehabilitate Platonism and to defend its unity, was led back to the study of the Old Academy[4] and of Plato himself.[5] Yet at the same time he seems not to have remained entirely unaffected by Stoic and Peripatetic doctrines and methods.[6]

Philo's contention that the philosophy taught in the Academy had never altered was flatly denied by his pupil. Antiochus argued that there were two distinct Academies, the Old which maintained Platonic dogmatism and the New which abandoned it. But he boldly went further. Pursuing in another direction the historical method which Philo had shown him, Antiochus came to the conclusion that the Old Academy and the Lyceum were fundamentally a single School.[7] His treatment of the Porch was no less drastic. Zeno, he held, was not the producer of an original system but merely reformed the Platonism which he had taken over from the Old Academy.[8]

This eclectic method of interpreting his predecessors brought Antiochus into popularity. He was the philosopher whom Lucullus chose as companion on his campaigns in Asia Minor. The learned Varro greatly esteemed his syncretism.[9] Cicero, with a rhetorician's

---

[1] III, 41: "Metrodorus (presumably not M. Scepsius but M. Stratonicaeus: *Luc.* 16; *De O.* I, 45; D. L. x, 9) primus dicitur esse confessus, non decreto placuisse Academicos nihil posse comprehendi, sed necessario contra Stoicos huiusmodi eos arma sumpsisse."

[2] He could have thus excused his own apparent inconsistency.

[3] Stob. II, 41; *Soph.* 230 c.

[4] Brochard (p. 195) suggests that he adapted not the New to the Old, but the Old to the New.   [5] Aug. *loc. cit.*

[6] I find no evidence to justify Kroll's statement (*Rh. M.* 1903, 576): "Philon konnte und wollte sich nicht, wie Antiochos, als einer Fortsetzer peripatetischer Schulübung hinstellen."

[7] *A. Po.* 17.   [8] *Ibid.* 34.

[9] Cf. Cic. *Ep. Att.* XIII, xii, 3. He seems aware of its difficulties also. Cf. *A. Po.* 7.

love of hyperbole but not without sincerity, eulogized him as "nobilissimus et prudentissimus"[1] and as "politissimus et acutissimus omnium nostrae memoriae philosophorum".[2] On the philosophy of the next two centuries Antiochus exercised a decisive influence. After his day we hear almost nothing further of the Sceptical Academy.[3] Henceforward Plato was not simply read within the precincts of the Academy, but was studied elsewhere besides, in close relation to, and often from the standpoint of, the other dogmatic Schools. It is of course true that the Middle Stoics had begun the eclectic treatment of Plato. But it remained for Antiochus as a professing Academic to assert, not only that the Academy and the Lyceum had been fundamentally the same School, but also that Plato rather than Zeno was the real progenitor of Stoicism.

To many ancient as probably to most modern observers Antiochus, despite the fact that he became head of the Academy and professed to restore to it its rightful heritage, is too much of a Stoic to merit the name of Platonist. Numenius, referring to the views which Antiochus adopted from his Stoic teacher Mnesarchus, says: μυρία ξένα προσῆψε τῇ 'Ακαδημίᾳ,[4] and Cicero (though respecting Antiochus as one of his old instructors in philosophy) is forced to declare of him: "Appellabatur Academicus; erat quidem, si perpauca mutavisset, germanissimus Stoicus."[5] Whether Antiochus himself, however, felt any difficulty in his position is exceedingly doubtful. Plato to him was the type of dogmatist, just as Socrates was the type of Sceptic.[6] He was combating the heresy which he saw had invaded Plato's School in the time of Arcesilaus. The victories which Scepticism had won in the past were due largely to the disunity

[1] *Brut.* 315.   [2] *Luc.* 113.

[3] Aenesidemus, Tubero and Favorinus were three Sceptical Academics.

[4] Euseb. *PE.* 739 D.

[5] *Luc.* 132. Cf. also S. E. *Hyp.* I, 235 (perhaps representing the standpoint of Aenesidemus).

[6] "Ita disputat, ut nihil affirmet ipse, refellat alios", etc., *A. Po.* 16 (note also § 18). Plato learned Pythagorean dogma "eaque quae Socrates repudiabat", *Fin.* V, 87 (cf. Field, 223). Yet in the *Lucullus* Socrates is ranked with Plato (§ 15, cf. § 74). Cicero himself has no doubt of Socrates's scepticism: *A. Po.* 44; *Div.* II, 150; *ND.* I, 11 (note also Tubero, *Rep.* I, 16).

prevailing among the forces of dogmatism. Thus he introduced Stoic dogma into the Academy, precisely in order to support his conception of Plato as the positive thinker.[1] And if, furthermore, Philo of Larissa vacillated between the only two positions which Antiochus would recognize, that held by Arcesilaus and that held before Arcesilaus,[2] then, in order to contrast his own attitude with that of his former teacher, Antiochus could hardly fail to exaggerate the unity of the dogmatic philosophy which he claimed to represent.

It was at Alexandria that Antiochus wrote the work entitled *Sosus*, in which he finally broke with Philo.[3] After what seems to have been a comparatively short sojourn in that city, he returned to Athens as Philo's successor, but left behind him in Alexandria a group of adherents by whom the tradition was carried on.[4] Consequently, although after the death of Antiochus the Athenian Academy fell into decay,[5] the dogmatism which he had taught continued to live on in the Egyptian capital, which especially because of its Museum was a congenial home for the study of Plato according to the methods prescribed by the Academy's greatest eclectic.

One of the earliest representatives of the eclectic Academy at Alexandria was Eudorus.[6] Besides following the method popularized by Antiochus of conflating Platonic with Aristotelean[7] and Stoic doctrines, Eudorus, following the example of Xenocrates and Posidonius, showed an inclination to Pythagorean speculations.[8] Somewhat later, in the time of Augustus, there appears to have existed at Alexandria an eclectic sect (ἐκλεκτική τις αἵρεσις)[9] founded by a certain Potamo, whose epistemology, as we shall see,

[1] Cf. Strache, *Ant.* 6. Cf. also de Faye in *Hibbert Journal*, 1924.
[2] Goed. 123 thinks Philo was not in any sense a dogmatist.
[3] *Luc.* 11. Brochard (p. 202) suggests that his anger ("stomachari coepit") was aroused by Philo's reconciliation of Plato and Carneades.
[4] Susemihl, II, 295.
[5] Cf. Cic. *ND.* I, 11: "Nunc propemodum orbam (sc. rationem Academiae) esse in ipsa Graecia intelligo"; Sen. *NQ.* VII, 32, 2: "Academici et veteres et minores nullum antistitem reliquerunt."
[6] Simplicius (*Cat.* 187, 10), like Arius Didymus (Stob. II, 42, 7), calls him an Academic. The Platonists Theomnestus, scholarch about 44 B.C., and Ammonius, teacher of Plutarch, were from Egypt.
[7] But he criticized Aristotle's logic. Cf. Simpl. *Cat.* 174, 14, etc.
[8] Cf. Dodds, *CQ.* XXII, 139.   [9] D. L. *Proem.* 21.

has some resemblance to that which we meet in Chapter IV of the *Didaskalikos*. Potamo's eclecticism was evidently modelled on that of Antiochus. That he was at the same time not disposed to neglect Plato's own writings may be inferred from the fact that he wrote a commentary on the *Republic*.[1]

But a more important eclectic philosopher of Alexandria is Arius Didymus, the greatly respected friend of the Emperor Augustus.[2] Arius was taken to Rome by the Emperor, who made him his court philosopher. On the death of Drusus, Livia found the philosopher's comfort of great avail.[3] Unfortunately only a small proportion of his output has survived[4] and from this it is hardly possible to judge his value as an independent thinker. But in an age which is hardly characterized by outstandingly original contributions to thought,[5] Arius could not have failed to be accounted a leading philosopher, and his reputation was in fact not swiftly forgotten.[6]

Though Arius was not a member of the Academy,[7] he highly appreciated the most recent developments in Academic philosophy. He praised the work of Eudorus.[8] He regarded Philo as an ingenious thinker and placed him among those responsible for considerable advances in philosophy. But more important for the present investigation is the fact that Arius, as a doxographer, was strongly influenced by the eclecticism of Antiochus. In the fragments (collected by Diels) of that part of his Ἐπιτομή which dealt with physics, this influence is less obvious than in the long chapter of Stobaeus

[1] The early Empire was the great age of Platonic commentary, contributed to by Eudorus, Plutarch, Tauros, Harpocration, and (among the Peripatetics) Adrastus and (probably) Ptolemy of Alexandria.

[2] Plut. 814 (*DDG.* 80).

[3] Sen. *Ad Marc.* 4.

[4] G. Haenel (*Cat. Manuscrt.* 476) gave under Toulouse, 173: "Arii philosophi tr. de coelo et mundo." Inquiry confirmed my suspicion that the philosopher is not Arius Didymus but Aristotle.

[5] I am here, of course, excluding religious teaching from consideration.

[6] Besides Seneca, M. A. viii, 31 mentions him (side by side with Maecenas), and he was used by Eusebius and by Priscian (*Solut.* 553, 38).

[7] The Didymus mentioned by Suidas is not Arius (*DDG.* 86). I find nothing to justify Goedeckemeyer's statement (p. 205) that he remained "auf dem Boden der damaligen akademischen Skepsis".

[8] Stob. II, 42, 7.

(II, vii, in Wachsmuth's edition) excerpted from the same Ἐπιτομή and dealing with ethics.

Arius reports the physical views of Aristotle and of a number of Stoics: Zeno, Cleanthes, Chrysippus, Panaetius, Mnesarchus, Apollodorus and Posidonius.[1] Only one of the physical fragments concerns Plato, but to the student of the *Didaskalikos* this is the most interesting of all, for it appears to be the original passage of which the opening of Chapter XII is an abridgement. Yet in neither case can we suppose dependence on Antiochus, for (as we shall subsequently see) Antiochus does not believe that the Ideas exist transcendentally, whereas Arius, both in the original and in the abridged passage, while regarding them from the logical point of view as Universals, at the same time gives them the ontological sense of suprasensible Exemplars, and elsewhere explicitly teaches that the Platonic Idea is θεῖον καὶ χωριστόν.[2]

In the remains preserved by Stobaeus of that part of the Ἐπιτομή which was devoted to Ethics, it is often possible to detect the influence of Antiochean syncretism. In the account of "The Ethics of Aristotle and the other Peripatetics,"[3] so strong are the resemblances to parts of *De Finibus* v, that Madvig could seriously regard it as the work of Antiochus himself—an ascription, however, which is hardly likely to supplant Meineke's judgment that the whole chapter was written by Arius Didymus. The debt to Antiochus throughout this chapter has been emphasized by Strache, whose enthusiasm, however, has sometimes led him too far.[4]

We may allow that Arius "in seiner Gesamtanschauung wie im einzelnen stark von Antiochos beeinflusst ist",[5] yet we must not overlook the important fact that he quotes Plato, Aristotle, and individual Stoic writers, sometimes giving the exact reference,[6] and probably, therefore, using them at first hand. Moreover, though Antiochus is named in none of the extant fragments, Posidonius and Panaetius are referred to more than once, and Mnesarchus, the

---

[1] *DDG*. 77.   [2] Stob. II, 55, 15.   [3] *Ibid*. 116, 19–152, 25.

[4] Diels, editing his posthumous *Ant.*, wrote, "wenn auch die jugendliche Vorliebe für das Einquellenprinzip ihn etwas zu weit (sc. in *Diss.*) getrieben hat".

[5] Pohlenz, Strache's critic, in *Ph. Wo.* 1911, 1497.

[6] Cf. Stob. II, 49, 54, 10 (for Aristotle 52, 10).

successor of Panaetius and teacher of Antiochus, is mentioned once. Again, the admiration which Arius felt for Philo is not to be forgotten. From Philo he may have learnt to stress the unity of Plato's thought: Πλάτων πολύφωνος, ούχ ὡς τινες οἴονται πολύδοξος,[1] and even the solidarity of the Academy.[2]

With a greater respect for history than was shown by Antiochus, Arius admits that differences exist between the Academy and the other Schools. He is, indeed, not always a trustworthy doxographer, but neither is he a thoroughgoing eclectic like Antiochus. His independent importance in the History of Platonism will become clear, when we investigate the *Didaskalikos* in relation to Antiochus.

[1] Stob. II, 55, 5. Cf. 49, 25.

[2] Insisted on in *Tht. Komm.*: from passages like *Th.* 150 C some οἴονται 'Ακαδημαϊκὸν Πλάτωνα ὡς οὐδὲν δογματίзοντα ("in Theaeteto adimit sibi scire", Tert. *An.* 17). δείξει μὲν οὖν ὁ λόγος καὶ τοὺς ἄλλους 'Ακαδημαϊκοὺς ὑπεξηρημένων πάνυ ὀλίγων καὶ δογματίзοντας καὶ μίαν οὖσαν 'Ακαδήμειαν κτα. Cf. further *Prol.* Herm. VI, ch. x, p. 205.

V

THE SOURCES AVAILABLE FOR THE STUDY OF ANTIOCHUS

In three of his philosophical works—*Posterior Academics, Lucullus,* and *De Finibus* v—Cicero writes explicitly from the standpoint of Antiochus. These are our three most trustworthy sources.[1] But it is impossible not to admit the existence of others, especially in Cicero. Cicero had little ambition to be an original thinker.[2] The four philosophers to whom he was chiefly indebted were Panaetius, Posidonius, Philo and Antiochus. Yet, despite the strenuous *Quellenforschung* which has been pursued during the past six decades, the extent to which they were followed individually is still a matter of debate. ἄλλος εἰς ἄλλα πη βλέψας ἕτερα δοξάσει.

The works of Cicero where dependence on Antiochus is by general consent admitted are as follows: (1) *De Legibus* (in part). Schmekel argued for Panaetius as the source.[3] But there are certain passages which are more characteristically Antiochean.[4] Hoyer and Theiler[5] regard Antiochus with favour, whereas Isaak Heinemann rejects him.[6] Possibly both Antiochus and Panaetius were turned to account by Cicero in this work. (2) *De Finibus* II and IV, and (in part) I and III. The attack in II against Epicurus is developed from the standpoint of Antiochus, while IV is derived either from him directly or from the Peripatetic Staseas, whom he influenced.[7] (3) *Tusculans* III and IV. Pohlenz supposes that Cicero in III follows to some extent the view which, after the publication of the περὶ

---

[1] One proviso is necessary. Varro's account in *A. Po.* 15–42 is *doxographical*, albeit the standpoint is Antiochean. Antiochus obviously (from *Luc.* 12–64) did not himself believe "sensus omnes hebetes", etc. of § 31.

[2] *Fin.* I, 6; *Off.* I, 6 do not alter the case.

[3] 55 sqq.   [4] E.g. I, 38. 55.

[5] 44 sqq.   [6] II, 52, etc.

[7] So Heinemann, I, 46: to be used for Antiochus with the same caution as περὶ κόσμου for Posidonius.

παθῶν of Posidonius,[1] Antiochus was prompted to adopt from Chrysippus, that the affections must be eradicated. Pohlenz supposes that in IV the ultimate basis is the θεραπευτικός of Chrysippus, Antiochus, however, being a mediating influence.[2] Book V is divided between Antiochus and Posidonius. Usener would draw no hard and fast distinction, since, according to his view, Antiochus himself, though the immediate source of a portion, was indebted to Posidonius. (4) *De Fato*. I. Heinemann, Strache and Lörcher agree in seeing here the influence of Antiochus.[3] (5) *Topica*. Wallies's view has been generally accepted that §§ 6–78 must be derived from Antiochus. Kroll would go further and add the last part of the treatise.[4] (6) *De Oratore*. Against von Arnim's attempt to connect this work with Philo of Larissa,[5] Kroll argues in favour of Antiochus, with particular reference to III, 54–143.[6] (7) *Partitiones Oratoriae*. Many correspondences can be found between this and *De Oratore*. Antiochean influence in the one cannot be assumed without assuming it in the other also.[7]

The difficulty of regarding Antiochus as the only possible source in these cases is not to be minimized. The attempt to derive from him (1) to the exclusion of Panaetius, or (3) to the exclusion of Chrysippus and Posidonius, or even (5), (6), (7) to the exclusion of Philo, is not likely to succeed. The principle of *Entweder Oder* in all these cases is unsound, for exactly how much Antiochus *differed* from his Stoic predecessors or even from the later Philo, we simply cannot say. For this reason, Finger's endeavours[8] to pick out exclusively Antiochean passages in *De Natura Deorum* II and III, and in *De Legibus* I, are unsuccessful.

[1] *Hermes*, 1906, 338.

[2] *Ibid.* 351. Philippson (*Hermes*, 1932, 293) differs.

[3] But Schmekel (pp. 155–84) urges Clitomachus (as *rapporteur* of Carneades), and his view is favoured in *UPG*. 473.

[4] *Rh. M.* 1903, 591. I. Heinemann, I, 46, conjectures that Cicero depended not immediately on Antiochus but on Staseas.

[5] *Dio v. Pr.* 97.

[6] *Rh. M.* 1903, 576.

[7] Sternkopf's Dissertation (named in *UPG*. 149*) I have not seen (Jensen, *ABA*. 1918, 47, n. 2, does not accept his findings). Cf. also Kroll, *NJ*. 1903, 684 sqq.

[8] *Rh. M.* 1931, 151–200, 310–20; 1932, 156–77, 243–62.

Besides Cicero, Sextus Empiricus has been held to be indebted to Antiochus. Hirzel believes that a large part of the seventh book, *Adversus Mathematicos*,[1] is derived from an Antiochean source, probably τὰ κανονικά.[2] Whether Antiochus is followed to the extent claimed by Hirzel is doubtful. It appears evident, nevertheless, that Sextus in many places is writing with Antiochus's book open before him. And, if so, then parallel passages elsewhere in Sextus must also be included as Antiochean. From the fragments of Varro preserved in the *De Civitate Dei* we may also glean information of Antiochus. But here again, as when dealing with Cicero, we need to exercise caution. For Varro followed not only Antiochus but also Panaetius[3] and Posidonius.[4]

When we have added the long chapter of Stobaeus which, as already mentioned, is excerpted from the *Epitome* of Arius Didymus, the list of works which it is usual to regard as being in some degree or other inspired by Antiochus is completed. But there remains to discuss another writing whose fundamentally Antiochean character seems to have been hitherto quite unsuspected,[5] namely the eighth of the *Miscellanies* of Clement of Alexandria.

In a useful monograph von Arnim has pointed out that, although the Stoic theory of causes is adopted and resemblances to Chrysippean doctrine appear, "nec tamen ex ipso Chrysippo Clemens hausisse putandus est, quia praeter Cleanthem etiam Archedemus laudatur. Recentiore igitur fonte usus est."[6] In tracing the source more exactly, we may first observe the following points. The logics of Aristotle and Stoicism are commingled in truly eclectic fashion. For this we cannot hold Clement himself responsible. The only philosophies which he is striving to blend are the Greek and what he calls the Barbarian, that is to say, the Christian religion. The Aristotelean and the Stoic view are not always harmonized successfully. Stählin rightly speaks of "eine unklare Verbindung der aristo-

---

[1] Sextus Empiricus does not (as Hirzel suggests) delay his attack till § 262.

[2] Cf. VII, 201.

[3] *DDG.* 295; *CD.* 6, 5.

[4] Cf. Schmekel, 104 sqq.

[5] Cf. Gabrielsson, *Über d. Quellen d. Clemens Alexandr.* I, 218.

[6] *De Oct. Clem. Strom. Libro* 16.

31

telischen und der stoischen Lehre vom αἴτιον". Moreover, the refutation of Scepticism is significant.[1]

Considering the book in detail, we remark in Chapter 1 the exegesis in a truly Antiochean sense of the Scriptural text: "Seek, and ye shall find; knock, and it shall be opened unto you; ask, and it shall be given you."[2] We cannot find, unless we have sought, we cannot seek, unless we examine, we cannot examine, unless we practise interrogation, we cannot go through the whole investigation, without gaining knowledge as a result. It is the province of the seeker to discover. The *Lucullus* supplies us with an excellently parallel passage.[3] Clement further says that the inquirer must keep not only to Holy Scripture but also to Common Notions (κοιναὶ ἔννοιαι), whence he may advance by means of scientific demonstration to knowledge: δι' ἀποδείξεως ἐπιστημονικῆς ἀφιλαύτως καὶ φιλαλήθως εἰς γνῶσιν προσιόντα καταληπτικήν.[4] Both in Chapter 1 and later, Clement's use of ἀπόδειξις suggests dependence on Antiochus rather than directly on Aristotle.[5]

In the next chapter Clement stresses the importance of clear definition as a preliminary to demonstration. The terms used in demonstration cannot be sounds signifying nothing, λέξεις ἀσήμαντοι like "βλίτυρι".[6] They must convey a meaning, and the commonly accepted meaning is of fundamental importance to the inquiry in which they are employed: οὐκ ἂν ἐφ' ἑτέραν ἀρχὴν ὁμολογουμένην μᾶλλον ἀναγάγοι τὸν λόγον ἢ τὸ πᾶσι τοῖς ὁμοεθνέσι τε καὶ ὁμοφώνοις ἐκ τῆς προσηγορίας ὁμολογούμενον σημαίνεσθαι. Similar passages can be found in the Ciceronian treatises which we have already connected with Antiochus.[7]

---

[1] Chapter v. At the beginning of the first chapter we are told that it is only the more recent Greek philosophers who have indulged in vain logomachies—seemingly a hit at the philosophers of the Middle Academy. Cf. τὰς ἀγοραίους εὑρησιλογίας (2, 5) with *RP.* 442 *fin.*: περὶ δὲ τὰς... εὑρεσιλογίας κενοδοξοῦντες κατατρίβουσι τοὺς βίους.   [2] 2, 1.

[3] *Luc.* 26; Clem. VIII, 2, 2.   [4] 2, 5. Cf. *Luc.* 26 and 30.

[5] Thus for Aristotle ἀπόδειξις is συλλογισμὸς ἐπιστημονικός (*An. Post.* 71 b 9 sqq. Cf. Ross, 43), whereas in Clem. VIII, 14, 1 sqq. it is used in as wide a sense as συλλογισμός in Aristotle, being defined as λόγος ἐξ ἑτέρων ἕτερόν τι πιστούμενος.

[6] Cf. *SVF.* II, 149; S. E. *AM.* VIII, 133; Porph. *Cat.* 102, 8.

[7] *Fin.* II, 3. Similar are *Off.* I, 7 and *Part. Or.* 126.

The rejection of the Stoic definition of "sun"[1] in favour of that in the *Theaetetus*[2] cannot be attributed certainly to Antiochean influence. But in a section of the Scholia to Dionysius's *Grammatike*, where traces of that influence seem to be distinguishable,[3] a similar view is expressed.[4] The definition of ἀπόδειξις, with which the next chapter opens, is in the manner of Stoicism[5] rather than Aristotle,[6] and of Antiochus also.[7]

The form in which Clement expresses the distinction between apodictic and syllogism[8] is not directly derived from Aristotle. For Aristotle does not use περαίνειν in the sense of ἀποδεικνύειν.[9] The method of expressing the contrast, which Aristotle had drawn between διαλεκτικὸς συλλογισμὸς ὁ ἐξ ἐνδόξων συλλογιζόμενος and ἀποδεικτικὸς συλλογισμός, seems quite Antiochean.[10]

Clement further declares: ἐπὶ τὴν ἀναπόδεικτον πίστιν ἡ πᾶσα ἀπόδειξις ἀνάγεται.[11] Now Aristotle had pointed out that the premises of demonstration must be immediate or indemonstrable.[12] But Clement's predilection for πίστις is not directly due to Aristotle.[13]

[1] *SVF.* I, 501, II, 650 sqq.   [2] 208 D.

[3] E.g. 659, 16 sqq.; 660, 34 (*A. Po.* 33); 663, 16; 668, 17 (cf. Ar. Did. *DDG.* 447). It is naturally an influence exercised indirectly.

[4] Partly given in *SVF.* II, 656.   [5] *Ibid.* II, 266–8.

[6] Yet *Rhet.* 1358 a 1 (πίστεις ἀποδεικτικαί) and 1414 a 35 should not be overlooked.

[7] *Luc.* 26, 27. Perhaps *Div.* II, 103 may be inspired by Antiochus: "conclusio rationis ea probanda est, in qua ex rebus non dubiis id quod dubitatur efficitur."   [8] 6, 2.   [9] Cf. Waitz on *An. Pr.* xxiii.

[10] *Fin.* V, 9 (cf. "ad probandum et ad concludendum", *A. Po.* 32). Cf. *Inv.* I, 74: "argumentatio nomine uno res duas significat, ideo quod et inventum aliquam in rem probabile aut necessarium argumentatio vocatur" (note in § 72: "Si peperit virgo non est: peperit autem" as "perspicuum". So Clement: to be with child is demonstrative proof of being a virgin no longer).

[11] 7, 2. Aristotle uses ἀναπόδεικτος with ἐπιστήμη, ὁρισμοί, ἀρχαί, πρότασις, but not with πίστις.   [12] *Top.* 100 a 30.

[13] In *Strom.* II, 15, 5 Aristotle "says" that π. is ἑπόμενον τῇ ἐπιστήμῃ κρῖμα. But Aristotle, *An.* 428 a 20, writes δόξῃ ἕπεται πίστις. Aristotle's ὑπόληψις σφόδρα (*Top.* 126 b 18) may be compared with: ps.-Plat. *Deff.* 413 C; "firma opinio", Cic. *Part. Or.* 9 (probably Ant.); κατάληψις ἰσχυρά, βεβαιοῦσα τὸ ὑπολαμβανόμενον (*SVF.* III, 548 = Ar. Did. Cf. Witt, *Am. Cor.* 331). For π. in Plato cf. *Rep.* 534 A, 601 E; *Gorg.* 455; *Laws* 966 CD (and Inge, *Faith*, 3).

In the first place, both here and elsewhere he writes with the Christian or Evangelical meaning in mind. Secondly, he is influenced by the Antiochean doctrine, that πίστις is the attitude of mind which is produced by the καταληπτικὴ φαντασία possessing ἐνάργεια. Antiochus deduced this doctrine from Zeno: "Visis non omnibus adiungebat *fidem* (sc. Zeno), sed iis solum quae propriam quamdam haberent declarationem (i.e. ἐνάργειαν) earum rerum, quae viderentur."[1] He himself certainly gave it prominence and contrasted it with the doctrine of Epicurus.[2] Clement later states: εἶεν δ' ἂν καὶ ἄλλαι τῶν ἀποδείξεων ἀρχαὶ μετὰ τὴν ἐκ πίστεως πηγήν, τὰ πρὸς αἴσθησίν τε καὶ νόησιν ἐναργῶς φαινόμενα.[3] τὰ μὲν γὰρ πρὸς αἴσθησιν συμβάντα ἐστὶν ἁπλᾶ τε καὶ ἄλυτα, τὰ δὲ πρὸς νόησιν ἁπλᾶ τε καὶ λογικὰ καὶ πρῶτα, τὰ δὲ ἐξ αὐτῶν γεννώμενα σύνθετα μέν, οὐδὲν δ' ἧττον ἐναργῆ καὶ πιστὰ καὶ λογικώτερα τῶν πρώτων. This may be connected with another passage which is based on Antiochus: ἐκ δὲ αἰσθήσεως καὶ τοῦ νοῦ ἡ τῆς ἐπιστήμης συνίσταται οὐσία,[4] κοινὸν δὲ νοῦ τε καὶ αἰσθήσεως τὸ ἐναργές.[5] This view we shall have occasion to study again later.

Clement proceeds to say that the man who practises demonstration must make perfectly sure that the premises which he assumes have themselves been proved true. Such verification Antiochus had favoured.[6] Another hint of Antiochean influence is given, when Clement remarks that the logical nomenclature used is not of funda-

[1] *A. Po.* 41. That ἐνάργεια was originally Epicurean rather than Stoic has been shown by F. H. Sandbach (*CQ*. xxiv, 50). Epicurus likewise used πίστις βέβαιος (D. L. x, 85).

[2] *Luc.* 19. Cf. S. E. *AM.* vii, 257; Aristocles ap. Euseb. *PE.* 762 c.

[3] Cf. Ph. Al. *Op. M.* 84; *Cong. Er.* 178; *Vit. Mos.* ii, 12 (and i, 280 with *SVF.* ii, 266); *Jos.* 149; *Flac.* 35; Plut. 756 b; Aspas. 74, 21; Galen, *HP.* 734. Plotinus has τὰ ἐπὶ τῆς αἰσθήσεως, ἃ δὴ δοκεῖ πίστιν ἔχειν ἐναργεστάτην ἀπιστεῖται...(v, v, 1); ὁ θεὸς οὐχ ὁρώμενος ἀπιστεῖσθαι ποιεῖ ὡς οὐκ ὢν τοῖς ἐναργὲς νομίζουσι μόνον ὃ τῇ σαρκὶ μόνον ἴδοιεν (v, v, 11). But (despite other slighting of πίστις, e.g. ii, 211, 2; 296, 11; 454, 11) Plotinus can write ὅσῳ ἐναργεστέρα ἡ πίστις, ἡσυχικωτέρα καὶ ἡ θεωρία (iii, viii, 6), and use πιστεύειν mystically (ii, ix, 17, 1, iv, 15, v, iii, 17, v, viii, 11). Cf. Arnou, *Désir de Dieu* 22. Further: Schlatter, *Glaube in NT.*; Reitzenstein, *HM.* 234; Theiler, *VN.* 140.

[4] Cf. S. E. *AM.* vii, 218 (Antiochean, Hirzel, iii, 508–9).

[5] *Strom.* ii, 13 (§ 13, 5 suggests *Luc.* 17).

[6] *Luc.* 44.

34

mental importance: τῶν δὲ ὀνομάτων ἀφροντιστεῖν, whether we adopt προτάσεις (with the Peripatetics) or ἀξιώματα or λήμματα (with the Stoics).[1]

To exemplify the need of beginning an inquiry with clear definition, without which the mind is often confused and disturbed,[2] Clement raises the question whether the foetus is an animal. What is meant by "animal"? Plato includes plants as animals. Aristotle will allow only that they possess vegetative life. Stoicism will not grant that the power of vegetation is life.[3] It is only when the question is put in the form, Does the substance which is in the foetal state possess the power of movement and of sensation? that the equivocation which arises through the use of ζῷον can be removed. Moreover, before the question can be argued and brought to a conclusion, ἔμβρυον must also be defined. For this term belongs to the class of πολυώνυμα, another example being κύων. There are land dogs and sea dogs, the constellation of the Dog, Diogenes the Cynic, and all the other dogs. Now though Aristotle, in discussing the kinds of homonymy and amphiboly, instanced ἀετὸς καὶ κύων,[4] yet Clement's classification is derived from a source where what Aristotle had only implied was carefully worked out. To the same source must be due a similar statement in a passage of the Scholia to the *Grammatike* of Dionysius Thrax,[5] a passage which we are about to connect with Antiochus.

Chapter v (=*SVF.* ii, 121) has already been shown to contain a refutation of Pyrrhonian Scepticism. The standpoint is that of Antiochus.[6] Although it is possible that in the present chapter Aristocles is a mediating influence,[7] yet Antiochean doctrine under-

---

[1] Cf. *supra*, p. 8, n. 6; *SVF.* ii, 237; Apul. π. ἑρμην. 176, 16.
[2] Cf. Cic. *Fin.* ii, 4.
[3] Cf. *SVF.* ii, 708 sqq. (and also 804 sqq.).
[4] Soph. *El.* 166 a 16.   [5] 679, 25 sqq. Cf. also S. E. *AM.* xi, 29.
[6] *Luc.* 29. Cf. 109. Cf. also the Epicurean attack in Lucr. iv, 469 sqq.
[7] Aristocles was a stoicizing and platonizing Peripatetic, who is dated to the latter half of the second century A.D. We shall have to consider his importance later. Cf. with Clement's καὶ μὴν καὶ ἀποφαίνεται ὅτι ἐπέχει the words of Aristocles (Euseb. *PE.* 759 c sqq.): λέγοντες ὡς περὶ οὐδενὸς ἀποφαίνεσθαι δέοι, κἄπειτα ἀποφαινόμενοι· καὶ ἀξιοῦσι μὲν μηδενὶ συγκατατίθεσθαι, πείθεσθαι δ' αὐτοῖς κελεύουσιν· εἶτα λέγοντες μηδὲν εἰδέναι πάντας ἐλέγχουσιν ὡς εὖ εἰδότες.

lies the discussion and, in particular, the statement τὸ μὲν δόγμα ἐστὶ κατάληψίς τις λογική · κατάληψις δὲ ἕξις καὶ συγκατάθεσις τῆς διανοίας seems appropriate to Antiochus himself.[1] And when Clement adds that not only sceptics but every dogmatist also ἔν τισιν ἐπέχειν εἴωθεν, ἤτοι παρὰ γνώμης ἀσθένειαν ἢ παρὰ πραγμάτων ἀσάφειαν ἢ παρὰ τὴν τῶν λόγων ἰσοσθένειαν,[2] the view is typically Antiochean.[3]

In Chapter VI Aristotle exercises great influence, yet he is not directly Clement's source. For intimately interwoven with Aristotelean doctrine is a theory of Division, in which neither Aristotle[4] nor the Old Lyceum[5] had shown interest. The theory of διαίρεσις, to which Plato had devoted attention especially in the *Sophist*, the *Politikos* and the *Philebus*,[6] was upheld by Speusippus,[7] and the Old Academy generally,[8] nor was it neglected by the Middle Academy.[9] A division which Carneades used was adopted by Antiochus.[10] Stobaeus preserves Philo's διαίρεσις τοῦ κατὰ φιλοσοφίαν λόγου, as reported by Arius Didymus.[11] Antiochus, however, was probably the first Academic to link with the traditional διαίρεσις the Aristotelean theory of Definition by the aid of Demonstration. And on this side his eclecticism is of permanent importance both for Platonism and for Peripateticism.[12]

[1] *Luc.* 27 (not given in *SVF.*).

[2] ἰσοσθένεια is common to Sceptic and Epicurean (D. L. IX, 74. 101, X, 32).   [3] *Luc.* 53.

[4] Cf. ἔστι γὰρ ἡ διαίρεσις οἷον ἀσθενὴς συλλογισμός, *An. Pr.* 46 a 33 (*RP.* 310 B); *An. Post.* II, 13; Ross, 52; II, 5, 1 (Shorey, *CP.* 1924, 6, n. 1).

[5] "Differentiae divisionum", says Boethius, *De Div.* Migne, LXIV, 891–2, were studied most carefully by the later Peripatetics, but neglected by the earlier.

[6] Relevant passages noted by Jackson (*JP.* xv, 285).

[7] Cf. *FPG.* III, 94; *RP.* 284 B.

[8] Athen. 59 D (cited by Mutschmann, ps.-Arist. *Div.* XVI).

[9] Cf. *Luc.* 43; "Oratoriae partitiones quae quidem e media illa nostra Academia effloruerunt", *Part. Or.* 139.

[10] *Fin.* v, 16. Chrysippus wrote περὶ διαιρέσεων and πιθανὰ πρὸς τὰς διαιρέσεις καὶ τὰ γένη καὶ τὰ εἴδη. . . .   [11] II, 39, 23.

[12] Though in Cicero's day "Peripatetici...spinas partiendi et definiendi praetermittunt" (*Tusc.* IV, 9) the situation soon altered, perhaps when Ariston of Alexandria, Antiochus's pupil, went over to the Peripatetic School.

In the present chapter Clement, before entering into the theory of Division, declares that the Universal is summed up by Sensation from the Particular.[1] So, too, for Antiochus the Mind, which is the source of the sensations and is itself Sensation, systematizes analogically[2] all those sense-presentations which it does not either make use of immediately or store up as the source of memory—and thence are formed Universals: "Cetera (sc. visa) similitudinibus construit, ex quibus efficiuntur notitiae rerum; quae Graeci tum ἐννοίας tum προλήψεις[3] vocant."[4]

Clement agrees with Plato and Aristotle in recognizing the logical principle that "Divisio non facit saltum".[5] The term προσεχῆ εἴδη,[6] however, which we shall find in the *Didaskalikos*,[7] appears to be characteristically Stoic.[8] Clement proceeds to mention three types of Division, that of a genus into species, that of a whole into parts, and that of a subject into accidents. Of these only the first is logically valuable. For definition must state essential attributes and be reached by the exclusion, at every stage, of members of co-ordinate species. The scheme which Clement follows appears more completely in the passage of the Scholia to the *Grammatike* of Dionysius Thrax,[9] to which reference has already been made. There we find mentioned the Division (A) of a genus into species (and of a species into its individual members), (B) of a whole into its parts (which may be either similar or dissimilar), (C) of an ambiguous term into its meanings, and (D) of a subject into accidents (and of accidents into subjects). Clement distinguishes (A) from (B) by pointing out that, whereas the genus exists in the

[1] 17, 6. Cf. also § 17, 4 with Arist. *RP*. 310 A.
[2] κατὰ τὴν ἀπὸ τῶν περιπτωτικῶς πεφηνότων ἀναλογιστικὴν μετάβασιν, S. E. *AM*. XI, 250.
[3] For their distinction cf. F. H. Sandbach, *CQ*. XXIV, 46.
[4] *Luc*. 30. Cicero in *Top*. 30, "genus est notio ad plurimas differentias pertinens", by "notio" translates ἔννοια, πρόληψις.
[5] Cf. *Met*. Z, 12 (especially δεῖ γε διαιρεῖσθαι τὴν τῆς διαφορᾶς διαφοράν). Here διαίρεσις is given more importance than in *An. Post*. II, 5 and 13. Cf. Ross, 57. 52.
[6] VIII, 18, 2 (and 7).   [7] 57, 6.
[8] D. L. VII, 61 is assigned conjecturally to Diogenes of Babylon by v. Arnim (fr. 25). Cf. also S. E. XI, 15.
[9] 679 Bekker.

species, the whole cannot exist in the part: the man is not in his hand or foot.[1] Compare now the Antiochean view as given in Cicero's *Topica*: "In partitione quasi membra sunt, ut corporis caput humeri manus latera crura pedes et cetera; in divisione formae sunt quas Graeci εἴδη vocant."[2] When Clement later remarks that ἐκ τῆς τοῦ ὅρου ἀγνοίας καὶ τὰς πολλὰς ἀμφισβητήσεις γίνεσθαι καὶ τὰς ἀπάτας συμβαίνει, he again expresses a view which Cicero adopts from Antiochus, in criticizing Epicurus.[3]

Chapter VII alleges two main causes of Scepticism. One is the fickleness of the human mind. The other is the apparent discrepancy which exists in things. Such is the view taken by Antiochus.[4] The combination in the next chapter of Aristotle's ten categories with Xenocrates's two[5] is significant.[6] Significant also is the mention of πολυώνυμα.[7] Porphyry points out that this term is not Aristotelean.[8] Boethus of Sidon says that Speusippus adopted the division of ἑτερώνυμα into ἰδίως ἑτερώνυμα, πολυώνυμα and παρώνυμα, examples of πολυώνυμα being ἄορ, ξίφος, φάσγανον.[9] Clement chooses the same examples. There can be little doubt that Boethus, in reporting Speusippus, is at the same time giving the view of Antiochus.[10] And if further proof be needed that Clement is here following the last-named we may note that the example chosen to illustrate a homonym derived from similarity of function is πούς. Thereby the ship sails and thereby we walk. Compare now what Cicero says in the *De Oratore*: "Si res suum nomen et vocabulum

[1] But see p. 137, *infra*.

[2] 30.

[3] *Fin.* I, 22. A similar standpoint is adopted in *Fin.* II, 30, III, 40. Cf. also *Tusc.* V, 72.

[4] *Luc.* 46. Stählin compares *PE.* 760 C also (Aristocles attacking Aenesidemus).

[5] fr. 12. Cf. Plato, *Phil.* 51 C. The Peripatetics Andronicus and Aspasius (12, 2) adopted them.

[6] 24, 1. [7] 24, 5.

[8] *Cat.* 60, 35 (cf. 69, 2). Aristotle has συν. παρ. ὁμ. Simplicius (*SVF.* II, 150) does not actually say that the Stoics use the term πολυώνυμα, but he suggests it.

[9] Cited by Prantl, 547.

[10] His treatment of the Aristotelean Universal and of the Platonic Idea (see *UPG.* 560) is obviously due to following Antiochus.

proprium non habet, ut pes in navi. . . ."[1] The other examples of
the various kinds of equivocal terms which Clement gives are the
same as those chosen by Porphyry in his *Commentary* on the *Categories* of Aristotle.[2] Porphyry may plausibly[3] be supposed to have
derived them from Peripateticism, in the form in which it had been
resuscitated by Antiochus.[4]

Clement deals lastly with the theory of Causes. The Stoic and
Peripatetic elements of which this is composed are not perfectly
harmonized—and Clement, or the authority whom he follows,
recognizes that they are occasionally incompatible.[5] Comparison
of the whole chapter with a passage in Cicero's *Topica*[6] will enable
us to see that they have a common source, which cannot be other
than Antiochean.[7]

προκαταρκτικὰ μὲν τὰ πρώτως ἀφορμὴν παρεχόμενα εἰς τὸ γίγνεσθαί τι, καθάπερ τὸ κάλλος τοῖς ἀκολάστοις τοῦ ἔρωτος· ὀφθὲν γὰρ αὐτοῖς τὴν ἐρωτικὴν διάθεσιν ἐμποιεῖ μέν, οὐ μὴν κατηναγκασμένως· συνεκτικὰ δὲ ἅπερ συνωνύμως καὶ αὐτοτελῆ[9] καλεῖται, ἐπειδήπερ αὐτάρκως δι᾽ αὐτῶν ποιητικά ἐστι τοῦ ἀποτελέσματος.	Alia (sc. generis causarum sine quo non efficitur) praecursionem[8] quamdam adhibent ad efficiendum et quaedam afferunt per se adiuvantia, etsi non necessaria, ut amori congressio causam attulerat, amor flagitio. Unum (genus causarum) quod vi sua id, quod sub eam vim subiectum est, certo efficit.

[1] III, 159. Cf. also Sen. *Ben.* II, 34 (where "dog" appears too: cf.
supra, p. 35).

[2] Cf. 24, 8–9 with Porphyry, *Cat.* 64. 67, 8. 66, 4.

[3] Prantl (p. 686) points out that Boethius in his *De Div.* follows
Porphyry, who in his turn is probably dependent on Andronicus.

[4] See the very just remarks of Giambelli, *Riv. Filol.* 1892, 485.

[5] Cf. *SVF.* II, 345.

[6] §§ 58–64 (without strict adherence to Cicero's order). Strangely
neglected by v. Arnim.

[7] Antiochus himself followed Chrysippus (cf. Theiler, *VN.* 27) and
Plato, *Ph.* 99 (Zeller, II, 2³, 331); *Tim.* 46.

[8] "In rhet. lang. *a preparation* of the hearer", Lewis and Short. But
the reference is to antecedent *causes* (προκαταρκτικά).

[9] Cf. *Did.* 63, 28; 64, 28.

39

ὁ μὲν πατὴρ αἴτιόν ἐστι προκαταρκτικὸν τῆς μαθήσεως, ὁ διδάσκαλος δὲ συνεκτικόν, ἡ δὲ τοῦ μανθάνοντος φύσις συνεργὸν αἴτιον,

Non enim si sine parentibus filii esse non possunt, propterea causa fuit in parentibus gignendi necessaria. | Sunt aliae causae quae plane efficiant,[1] nulla re adiuvante, aliae quae adiuvari velint, ut sapientia efficit sapientes sola per se; beatos efficiat necne sola per se, quaestio est. |

ὁ δὲ χρόνος τῶν ὢν οὐκ ἄνευ λόγον ἐπέχει.

Huius generis causarum sine quo non efficitur alia sunt quieta nihil agentia, . . . ut locus, tempus, ...

εἰ μέν τί ἐστιν αἴτιον καὶ ποιητικόν,[2] τοῦτο πάντως ἐστὶ καὶ δι᾽ ὅ, εἰ δέ τί ἐστι δι᾽ ὅ, οὐ πάντως τοῦτο καὶ αἴτιον. e.g. Medea οὐκ ἂν ἐτεκνοκτόνησεν εἰ μὴ ὠργίσθη, εἰ μὴ ἐζήλωσεν, εἰ μὴ ἠράσθη, εἰ μὴ Ἰάσων ἔπλευσεν, εἰ μὴ Ἀργὼ κατεσκευάσθη, εἰ μὴ τὰ ξύλα ἐκ τοῦ Πηλίου ἐτμήθη.

Hoc igitur, sine quo non fit, ab eo, a quo certo fit, diligenter est separandum. Illud enim est tamquam "Utinám ne in nemore Pélio—secúribus | caesá cedidisset ábiegna ad terrám trabes!" Nisi enim cecidisset abiegna ad terram trabes, Argo illa facta non esset, nec tamen fuit in his trabibus efficiendi vis necessaria.[3]

(Aristotle's four causes). The brass in relation to the statue is the material cause, i.e. the cause *sine qua non*, or αἴτιον συνεργόν, but not συνεκτικόν.[4]

Alterum (genus causarum) quod naturam efficiendi non habet, sed sine quo effici non possit, ut si quis aes causam statuae velit dicere, quod sine eo non potest effici.

(Some causes are evident, some are grasped by a process of reasoning, some are occult— ἄδηλα—some are inferred by analogy). Of those which are

Aliae (causae quae non sunt constantes) sunt perspicuae, aliae latent . . . latent quae subiectae sunt fortunae. Cum enim nihil sine causa fiat, hoc ipsum est

---

[1] Cf. *Part. Orat.* 94.
[2] In *Fin.* III, 55 "efficientia" = ποιητικά.
[3] Cf. Cic. *Fat.* 35.
[4] σ. is found in περὶ κόσμου, VI.

occult τὰ μὲν πρὸς καιρὸν ἄδηλα   fortunae eventus, obscura causa,
. . . τὰ δὲ φύσει ἄδηλα.   quae latenter efficitur. [ea quo-
rum obscurae causae, ut in terris
mundoque admirabilia.[1]]

While the general character of Clement's book is unmistakably
Antiochean, the fact that not every detail exactly accords with what
we learn of Antiochus from Cicero is not to be overlooked. But
to establish a direct relation is no part of our purpose. Before
Clement wrote, the eclecticism which Antiochus had taken over
from the Middle Stoa and brought into popularity had undergone
two centuries of development and modification, in the hands of
Platonists, Stoics and Peripatetics. In particular, the criticism which
the Alexandrian Sceptic Aenesidemus, a member of the Academy
subsequently to Antiochus, had directed against the revived dogmatism, had in turn been refuted by one who seems to have been
a staunch supporter of Antiochus in the second century, the Peripatetic Aristocles.[2] And in the present book Clement may well be
directly following him or a similar Peripatetic authority.

[1] *Part. Orat.* 56. In *Luc.* 32 and 54 "incerta" = ἄδηλα.
[2] Cf. e.g. 19, 20, 29 with *PE.* 768 A, 764, 768 D, respectively.

vi

THE *DIDASKALIKOS* IN RELATION TO ANTIOCHUS

A. THE INTRODUCTION

Our writer opens with a well-known definition of σοφία, which seems to have been popularized by the Middle Stoics,[1] and which Antiochus adopted.[2] The contrast between the flux of sensible things and the permanence of intelligible reality need be due to no other than a Platonic source. But, although this must have been somewhat strange in a system which was based on Stoic sensationalism,[3] Antiochus probably sought to give it prominence, and certainly recognized its importance for Plato and the Old Academy.[4] Our writer declares also that the philosopher will be unruffled by pleasure (52, 11–14). Later he will admit that some pleasures participate to a limited degree in the Good, but here his attitude is similar to that which Antiochus himself evinced[5] and claimed to discover in the Old Academy: "Fuga desidiae voluptatumque contemptio."[6] Further, the philosopher possesses a natural aptitude for the knowledge of truth.[7] Antiochus pointed out that Plato's successors in the Academy and the Lyceum "naturae celeritatem ad discendum et memoriam dabant",[8] and contrasted with their

---

[1] Plato already has κατ' ἀνθρώπινα καὶ κατὰ θεῖα πράγματα (*Sym.* 186 B, where Taylor, *PMW*. 217, 1, would limit the meaning of θ. π. to "physics"). See *SVF*. II, 35, 36. 1017; Cic. *Off.* II, 5; Hobein, *Diss.* 52.

[2] *Tusc.* IV, 57; *Fin.* II, 37; Stob. II, 145, 19.

[3] Cf. p. 29, n. 1, *supra*. Reid on *A. Po.* 31 is sounder than Hirzel, III, 502.

[4] *A. Po.* 31.

[5] *Fin.* V, 57; II, 106; *Tusc.* V, 101; Clem. *Strom.* II, 118, 5 (Hoyer 12).

[6] *A. Po.* 23. But Eudoxus ought to be excepted (Arist. *EN.* 72 b 9).

[7] Cf. Stob. II, 126, 1: "τάχα ἂν φυσικάς τις ἀρετὰς ἔχοι"; Plot. I, iii, 6.

[8] *A. Po.* 20. Cf. also *Tusc.* V, 68 (which Gerhäusser would derive from Posidonius's *Protrepticus*), but not so Plotinus. (Generally οὐχ οἱ αὐτοὶ μνήμονες καὶ ἀγχίνοι, IV, vi, 3.)

view that of Zeno.[1] But he himself believed that a reconciliation between the two views was not impossible.[2] Besides dividing the virtues into the natural and the moral, Antiochus subdivided the moral into those which are capable of development (exercitationis assiduitate, ἐξ ἐπιμελείας περιγίνεσθαι) and those which are in themselves perfect (virtus quasi perfectio naturae, ἐκ τελειότητος ὑπάρχειν).[3] In the *Didaskalikos*, though perhaps not quite so distinctly, the same contrast appears.[4]

There follows a discussion of the Two Lives.[5] Theoretic activity is indeed superior, since its objects are the divine nature, the first unmoved causes, the movements of the heavenly bodies, and the constitution of the universe. But practical activity is also necessary and the best branches of it are legislation, statecraft, and education. Antiochus took a similar view, as we learn from Cicero.[6]

We may also compare a passage from Arius Didymus's account of "Aristotelean and Peripatetic Ethics", where the philosopher-sage is said to choose the life of Virtue, whether this involves being a general, a king's counsellor, a legislator, or a servant of state. If none of these posts is open to him, he will devote himself to public speaking, or to contemplation, or to what holds an intermediate position between the two—education. If he has his way, he will put into practice as well as contemplate what is morally fine. But if prevented by circumstances from engaging in both spheres of life, then he will confine himself to the practical alone, setting value on the theoretical but being roused to political action owing to his interest in the common weal. The political life, which may be identified with the practical, will attract him, not because circum-

---

[1] *A. Po.* 38 (*SVF.* I, 199). [2] *Fin.* v, 36.

[3] *A. Po.* 20–1; Stob. II, 136, 16 sqq. The passages are compared by Strache, *Diss.* 55.

[4] See also p. 10, n. 8, *supra*.

[5] See p. 8, n. 2, *supra*. See further *Tusc.* v, 9 (probably Posidonius, reporting Heraclides's story of Pythagoras); Sen. *Ep.* 92, 10: "philosophia et contemplativa est et activa" (and as *contemplativa* must have δόγματα). Hoyer discovers Antiochus in this *Letter*, § 14, and his view is accepted by Strache, *Diss.* 43 and somewhat haltingly by Theiler, *VN.* 27, 2. But the claims of Posidonius are strong here as elsewhere in the *Letter*.

[6] *Fin.* v, 51, 53, 58.

stances force him to it, but because to enter it is his principal duty (προηγουμένως, μὴ κατὰ περίστασιν).[1]

In the *Didaskalikos* the Sage is said to enter public life, when he sees statesmen governing badly, and to regard himself when general, judge, or ambassador,[2] as the victim of circumstances (περιστατικὰ μὲν ἡγούμενος τὸ στρατηγεῖν, τὸ δικάζειν, τὸ πρεσβεύειν...), from which Strache infers that the point of view is different.[3] It is, however, very doubtful whether any fundamental difference exists. For the Sage enters the sphere of action because he is constrained to apply the results of his contemplation to the improvement of men's characters (μελετῆσαι εἰς ἀνθρώπων ἤθη)[4] and considers that the tasks of legislating, laying down a constitution, and educating youth, are of principal importance, when the practical is taken by itself (ἄριστα δ' ἐν πράξει καὶ ὡς ἐν ταύτῃ προηγούμενα τὸ περὶ νομοθεσίας καὶ πολιτείας κατάστασιν καὶ παιδείαν νέων). Our writer regards both lives as important. The value of the contemplative life lies in the fact that it is completely free, whereas the other, while no less necessary, is subject to restraint. Antiochus approved of the important place assigned to θεωρία by Aristotle and Theophrastus.[5] But, true to the doctrine of the Academy and the Stoa, he refused to subordinate πρᾶξις completely to θεωρία.[6]

We have already noticed that the tripartite division of philosophy given in Chapter III has some similarity to that of Zeno.[7] But the

[1] Stob. II, 143, 24 sqq. Cf. πολιτεύεσθαι, νομοθετεῖν, παιδεύειν, in *SVF.* III, 611 (Ar. Did. also).

[2] Cf. Ph. Al.'s *Legatio ad Gaium.*

[3] He criticizes Freudenthal (p. 297) for comparing the two passages, *Diss.* 86. "Cum hic (sc. in Stob.) Antiochia ratione vita ex umbratili et negotioso temperata utilior esse dicatur sola theoretica...illic (in *Did.*) manifesto practica vita contemplativae postponitur."

[4] After *Rep.* 500 c.

[5] *Fin.* V, 11. Cf. Stob. II, 117, 13. Apparently Panaetius criticized Plato's view (*Off.* I, 28; *Rep.* 540 B): "philosophos ad rempublicam ne accessuros quidem nisi coactos." Plotinus approves practical virtues which, in this World, τὸ καλῶς ἐνεργοῦσι, προηγούμενον τοῦτο ἀλλ' οὐχ ὡς ἀναγκαῖον τιθέμεναι, and his Sage τάχα ποτὲ περιστατικῶς ἐνεργήσει κατά τινας αὐτῶν (I, ii, 7). For προηγούμενον and περιστατικόν cf. Epict. III, 14, 7; Elter, *Gnom.* 471.

[6] *CD.* 19, 3.   [7] p. 11, n. 3, *supra.*

terminology is different. Zeno, and indeed the Stoics generally, spoke of the three main departments as λογικόν, φυσικόν, ἠθικόν. In the *Didaskalikos* three branches of γνῶσις are mentioned, διαλεκτική, θεωρητική, πρακτική.[1] Under the influence of Aristotle, as we have seen, physics becomes a species of Theoretic. The obvious reason for this alteration in nomenclature is the desire to preserve the contrast which has been made in the previous chapter between θεωρητικόν and πρακτικόν. And Antiochus, who emphasized the theoretic aspect of physics,[2] appears from a passage in the *Civitas Dei* to have consciously combined with the customary Stoic trichotomy the antithesis which he had learnt from Aristotle; and to have attributed the combination to Plato.[3] There, as in the *Posterior Academics*, the arrangement is ἠθικόν, φυσικόν, λογικόν, which differs from that of Zeno. In *De Finibus* v the order in which the three departments are mentioned is that of Panaetius and Posidonius.[4]

The department of διαλεκτική is subdivided into τὸ διαιρετικόν, τὸ ὁριστικόν, τὸ ἀναλυτικόν,[5] τὸ ἐπαγωγικόν and τὸ συλλογιστικόν. The last named, strictly deductive logic, undergoes further division into τὸ ἀποδεικτικόν,[6] τὸ ἐπιχειρηματικόν[7] and τὸ ῥητορικόν. Antiochus explicitly distinguished these species, though he is not recorded to have subsumed ῥητορικόν, as our writer does, under συλλογιστικόν: "Argumentis et quasi rerum notis ducibus utebantur (sc. the Old Academy and the Lyceum) ad probandum (i.e. τὸ ἐπιχειρηματικόν, ratiocinatio[8]) et ad concludendum (i.e. τὸ ἀποδεικτικόν[9]) id quod explanari volebant: in quo tradebatur omnis

---

[1] ἠθικόν (a subdivision 53, 35) seems later (79, 30) as wide as πρακτική itself.

[2] Cf. *Fin.* v, 9; *A. Po.* 19.

[3] *CD.* 8, 4 (probably Varro, following Antiochus).

[4] φ.λ.η. (*Fin.* v, 9; Schmekel, 185, 238). In *Tusc.* v, 68, which Gerhäusser and Usener claim for Posidonius, the order is φ.η.λ.

[5] Prantl's conjecture.

[6] For Platonic ἀπ. cf. *Meno* 97 C–98 A; for Aristotelean ἀπ. p. 33, n. 6, *supra* and *An. Post.* 73 a 24, 81 a 38 sqq. Cf. also ps.-Plat. *Deff.* 414 E; *SVF.* II, 235. For ἀπ. + πίστις in *NT.* cf. *Cor.* I, 2, 6.

[7] "Dialectical syllogism", *Top.* 162 a 16. Cf. *Parv. Nat.* 451 a 19; *An. Pr.* 46 a 9.

[8] *Inv.* I, 57.   [9] Cf. p. 33, n. 10, *supra*.

dialecticae disciplina, id est orationis ratione conclusae. Huic quasi ex altera parte oratoria vis dicendi adhibebatur (i.e. τὸ ῥητορικόν)."[1]

The department of πρακτικὴ φιλοσοφία is divided, as in the *Eudemian Ethics*,[2] into ἠθικόν, οἰκονομικόν and πολιτικόν. Panaetius had dwelt upon the importance of the second of these branches[3] and Antiochus followed him.[4] In Arius Didymus's account of Peripatetic Ethics, after the subject of Ethics (ὁ ἠθικὸς τόπος) has been discussed,[5] we learn of the other two: ἀναγκαῖον ἐφεξῆς καὶ περὶ τοῦ οἰκονομικοῦ τε καὶ πολιτικοῦ διελθεῖν.[6] There is nothing to prevent our supposing that Arius derived the trichotomy from Antiochus.[7]

Reference has been made to the fact that the division of theoretical philosophy into physics, theology and mathematics goes back to Aristotle.[8] We shall do well to observe the place accorded to astronomy. Aristotle had distinguished physics from mathematics, because the former science deals with natural bodies, which have a separate existence (χωριστά)[9] but are not unchangeable (ἀκίνητα), whereas the latter studies numbers and figures, which are unchangeable but have no separate existence—both thus differing from theology, whose objects are both χωριστά and ἀκίνητα.[10] For Aristotle, therefore, astronomy comes within the province of physics rather than of mathematics.[11] In the present chapter the same view of astronomy is adopted (54, 1–2), but later it is included among the mathematical sciences, being described in Platonic fashion as a kind of τέταρτον μάθημα.[12] The term ἀποκατάστασις is not derived

---

[1] For "περὶ τὸ ἐνθύμημα" cf. *An. Pr.* 70 a 10; Cic. *Top.* 55.

[2] 18 b 13.   [3] *Off.* II, 87. Cf. Strache, *Diss.* 69.

[4] Cf. *Fin.* v, 67 sqq.   [5] Stob. II, 147, 26 sqq.

[6] Chalcidius, *in Tim.* 265, divides "activum" into "moralis", "domestica", "publica".

[7] Cic. *Tusc.* I, 2 can hardly be used for Antiochus.   [8] p. 8, n. 3, *supra*.

[9] ἰδίαν ὑπόστασιν ἔχει, in the language of later philosophy (cf. Witt in *Am. Cor.*).

[10] *Met.* 25 b 18 sqq. For ἀχώριστα εἴδη cf. *Did.* 55, 35.

[11] Cf. *Cael.* II, 2 and Ross, 70. The later Peripatetics sometimes made αστρ. subordinate to μαθ. and not to φυσ. (cf. Baumstark, *Ar. Syr.* 199; Ammon. *CommPorph.-Isag.* 11, 22). D. L. v, 28 divides θεωρ. simply into φυσ. and λογ. Chalc. 264 does not differentiate μαθ. and φυσ.

[12] *Did.* 61, 23; *Rep.* 528 E.

46

from Plato. It occurs, however, with a different meaning,[1] in the un-Platonic dialogue *Axiochus*. In the *Didaskalikos* the sense appears to be quite general. Parallel perhaps is Cicero's phrase in *Laws* 1: "perpetui cursus (περίοδοι) conversionesque caelestes (ἀποκαταστάσεις)."[2]

B. EPISTEMOLOGY

Antiochus showed himself a true follower of Zeno in the importance which he attached to Epistemology.[3] Against his own predecessors in the Academy and the Pyrrhonian Sceptics, who had denied the Stoic κριτήριον whether conceived as αἴσθησις or as νοῦς,[4] he zealously maintained that a καταληπτικὴ φαντασία, a sense-presentation containing its own guarantee of truth, is possible: "Habeo regulam, ut talia visa (i.e. φαντασίας) vera iudicem, qualia falsa esse non possint."[5] The very denial of the possibility of knowledge is a δόγμα, and a δόγμα involves the recognition of a criterion. Nevertheless, as against the Epicurean sensationalism, Antiochus denied that in every circumstance αἴσθησις must be infallible. For, as an instrument of knowledge, it requires the right adjustment in order that it may supply true results. When such an adjustment is effected, there is no one "qui in sensibus sui cuiusque generis iudicium requirat acrius".[6] Antiochus further stressed the inevitability of judgment. The mind cannot remain suspended, but must yield its assent to self-evident presentations: "Ut enim necesse est lancem in libra ponderibus impositis deprimi, sic animum perspicuis cedere."[7] To pass judgment means that there are objects which may be judged: "Nihil possumus iudicare, nisi quod est nostri iudicii."[8]

At the opening of Chapter IV our writer agrees with Antiochus in regarding judgment as logically entailed by the existence of a subject which judges and an object which is judged: ἐπεὶ οὖν ἐστί

---

[1] 370 B: the return of sun or moon after eclipse.
[2] § 24. More varied is *ND.* II, 51 (which Finger, however, assigns to Antiochus and not Posidonius).
[3] *Luc.* 29.   [4] See Goed. 55.
[5] *Ibid.* 58. Cf. also *Brut.* 152 (typically Antiochean). "Regula" in *Fin.* I, 63 = the Epicurean κανονικόν.
[6] *Luc.* 19.   [7] *Ibid.* 38.   [8] *Fin.* II, 36.

τι τὸ κρῖνον, ἔστι δὲ καὶ τὸ κρινόμενον, εἴη ἄν τι καὶ τὸ ἐκ τούτων ἀποτελούμενον, ὅπερ εἴποι ἄν τις κρίσιν. The judgment itself is properly speaking the criterion, but if criterion be taken in a wider sense, τὸ κρῖνον may also be included, by which may be meant either the agent (τὸ ὑφ᾽ οὗ) or the instrument (τὸ δι᾽ οὗ). Then νοῦς is the agent and λόγος φυσικός the criterion. The contrast in this form, however, is afterwards neglected, the λόγος being treated indifferently as judge and as criterion. The real antithesis in this chapter is rather between λόγος as ἐπιστημονικός [1] (i.e. human λόγος as dealing with intelligibles) and λόγος as δοξαστικός (i.e. human λόγος as dealing with sensibles).

The distinction between agent and instrument was clearly drawn by the eclectic Potamo of Alexandria: δύο κριτήρια τῆς ἀληθείας εἶναι, τὸ μὲν ὡς ὑφ᾽ οὗ γίγνεται ἡ κρίσις, τουτέστι τὸ ἡγεμονικόν· τὸ δὲ ὡς δι᾽ οὗ, οἷον τὴν ἀκριβεστάτην φαντασίαν.[2] Here Potamo followed Antiochus. For the latter, while identifying νοῦς and αἴσθησις, held that a "vis naturalis" characterizes the mind when it operates as sensation, and that thus αἴσθησις can be regarded as the instrument of νοῦς,[3] or (to quote from the Antiochean portion of Sextus Empiricus's *Adversus Mathematicos* VII): φαίνεται πρῶτα κριτήρια τῆς τῶν πραγμάτων γνώσεως ἥ τε αἴσθησις καὶ ὁ νοῦς, ἡ μὲν ὀργάνου τρόπον ἔχουσα, ὁ δὲ τεχνίτου.[4]

It would seem that Antiochus taught[5] that the word criterion may be used in three different senses, κοινῶς, ἰδίως, or ἰδιαίτερον,[6] since criteria may be natural, artificial or logical. The faculties of sight, hearing and so forth are φυσικὰ κριτήρια, measuring instru-

---

[1] For the term see Arist. *EN*. 39 a 6 sqq.; *An*. 431 b 27; Plut. 443 E.
[2] D. L. *Proem*. 21.
[3] "Mens ipsa, quae sensuum fons est, atque etiam ipsa sensus est, naturalem vim habet, quam intendit ad ea quibus movetur" (*Luc*. 30); "(Mens) et sensibus utitur et artes efficit, quasi sensus alteros" (*ibid*. 31); "Cum vim quae esset in sensibus explicabamus, simul illud aperiebatur comprehendi multa et percipi sensibus..." (*ibid*. 37). *SVF*. II, 849 may perhaps contain Antiochean doctrine. Cf. also Chrysippus, *SVF*. II, 255, 15, with which III, 257 is in formal contradiction. Contrast *ibid*. the view of Posidonius (and of Cleanthes also?), *SVF*. I, 571. (Note δύναμις, *Did*. 54, 31.)
[4] § 226.　　　　　　　　　　[5] *Ibid*. § 31 sqq.
[6] Cf. Galen, *DDG*. 606, 10. The terms appear in Porph. *Isag*. 8, 8.

ments are τεχνικὰ κριτήρια, while by λογικὰ κριτήρια only those employed by the philosopher are meant. But here another trichotomy may be performed. For the logical criterion may be regarded either as the agent or as the instrument or as the application and the state of the critical faculty: τὸ μέν τι εἶναι κριτήριον ὡς ὑφ' οὗ, τὸ δὲ ὡς δι' οὗ, τὸ δὲ ὡς προσβολὴ καὶ σχέσις. For, just as in the operation of weighing we need the balance,[1] the person who weighs, and the adjustment, so in philosophy, in order that we may distinguish truth from falsehood, we need the agent (ἄνθρωπος, ὑφ' οὗ γίνεται ἡ κρίσις), the instrument (sensation and discursive reason, δι' ἧς γίνεται τὰ τῆς κρίσεως) and the test supplied by presentation (τῇ σχέσει τῶν προειρημένων ὀργάνων ἡ προσβολὴ τῆς φαντασίας).

It is noteworthy that in the chapter which we are considering the writer favours repeated dichotomy.[2] The first differentiation of λόγος is into the divine and the human. It is not easy to see how the two species exclude one another. The intended antithesis between the divine as παντελῶς ἄληπτος and the human as κατὰ τὴν τῶν πραγμάτων ἀδιάψευστος[3] can be obtained only by some forcing of πραγμάτων. The same distinction appears in a much clearer form in a passage of Sextus Empiricus: ἄλλοι δὲ ἦσαν οἱ λέγοντες κατὰ τὸν Ἐμπεδοκλέα κριτήριον εἶναι τῆς ἀληθείας οὐ τὰς αἰσθήσεις ἀλλὰ τὸν ὀρθὸν λόγον, τοῦ δὲ ὀρθοῦ λόγου τὸν μέν τινα θεῖον ὑπάρχειν τὸν δὲ ἀνθρώπινον, ὧν τὸν μὲν θεῖον ἀνέξοιστον (cannot be revealed to man) τὸν δὲ ἀνθρώπινον ἐξοιστόν. But Empedocles, we learn, is confident μὴ εἶναι εἰς τὸ παντελὲς ἄληπτον τὴν ἀλήθειαν, ἀλλ' ἐφ' ὅσον ἱκνεῖται ὁ ἀνθρώπινος λόγος ληπτὴν ὑπάρχειν: he declares that τὸ δι' ἑκάστης αἰσθήσεως λαμβανόμενον πιστόν ἐστι, τοῦ λόγου τούτων ἐπιστατοῦντος—καίπερ πρότερον καταδραμὼν τῆς ἀπ' αὐτῶν πίστεως.[4] Here the view fathered upon Empedocles that sense-perception with the aid of reason is trustworthy and the emphasis laid on πιστόν and πίστις are not without significance. We

---

[1] Cf. *Luc.* 38.   [2] 54, 11. 18. 22.

[3] Cf. S. E. *AM.* VII, 191, 199. § 199 resembles *Luc.* 20 (cf. also Eus. *PE.* 764 for Aristocles). ἀδιάψευστος was used by Stoicism (*SVF.* I, 624—Sphaerus—and M. A. IV, 49) in opposition to the Sceptical view (cf. S. E. *AM.* VII, 159).

[4] *AM.* VII, 122 sqq.

need only recall *De Finibus* IV, 8–9: "Quasi denuntiant ut neque sensuum fidem sine ratione nec rationes sine sensibus exquiramus, atque eorum alterum ab altero separemus", or the doctrine which Antiochus discovered in the Old Academy, that the criterion of truth "oritur a sensibus, tamen non est in sensibus".[1] The passage of Sextus to which attention has been directed may on these grounds be attributed to Antiochus or to his School.[2]

The distinction which is now drawn between ἐπιστημονικὸς λόγος as ἀδιάψευστος and δοξαστικὸς λόγος[3] as merely πιθανός may appear at first to be due rather to Xenocrates than to Antiochus. For the latter, according to Cicero, followed Stoicism in maintaining that the philosopher does not opine.[4] In *Tusculans* IV, a book which on other grounds may be connected with Antiochus, there is the same agreement with Stoicism.[5] In view of these passages it is rather surprising to find that Antiochus recognized with Plato true opinions: "Beatum cui etiam in senectute contigerit ut sapientiam verasque opiniones assequi possit!"[6] His standpoint, as described by Varro in the *Posterior Academics*, is, that Plato and Zeno alike opposed δόξα to ἐπιστήμη.[7]

Yet Antiochus did not always thus degrade δόξα. In a passage of Sextus Empiricus, where the signs of Antiochean influence are many, δόξα is an approved term: ὅταν γὰρ εἴξῃ ἡ ψυχὴ τῇ ἀπὸ τῆς αἰσθήσεως ἐγγενομένῃ φαντασίᾳ καὶ τῷ φανέντι συγκατάθηται, λέγεται δόξα.[8] The context makes evident that in this case δόξα, albeit subsequent (ὑστερογένης) to αἴσθησις and φαντασία, is not regarded after the fashion of the Porch as ἀκαταλήπτῳ συγκατάθεσις or ὑπόληψις ἀσθενής,[9] but has the wider meaning which it sometimes

---

[1] *Fin.* IV, 9; *A. Po.* 30.

[2] Theiler, *VN.* 55, n., has called attention to the similarity between *Did.* 154, 10 sqq. and the passages which are dealt with here.

[3] Plotinus in referring to the sensitive phase of Universal Soul uses the term: ἡ δὲ αἰσθάνεσθαι πεφυκυῖα καὶ ἡ λόγον δοξαστικὸν δεχομένη, II, ii, 3.

[4] *Luc.* 67 = *SVF.* II, 110.   [5] 15. 26 (*SVF.* III, 380, 427).

[6] *Fin.* v, 58.

[7] 30 (with *hebetes* contrast "nemo qui in sensibus iudicium requirat acrius", *Luc.* 19); 41.

[8] S. E. *AM.* VII, 225.

[9] *SVF.* III, 548 (Ar. Did.).

receives in Plato and Aristotle,[1] as well as in the treatise here under consideration, of judgment, κρίσις.

Antiochus would therefore appear to have been inconsistent in his use of δόξα. On the one hand, he could insist with Zeno that opinion is concerned only with the unknown and the false and therefore lacks conviction. Thus he rejected δόξα as being beyond the control of λόγος, and avoided the use of δοξάζειν with ὁ σπου-δαῖος: "Sapientem nihil opinari, id est, numquam assentiri rei vel falsae vel incognitae."[2] On the other hand, he could not fail to recognize that in the language of pre-Stoic philosophy δόξα had not been confined to this one meaning, and therefore, in token of his eclecticism, he sometimes accepted it as meaning δόγμα, the rational assent itself, which is the inevitable outcome of clear sense-presentations.

That this is the genuinely Antiochean view is further shown by the following passage, which we may again confidently ascribe to him or to his School, and which is of considerable importance for the present investigation.[3] Here we learn that reason (λόγος), in combination with the perspicuity (ἐνάργεια) of sensation, is clearly declared by Plato in the *Timaeus* (viz. 28 A) to be the criterion, when he defines τὸ ὄν as νοήσει μετὰ λόγου περιληπτόν, and τὸ γινόμενον (sc. as περιληπτόν: but Plato himself wrote δοξαστόν) δόξῃ μετὰ αἰσθήσεως. The passage proceeds as follows: περιληπτικὸν δὲ καλεῖσθαί φασι λόγον παρ' αὐτῷ οἱ Πλατωνικοὶ τὸν κοινὸν τῆς ἐναργείας καὶ τῆς ἀληθείας. δεῖ γὰρ τὸν λόγον ἐν τῷ κρίνειν τὴν ἀλήθειαν ἀπὸ τῆς ἐναργείας ὁρμᾶσθαι, εἴπερ δι' ἐναργῶν ἡ κρίσις γίνεται τῶν ἀληθῶν. ἀλλ' ἥ γε ἐνάργεια οὐκ ἔστιν αὐτάρκης πρὸς γνῶσιν ἀληθοῦς... ἀλλὰ δεῖ παρεῖναι τὸ κρῖνον τί τε φαίνεται

---

[1] In Plato, as v. Hartmann observes (*Plat. Log. d. Seins*, 93, n. 1), δ. is usually contrasted with ἐπιστήμη (γνῶσις). In *Rep.* 477 sqq. δ. is the faculty intermediate between ἐπ. and ἄγνοια; *ibid.* 511 D, the "state of mind" (cf. Prof. Cornford, *Mind*, 1932, 50) ranked third after νοῦς and διάνοια. But in *Tht.* 187 A δοξάζειν = πραγματεύεσθαι περὶ τὰ ὄντα (cf. *CQ.* XXVII, 101, 1). Cf. also *Soph.* 264 A; *Phil.* 38 B. So Stenzel, *Stud. z. Entw.* 86: Plato "einmal eine δόξα der Verifizierung unfähige, ein andermal die mit dem λόγος zusammengehende, verifizierte δόξα meint". For δ. in Aristotle, cf. *EN.* 42 b 14; *An.* 428 a 19; *RP.* 311 b; in Plotinus, *Enn.* I, i, 9.

[2] *Luc.* 59.   [3] S. E. *AM.* VII, 141 sqq.

μόνον καὶ τί σὺν τῷ φαίνεσθαι ἔτι καὶ κατ' ἀλήθειαν ὑπόκειται, τουτέστι τὸν λόγον. Thus λόγος comes to the aid of ἐνάργεια and ἐνάργεια is the starting-point for λόγος. Nor can λόγος test ἐνάργεια without the help of sense-presentation: πάλιν συνεργοῦ δεῖται ὁ λόγος τῆς αἰσθήσεως (Plato's δ ό ξ η μετ' αἰσθήσεως δοξαστόν)· διὰ ταύτης γὰρ τὴν φαντασίαν παραδεχόμενος ποιεῖται τὴν νόησιν καὶ τὴν ἐπιστήμην τἀληθοῦς, ὥστε περιληπτικὸν αὐτὸν ὑπάρχειν τῆς τε ἐναργείας καὶ τῆς ἀληθείας, ὅπερ ἴσον ἐστὶ τῷ καταληπτικόν.

This method of treating Plato is typically Antiochean. Antiochus, though head of the Platonic School, was prepared to criticize Plato and the Old Idealists for not remaining sensationalists.[1] Sensation must not be denied its place. It is the first step of the ladder, of which the last step leads to philosophic knowledge. Between the two come Universal Notions, discursive reason, and demonstration, but each of them depends on particular sense-experiences. "Efficiuntur notitiae rerum.... Eo cum accessit ratio (λόγος) argumentique conclusio (ἀπόδειξις) rerumque innumerabilium multitudo (τὰ κατὰ μέρος ἄπειρα[2]) tum et perceptio eorum apparet et eadem ratio perfecta his gradibus (ἐπιβάθραι[3]) ad sapientiam[4] pervenit."[5] Antiochus, if he employed the terms νόησις and ἐπιστήμη, did not recognize with Plato and Aristotle[6] a νοῦς which is capable of immediate intuition and entirely independent of sense-perception.

It has been shown that the Antiochean use of the term λόγος is two-fold, since λόγος is δόξα when dealing with sensibles and ἐπιστήμη when it operates with the intelligibles which it has derived from sense-experience. The appearance of λόγος δοξαστικός and λόγος ἐπιστημονικός in the treatise under examination is proof of

[1] *Fin.* IV, 42. Hirzel (III, 503, note to 500) rightly regards this as an Antiochean criticism of Plato.

[2] Borrowing the phrase used in *Did.* 78, 4–5.

[3] Cf. Clem. *Strom.* II, 13, 3: ἀλλ' ἡ μὲν αἴσθησις ἐπιβάθρα τῆς ἐπιστήμης, ἡ πίστις δὲ διὰ τῶν αἰσθητῶν ὁδεύσασα ἀπολείπει τὴν ὑπόληψιν κτα. The Plotinian ἐπαναβαίνειν ἀεὶ εἰς ἄπειρον (III, vi, 1) is a criticism of Stoic epistemology.

[4] Reid suggests as a translation "true form of philosophy".

[5] Cf. p. 32, *supra.* Locke's *Hum. Under.* II, i, 2 affords an excellent parallel.

[6] But Aristotle's epistemology is closer to the Stoic-Antiochean than Plato's is (cf. Ross, 54–5).

a measure of agreement between its author and Antiochus. Due allowance must, however, be made for the fundamentally different ways in which they explain νοῦς, νόησις and νοητά. For our writer ἐπιστήμη and δόξα have no common starting-point. Certainly δόξα is based on αἴσθησις, but the source of genuine knowledge (ἐπιστήμη)[1] is the intuitive apprehension of transcendent Ideas (νόησις τοῦ νοῦ νοοῦντος τὰ νοητά), which may be said to be transformed into ἐπιστήμη after the soul's incarnation.[2]

Yet, notwithstanding this important difference, our writer's epistemology and that of Antiochus are strikingly similar, as the following comparison will show:[3]

οἱ περὶ τὸν Ἀριστοτέλη καὶ Θεόφραστον καὶ κοινῶς οἱ Περιπατητικοί, διττῆς οὔσης κατὰ τὸ ἀνωτάτω τῆς τῶν πραγμάτων φύσεως, διττὸν τὸ κριτήριον ἀπολείπουσιν, αἴσθησιν μὲν τῶν αἰσθητῶν, νόησιν δὲ τῶν νοητῶν, κοινὸν δὲ ἀμφοτέρων, ὡς ἔλεγεν ὁ Θεόφραστος,[5] τὸ ἐναργές...ἀπὸ τῶν αἰσθητῶν κινεῖται ἡ αἴσθησις,[6] ἀπὸ δὲ τῆς κατὰ ἐνάργειαν περὶ τὴν αἴσθησιν κινήσεως ἐπιγίνεταί τι κατὰ ψυχὴν κίνημα...ὅπερ μνήμη τε καὶ φαντασία καλεῖται παρ' αὐτοῖς, μνήμη μὲν τοῦ περὶ τὴν αἴσθησιν πάθους, φαντασία δὲ τοῦ ἐμποιήσαντος τῇ αἰσθήσει τὸ πάθος αἰσθητοῦ, πρὸς ὃ καὶ ὁμοιότητα σῴζει.

Did. 54, 22:
διττὸς δὲ καὶ οὗτος,[4] ὁ μὲν περὶ τὰ νοητά, ὁ δὲ περὶ τὰ αἰσθητά.

Did. 54, 36:
ἀπ' αὐτοῦ (sc. αἰσθητοῦ) αἴσθησις ἡμῖν καὶ ἀπὸ ταύτης μνήμη. [(*Luc.* 30) "Naturalem vim habet (mens) quam intendit ad ea quibus movetur. Itaque alia visa sic arripit, ut his statim utatur: aliqua recondit; e quibus memoria oritur. Cetera autem similitudinibus construit...."]

---

[1] Also γνῶσις, 52, 26. Cf. ἐπ. ἁπλῆ in *Tht. Komm.* 15.
[2] 55, 27. Cf. "Platonic" *Deff.* 414 A.
[3] S. E. VII, 216 sqq. (condensed), with which Hirzel failed to compare *Did.*   [4] λόγος ἀνθρώπῳ δυνατός.
[5] fr. XXVII Wimmer (but cf. Hirzel, III, 508–9). See also fr. XIII (= Clem. *Strom.* II, 9): τὴν αἴσθησιν ἀρχὴν εἶναι πίστεως.
[6] As in Aristotle, *An.* 429 a 1.

[(Ant. S. E. *AM.* vii, 162) δυοῖν ἀντιλαμβανόμεθα, ἑνὸς μὲν αὐτῆς τῆς ἀλλοιώσεως, τουτέστι τῆς φαντασίας, δευτέρου δὲ τοῦ τὴν ἀλλοίωσιν ἐμποιήσαντος.]

τοῦτο δὲ πάλιν τὸ κίνημα, (§221) ὅπερ μνήμη τε καὶ φαντασία καλεῖται, εἶχεν ἐν ἑαυτῷ τρίτον ἐπιγινόμενον ἄλλο κίνημα τὸ τῆς λογικῆς φαντασίας, κατὰ κρίσιν λοιπὸν καὶ προαίρεσιν τὴν ἡμετέραν συμβαῖνον, ὅπερ κίνημα διάνοιά τε καὶ νοῦς προσαγορεύεται, οἷον ὅταν τις προσπεσόντος κατ' ἐνάργειαν Δίωνος πάθῃ πως³ τὴν αἴσθησιν καὶ τραπῇ, ὑπὸ δὲ τοῦ περὶ τὴν αἴσθησιν πάθους ἐγγένηταί τις αὐτοῦ τῇ ψυχῇ φαντασία, ἣν καὶ μνήμην πρότερον ἐλέγομεν καὶ ἴχνει παραπλήσιον ὑπάρχειν, ἀπὸ δὲ ταύτης τῆς φαντασίας ἑκουσίως ἀναϲωγραφῇ αὐτῷ καὶ ἀναπλάσσῃ⁴ φάντασμα, καθάπερ τὸν γενικὸν ἄνθρωπον. τὸ γὰρ

Did. 55, 7: κατά τινα ὁμοιότητα... 54, 29: αἴσθησίς ἐστι πάθος ψυχῆς,¹ διὰ σώματος ἀπαγγελτικὸν προηγουμένως τῆς πεπονθυίας δυνάμεως. δόξα δέ ἐστι συμπλοκὴ μνήμης καὶ αἰσθήσεως.² ὁπόταν γὰρ ἐντύχωμεν αἰσθητῷ τινι πρῶτον ...ἔπειτα ἐντύχωμεν τῷ αὐτῷ πάλιν αἰσθητῷ, τὴν προϋποκειμένην μνήμην συντίθεμεν τῇ ἐκ δευτέρου γενομένῃ αἰσθήσει καὶ ἐν ἑαυτοῖς λέγομεν φέρε Σωκράτης, ἵππος...καὶ τοῦτο καλεῖται δόξα. *Did.* 54, 31: ὁπόταν ἐν τῇ ψυχῇ διὰ τῶν αἰσθητηρίων κατὰ τὴν αἴσθησιν τύπος ἐγγένηται, ὅπερ ἐστὶν αἴσθησις.

Did. 55, 12: ὅταν δὲ τὰ δοξασθέντα ἐξ αἰσθήσεως καὶ μνήμης ἀναπλάσασα⁴ ἡ ψυχὴ τῇ διανοίᾳ ἀποβλέπῃ εἰς ταῦτα ὥσπερ εἰς ἐκεῖνα, ἀφ'

¹ The Stoic view (*SVF.* II, 54) denied by Plotinus (III, vi, 1, 1, IV, iii, 26). Chalc., *in Tim.* 194, follows *Tim.* 40 A: αἴσθησις ἐκ παθημάτων.

² *Did.* 54, 35. Arist. *An.* 428 a 28 writes: ἐκ τῆς τοῦ λευκοῦ δόξης καὶ αἰσθήσεως ἡ συμπλοκὴ φαντασία ἐστί (cf. 432 a 11). Plato has σ. εἰδῶν, on which cf. Stenzel, *Dial.* 65 sqq.

³ See Antiochus in § 161: (αἴσθησις) τραπεῖσα καὶ πως παθοῦσα κατὰ τὴν τῶν ἐναργῶν ὑπόπτωσιν (Antiochus interprets Carneades); Aristocles, *PE.* 768 B: ὑπ' ἐκείνων (sc. τῶν πραγμάτων) αὐτοὶ διατιθέμεθά πως. Cf. *AM.* vii, 162 (Antiochus's actual words).

⁴ In Aristotle (624 b 18) the verb has no psychological importance. Aenesidemus (Phot. *Bibl.* 212, 170 b 28), probably referring to Antiochus and Philo of Larissa, declares contemporary philosophers ἀναπλάσαι δόξας. Plotinus has φαντασίας οἷον ἀναπλάττουσι (vi, viii, 3).

δὴ τοιοῦτο κίνημα τῆς ψυχῆς κατὰ διαφόρους ἐπιβολὰς οἱ Περιπατητικοὶ τῶν φιλοσόφων διάνοιάν τε καὶ νοῦν ὀνομάζουσι, κατὰ μὲν τὸ δύνασθαι διάνοιαν, κατὰ δὲ ἐνέργειαν νοῦν.² (§ 226) φαίνεται πρῶτα κριτήρια τῆς τῶν πραγμάτων γνώσεως ἥ τε αἴσθησις καὶ ὁ νοῦς, ἡ μὲν ὀργάνου τρόπον ἔχουσα, ὁ δὲ τεχνίτου.³

ὧν ἐγένετο, ἀναζωγράφησιν τὸ τοιοῦτο ὁ Πλάτων καλεῖ, ἔσθ' ὅτε δὲ καὶ φαντασίαν.¹

Did. 54, 28: ἐπιστήμης τῆς περὶ τὰ νοητὰ καὶ δόξης τῆς περὶ τὰ αἰσθητὰ ἀρχαὶ νόησις καὶ αἴσθησις.

Here the number of resemblances is sufficient to justify the assumption that the general theory of the transition from sense-perception to knowledge which appears in the *Didaskalikos* is borrowed from Antiochus. Yet the passages by no means agree in every detail of terminology. Thus, for example, on the Antiochean view φαντασία is that which produces μνήμη. But in the *Didaskalikos* it is that which results from μνήμη.⁴ Moreover φαντασία is there equivalent to what Antiochus regards as νοῦς. The fact is significant. For our writer does not assent to the view that νοῦς is simply the actualization of what is first of all potential. For him νοῦς is strictly the active principle, νοῦς ποιητικός, which already knows all intelligible objects, and which therefore enables the instrumental principle, λόγος φυσικός, to perform its function. The activity of νοῦς is νόησις: νοῦ ἐνέργεια θεωροῦντος τὰ πρῶτα νοητά.⁵ And these intelligible objects are judged by νόησις in combination with ὁ ἐπιστημονικὸς λόγος.⁶

¹ Cf. *Soph.* 264 B.
² But active reason for Aristotle is not a product of passive reason. With the present passage cf. Ar. Did. *DDG.* 456, 5 sqq.
³ See p. 48, *supra.*
⁴ Yet μνήμη is inconsistently used, being later (55, 29) identified with ἐπιστήμη ἁπλῆ. And φαντασία later (78, 22) is put on a lower level than λογισμός and κρίσις (cf. φ. as πληγὴ ἀλόγου ἔξωθεν in Plot. 1, viii, 15).
⁵ 55, 18.
⁶ 56, 4–5. In 69, 21–2 both the intelligible and the sensible order of reality can be apprehended by νόησις. Galen, *HP.* 733, 14 holds that the two orders need different criteria (cf. Plut. *An. Pr.* 1024 F).

Another point is noteworthy. In the *Didaskalikos* sense-perception is described as a τύπος ἐν τῇ ψυχῇ. Hirzel, in tracing the passage which we have quoted from Sextus Empiricus back to Antiochus, lays emphasis on the fact that there sense-perception is termed not—as by the Stoics—an impression or imprint (τύπος, τύπωσις), but—as by Aristotle—a movement in the soul (κίνημα κατὰ ψυχήν).[1] From this Hirzel infers that Antiochus rejected the Stoic name. The fact that in the *De Memoria*[2] Aristotle himself describes what is produced by perception as a kind of impression of the percept which the movement resulting from sensation stamps upon the soul (ἡ γὰρ γινομένη κίνησις ἐνσημαίνεται οἷον τύπον τινά), leads Hirzel to suppose that when in the *Lucullus*[3] the Antiochean School is represented as approving of Zeno's definition: "Visum impressum effictumque...id nos a Zenone definitum rectissime dicimus", all that is meant is that Antiochus took Zeno in an Aristotelean sense.

Hirzel is forced to this explanation by reason of his treating *Adversus Mathematicos* VII, 227–42, as Antiochean throughout. But the sceptical criticisms which are brought against the Stoic theory, whether it be formulated by Zeno, Cleanthes, Chrysippus, or platonizing Stoics, are much more appropriate in the mouth of Sextus himself or—since this is also possible—of Aenesidemus.[4] Antiochus, we may be quite sure, had not the wish thus to criticize Stoic epistemology, but, while following Aristotle in his view of sense-perception as a combination of κίνησις and τύπος, at the same time maintained the Stoic doctrine of τύπωσις or ἀλλοίωσις ἐν ψυχῇ.[5] No real importance need, therefore, be given to the circumstance that the term τύπος is chosen in the *Didaskalikos* in place of the κίνημα of Sextus Empiricus. Antiochus doubtless

[1] *Op. cit.* III, 517.

[2] 450 a 25 sqq. Plotinus, as Bréhier remarks, in *Enn.* IV, vi, finds the Aristotelean no better than the Stoic view.

[3] § 18 (*SVF.* I, 59).

[4] Aenesidemus is negatively influenced by Antiochus, e.g. his Fifth Trope is a reply to the view expressed in *Luc.* 19. Cf. also his scepticism (Ph. Al. *Ebriet.* 172; S. E. *Hyp.* I, 38) about κρῖνον and κρινόμενον.

[5] Posidonius doubtless differed in holding that ἡ αἴσθησίς ἐστιν οὐκ ἀλλοίωσις ἀλλὰ διάγνωσις ἀλλοιώσεως (see Jaeger, *Nemes.* 15 sqq.; I. Heinemann, II, 457).

used either with complete indifference, justifying himself on the ground that though they employ other terms the Stoics say the same things as the Peripatetics, and *vice versa*.[1]

The equation of the Stoic φυσικὴ ἔννοια and the Platonic πτέρωμα ψυχῆς or ἐπιστήμη ἁπλῆ recalls what Antiochus asserted to be the doctrine of Plato's successors: "Scientiam nusquam esse censebant nisi in animi notionibus atque rationibus."[2] But again, whereas in the *Didaskalikos* ἔννοιαι are regarded as constituent parts of the ἐπιστημονικὸς λόγος because they have been brought by the soul from the intelligible into the sensible world, Antiochus maintained that they are the result of generalization from the experience of particular things belonging to the sensible world: ὁ ἀθροισμὸς τῶν τοιούτων τοῦ νοῦ φαντασμάτων καὶ ἡ συγκεφαλαίωσις[3] τῶν ἐπὶ μέρους εἰς τὸ καθόλου[4] ἔννοια καλεῖται.[5] Antiochus, as we have seen, argued that knowledge is the result of combining these general notions.[6] But that he regarded these as due to the recollection[7] of pre-natal Ideas appears most improbable.[8] It has been suggested by Theiler[9] that *Tusculans* I, 57 gives the Antiochean view. But to reject Posidonius—to whom this passage has been assigned by Schmekel[10]—in favour of Antiochus, on the strength of a verbal resemblance between § 58 and *Posterior Academics* 30 is to neglect altogether the fact that Antiochus did not believe in the existence of what Plato calls τόπος νοητός, and obviously ranged himself on the side of Aristotle when the latter attacked Plato's theory of Ideas: "Aristoteles primus[11] species, quas

---

[1] Cf. *Tusc.* IV, 6.

[2] As Theiler, *VN.* 41, suggests, Antiochus could appeal to Platonic passages like *Meno* 86 A sqq.

[3] Cf. Clem. *Strom.* VIII, 17, and contrast Plot. VI, v, 1: (ἀρχή) ἡ οὐκ ἐκ τῶν καθέκαστα συγκεφαλαιωθεῖσα.

[4] Contrast *Did.* 78, 4.

[5] S. E. *AM.* VII, 224 (cf. 345 and Reid on *Luc.* 21). Cf. *Luc.* 30.

[6] *Luc.* 30. (In *De Leg.* I, 44: "communis intelligentia (synonymous with 'natura') notas nobis res efficit, easque in animis nostris inchoavit.")

[7] As in *Did.* 55, 29, where, however, μνήμη is inappropriate. Cf. *Phil.* 34 sqq. and Plot. IV, iii, 25.

[8] Cf. Reid on *Luc.* 30 and Madvig on *Fin.* v, 59.

[9] *VN.* 42.   [10] Severely dealt with by R. M. Jones.

[11] Cf. *An.* 429 a 27.

paullo ante dixi, labefactavit; quas mirifice Plato erat amplexatus, ut in his quiddam divinum[1] esse diceret."[2] Strache's view, namely that Antiochus identified the Platonic Ideas with the κοιναί ἔννοιαι of Stoicism,[3] is preferable to that of Theiler. And there is scarcely ground for believing with Theiler that Antiochus accepted the doctrine of the soul's immortality on which Plato lays so much emphasis in the *Meno*. It is likely that, under the influence of Panaetius, he abandoned it altogether, thus differing from Posidonius,[4] who held that the soul exists both before birth and after death.

There now appears a distinction between First and Second Intelligibles.[5] The First Intelligibles are the eternal archetypal Ideas or objective Realities, which it is important to remember are intuitively apprehended not only by incarnate but by discarnate souls also. The Second Intelligibles are explained as being τὰ εἴδη τὰ ἐπὶ τῇ ὕλῃ ἀχώριστα ὄντα τῆς ὕλης, and thus have an obvious resemblance to the λόγοι ἔνυλοι of Aristotle, though their derivation from Plato himself is not so clear.[6] The distinction can be exactly paralleled[7] in Seneca's 58th *Epistle*: (ex idea) "quod artifex trahit et operi suo imposuit idos est. Alterum exemplar est...alterum forma ab exemplari sumpta et operi imposita....Idos in opere est, idea extra opus, nec tantum extra opus est, sed ante opus."[8] Here the theory of the Idea is genuinely Platonic, and the definition which Seneca has already given ("Idea est eorum quae natura fiunt exemplum aeternum") is that which Xenocrates is known to have formulated.[9] Theiler argues for Antiochus instead of Posidonius, the source usually assumed.[10] But in the *Posterior Academics* the

[1] *Soph.* 248 E–249 A; *Tim.* 37 C. Cf. Plot. v, v, 1 (against Stoicism: cf. *SVF.* I, 65).

[2] *A. Po.* 33.

[3] *Ant.* 17. Strache's "geschwunden" (*ibid.* 26) is not too strong.

[4] Both of course agree in conceiving the soul unplatonically as corporeal.

[5] 55, 34 sqq. Cf. 64, 10.

[6] Chalc. 342 uses *Rep.* 510 B to explain *Tim.* 51–2. See also Plut. *An. Pr.* 1001 C sqq., 1023 B; Witt, *CQ.* XXV, 104.

[7] As Freudenthal noted (p. 279, repeating, however, Zeller's misprint).

[8] § 18. See further *Hermet.* 272, 329, 392 sqq. and *Enn.* I, viii, 8, IV, iii, 20, vii, 8, VI, vii, 33 E, etc.

[9] *Supra*, p. 16.   [10] After Schmekel.

Idea (*Species*) appears only in a logical sense,[1] not as a formal cause, and in the *Topics* nothing is said about the existence of what Seneca refers to as "idea extra opus", but *species* and εἶδος (in the Aristotelean sense) are treated as equivalent terms.[2]

Corresponding to the distinction between First and Second Intelligibles appears one between First and Second Sensibles, viz. between ποιότητες and ποιά. The germ of this can be discovered in Aristotle,[3] who draws a contrast between ποιότητες and ποιά τὰ κατὰ ταύτας παρωνύμως λεγόμενα,[4] and anticipates our writer in making λευκότης distinct from τὸ λευκὸν τὸ κεχρωσμένον.[5] Antiochus, as reported in the *Posterior Academics*, interpreted Aristotle in a Stoic sense: "Qualitatum sunt aliae principes, aliae ex iis ortae. Principes sunt uniusmodi et simplices. Ex iis autem ortae variae sunt, et quasi multiformes. Itaque aer...et ignis et aqua et terra prima sunt. Ex iis autem ortae animantium formae earumque rerum, quae gignuntur e terra."[6] Zeller justly says that Cicero must have found ποιότης in his original.[7] But whether Cicero correctly reproduced his original is rendered doubtful by what appears later: "Cum ita moveatur illa vis quam qualitatem esse diximus, et materiam ipsam totam penitus commutari putant (i.e. the Old Schools, in the judgment of Antiochus) et illa effici quae appellant qualia, e quibus...effectum esse mundum."[8] From this it would appear that the four elements were called not ποιότητες but ποιά, that the Efficient Cause informing indeterminate Matter[9] was described as ποιότης, and that the concrete body produced by the conjunction of Matter and Form (συνδύασμά τι, as it is termed in the *Didaskalikos*[10]) received the name of οἷον ποιότης or (as would be more natural) ποιόν τι: "Sed quod ex utroque id iam corpus et quasi qualitatem quamdam nominabant." Like the Stoics, Antiochus

---

[1] "Tertia deinde philosophiae pars, quae erat in ratione et in disserendo", § 30, supplies the keynote.

[2] § 30.

[3] Cf. Ross, 24, n. 1.   [4] *Cat.* 10 a 27.

[5] *Top.* 109 b 3 sqq. Cf. Plot. vi, iii, 9: "In the Category of ποιόν there are λευκόν and τὶ λευκόν"; iv, vii, 14: αὐτὸ τὸ χρῶμα, οὐ ποτὲ μὲν λευκόν, ποτὲ δὲ οὐ λευκόν.

[6] 26.   [7] *Gesch. g. P.* iii, i⁴, 626, n. 1.

[8] 28. Here, Reid notes, Cicero uses "qualitas" appropriately.

[9] 24, 27.   [10] 66, 2.

conceived qualities as being substances and bodies, whence (as Plutarch remarks[1]) much confusion is apt to arise. Our writer regards neither whiteness in abstraction nor the whitish hue in the object as a substance. But by adopting the name ἄθροισμα, he shows himself once again in harmony with Antiochus—especially when he applies it to the congeries of qualities which contribute to the existence of the Sensible World. The word seems to have been used by Antiochus as a technical term.[2]

There now follows an elaborate criteriological scheme corresponding to the divisions already made in the two realms of Existence. If Antiochus denied the existence of Intelligible Objects which the mind apprehends intuitively, then we cannot suppose that the details of this scheme are all derived from his epistemology. Indeed, when we read that intellection in conjunction with scientific reason apprehends First Intelligibles by an act of insight,[3] we shall do well to recall the fact that Cicero specifically rebukes Antiochus for preferring Stoic sensationalism to the idealism of the philosophers whose heir he claimed to be.[4] At the end of the chapter again appears the antithesis already discussed between theoretical and practical philosophy.[5] When moral judgments are said to be formed by making φυσικὴ ἔννοια the standard, we may compare the Antiochean view in *De Finibus* v: "(natura) dedit talem mentem, quae omnem virtutem accipere posset, ingenuitque sine doctrina notitias parvas..."[6]—to which our actions should conform.

C. LOGIC

In Chapter v we leave epistemology for formal logic. Although these two branches of philosophy are not explicitly distinguished and διαλεκτική earlier has been described in a phrase wide enough

[1] τὰς δὲ ποιότητας αὖ πάλιν οὐσίας καὶ σώματα ποιοῦσι ταῦτα δὲ πολλὴν ἔχει ταραχήν (*SVF*. II, 380).

[2] Found in *Theaet*. 157, and adopted by Epicurus (D. L. x, 62) and Chrysippus (*SVF*. II, 841). For Antiochus cf. S. E. *AM*. VII, 277 (*Luc*. 21), 224, 345 sqq. With the ἄθροισμα of *Did*. 56, 2, cf. Galen, *HP*. 672, 14: τὸ αἰσθητὸν τουτὶ πῦρ ἀθρόον ἄθροισμα.

[3] *Did*. 56, 5, after *Tim*. 28 A (see also Numen. *PE*. 526).

[4] *Luc*. 142–3.   [5] Cf. 56, 15 with *CD*. 8, 4 referred to p. 45, *supra*.

[6] § 59 (cf. *CD*. 19, 3). Similar is *Luc*. 24. A Platonic basis for *Did*. 56, 18 could be found in *Phaedo* 76 D.

to include epistemology as ἡ τοῦ λόγου θεωρία,[1] yet both there and here the meaning of διαλεκτική appears to be strictly confined to logic. In accordance with the classification in Chapter III, Platonic division comes first and Aristotelean syllogism last. Division must show us what a thing is, before we consider a thing's properties. That this must be the order of inquiry was recognized both by Plato[2] and by Aristotle,[3] the latter pointing out the necessity of deciding the That before the What. The lines laid down by Aristotle were followed by Antiochus: "Aut sitne, aut quid sit, aut quale sit, quaeritur."[4] The sentence with which the chapter before us opens may be compared with an utterance of Varro preserved by Saint Augustine: "Nihil prodest hominis alicuius medici nomen formamque nosse, et quod sit medicus ignorare."[5]

Our writer proceeds[6] to say that the What may be revealed either *a priori* by division and definition, or *a posteriori*[7] by analysis. With this should be studied Chapter VI of Clement's Book on Logic, which we have already brought into connexion with Antiochus. In that chapter we have also found the three most important of the five kinds of διαίρεσις which are now enumerated in the *Didaskalikos*. These are: (1) of a genus into species, (2) of a whole into parts, (3) of a word into its several meanings, (4) of accidents into subjects, (5) of subjects into accidents. When we set this side by side with a passage from the *De Divisione* of Boethius,[8] we see that

---

[1] 53, 23. Sinko and the early editors translate λ. here by "sermo" (Sinko comparing Apul. 86, 5: "loquendi ratio"). But λ. must mean (as Cicero translates λ. in *A. Po.* 32) "oratio ratione conclusa", i.e. must be both ἐνδιάθετος and προφορικός. For the complete phrase cf. S. E. *AM.* VII, 112: τὴν κατὰ τὸν φιλόσοφον λόγον θεωρίαν; the title of Galen's treatise περὶ τῆς κατὰ Πλάτωνα λογικῆς θεωρίας (cf. *SVF.* II, 248); Plot. III, viii, 3 (φύσις τὴν θεωρίαν) τὴν ἐκ λόγου οὐκ ἔχει.

[2] *Phdr.* 237 B; Cic. *Fin.* II, 4. Cf. *Prol.* 147, 5; Stob. II, 42 (Ar. Did.).

[3] *An. Post.* II, 1.

[4] *Top.* 82. Cf. *Part. Orat.* 33. 62. Clem. *Strom.* VIII, vi.

[5] *CD.* 4, 22.　　[6] For the terms used in 56, 25, cf. Porph. *Isag.* 9, 12.

[7] Theiler (*VN.* 6) compares "retro legere", Sen. *Ep.* 58, 8. A better parallel appears in Galen, *HP.* 793.

[8] Migne, *PG.* 64, 877 B sqq. See further Baumstark, *Aristoteles bei den Syrern* (*UPG.* 560–1), 196; Cic. *Or.* III, 114 (*Div. Arist.* p. 62 Mutschmann), 115 (*DL.* III, 80–1); Ar. Did. Stob. II, 143; *DDG.* 607; S. E. *Hyp.* II, 213. Markedly different is Diog. Bab. fr. 25 v. Arnim.

the list of possible kinds of διαίρεσις may include, in addition to those mentioned in the *Didaskalikos*, that of an accident into accidents, which is the third species of *divisio secundum accidens*: "Huius est triplex modus, unus cum subiectum in accidentia separamus, alius cum accidens in subiecta dividimus, tertius cum accidens in accidentia secamus." This species is likewise admitted by the scholiast on Dionysius's *Grammatike*, whose scheme we have previously compared (p. 37) with Clement's.

Accepting Prantl's conjecture that Boethius was indirectly dependent on the Peripatetic Andronicus, we are not thereby prevented from assuming that Andronicus in his turn adopted the scheme in some form or other from the Academy, which (as we have seen) was the real home of διαίρεσις. Like other members of his School,[1] such as Boethus of Sidon, Aristo of Alexandria, and Staseas of Naples, Andronicus was eclectic. He followed Xenocrates in positing the two categories καθ' αὐτό and πρός τι,[2] and placed θερμόν in the category of ποιά or (borrowing a Stoic term) πώς ἔχοντα,[3] but θερμαντικόν in that of ποιητικά[4] or πρός τι.[5] This sort of eclecticism would hardly have been possible if Andronicus had not been affected by Antiochus.

The method of definition *per genus et differentiam*, which is next described, is similar to the dichotomy on which Plato himself laid emphasis in the later *Dialogues*.[6] The example chosen is of interest for our purpose. The genus is ζῷον, its differentiae being λογικόν and ἄλογον. The subaltern genus ζῷον λογικόν is differentiated as θνητόν and ἀθάνατον, whereby the *infima species*, ἄνθρωπος, is reached, since ζῷον λογικὸν θνητόν is coextensive with ἄνθρωπος, the *definiendum*. Two passages deserve to be brought forward for comparison. One has already been pointed out by Freudenthal,

---

[1] And perhaps certain Neopythagoreans too (S. E. *AM*. x, 261, 282). So Schmekel, 437, followed by *UPG*. 517.

[2] Xen. fr. 12. [3] *SVF*. ii, 369, 399.

[4] Contrast *Did*. 66, 31. [5] Simp. *Cat*. p. 263.

[6] Taylor observes (*PMW*. 347) that διαφορά first occurs in the Aristotelean sense in *Theaet*. 208. Plato, *Polit*. 262 sqq., recognizes the importance of determining the *fundamentum divisionis* prior to the dichotomy, and the distinction between εἶδος and μέρος (so in Cic. *Top*. 31).

who calls it Stoic but does not explain why.[1] This occurs in Sextus Empiricus, *Adversus Mathematicos* VII, 277: ὁ ἄνθρωπος οὔτε ᾳ̃όν ἐστι ψιλῶς οὔτε λογικὸν κατ' ἰδίαν οὔτε θνητὸν κατὰ περιγραφήν, ἀλλὰ τὸ ἐξ ἁπάντων ἄθροισμα. With this and with the text before us should be compared *Lucullus* 21. There the Antiochean theory of inference from the particular to the universal is under discussion, but, instead of descending step by step from the genus to the species, we move upwards (κάτωθεν ἀναλυτικῶς, to borrow a phrase already used in the *Didaskalikos*) by collecting attributes each of which is wider than the *definiendum* but the summation of which is coextensive with it, and therefore gather the differentiae in the reverse order. Nevertheless, in all three passages each step of the process corresponds, and the logician perceives the Tree of Porphyry.

In this account there is nothing for which a foundation cannot be discovered in Plato's writings,[2] apart from the use of certain terms which are either unknown to him (e.g. ἄμεσοι προτάσεις, αὐτοκίνητος[3]), or not employed by him in a technical sense (e.g. τὸ ζητούμενον, ἐναργές). The terms ἄμεσοι προτάσεις and ἐνάργεια remind us of what we have already encountered in Clement of Alexandria. In Clement we may also find τὸ ὁμολογούμενον and τὸ ᾳητούμενον used as technical terms.[4] In the present passage ἐναργές is associated with scientific axiom (what the writer describes as τὸ πρῶτον καὶ ὁμολογούμενον), whereas Plato is wont to apply it to δοξαστόν rather than to ἐπιστητόν.[5] Antiochus, perhaps following Theophrastus,[6] made τὸ ἐναργές the criterion of Sensibles and

[1] p. 281. The passage is not included by v. Arnim in *SVF*. Cf. also S. E. *AM.* IX, 338; Arist. *Met.* 38 a 8, 19; Clem. *Strom.* VIII, 17, 4. 18, 7; and Porphyry, *Quinque Voces*, p. 5.

[2] Cf. Prof. Cornford, *Mind*, 1932, 40 sqq.

[3] Found in Arist. *Phys.* 258 a 2. Apparently unused by Xenocrates (fr. 60).

[4] *Strom.* VIII, 3, 3; 6, 5. Plato often has τὰ ὁμολογούμενα.

[5] Cf. *Did.* 62, 12; *Rep.* 511 A: εἰκόσι δὲ χρωμένην...ὡς ἐναργέσι δεδοξασμένοις (yet these belong to geometry and kindred τέχναι). *Ibid.* 486 C; *Polit.* 286 A. See also Hirzel (III, 504, n. to 500) on *Tht.* 179 C; *Ph.* 83 C.

[6] p. 53, n. 5, *supra.* That ἐναργές was used by Carneades is denied by Zeller (against Hirzel). Cf. *RP.* 439 a. For ἐνάργεια in Stoicism see F. H. Sandbach, *CQ.* XXIV, 50.

Intelligibles alike,[1] and it acquires an importance in his theory of knowledge which it does not possess in the Platonic.

The chapter ends with a brief mention of ἐπαγωγή. Induction means either the process of reasoning from parallel cases, i.e. inference by analogy, or the inference from particular to universal, and its importance lies in its power to awaken the Innate Ideas which are dormant within us: χρησιμωτάτη δὲ ἡ ἐπαγωγή εἰς τὸ ἀνακινεῖν τὰς φυσικὰς ἐννοίας. The Platonic text on which this is based is without doubt *Meno* 85 sqq. Significant, however, is the combination of the Platonic ἀνακινεῖν, ἐπαγωγή, a characteristically Aristotelean term,[2] and the φυσικαὶ ἔννοιαι of Stoicism. Antiochus, regarding the inductive method as indispensable[3] and holding that Nature has implanted in the human mind the seeds from which knowledge may be developed,[4] agreed with Stoicism that these become Ideas as the result of training, which only operations based on sense-perceptions can supply.[5]

In Chapter VI the theory of syllogism is expounded with a care which in a Platonist is remarkable. Without the least apology our writer, after having stated that the method is used by Plato, introduces Aristotle's well-known definition of syllogism,[6] but nowhere recognizes that the formal study of the latter is entirely due to Aristotle. This attitude is obviously not inspired by any desire for exegetical originality. It is simply a part of the particular Platonic tradition followed in the *Didaskalikos*. And this tradition we have found to go back to Antiochus.

The treatment of categorical syllogism is quite in the manner of Aristotle himself. By regarding Plato's dialectical method of eliciting a conclusion by means of interrogation as essentially that of Aristo-

[1] *Fin.* IV, 8; *Luc.* 17, 45, etc.

[2] ἐπάγειν in Plato (e.g. *Polit.* 278 A) is not without importance. See also *supra*, p. 9, n. 3; Ross, 40, n. 1. Stoicism seems to have preferred ἀναλογία to ἐπαγωγή (cf. *SVF.* II, 87).

[3] Note that philosophy (*Tusc.* IV, 84) consists "ex rationum collatione" (cf. also § 27; *Top.* 42).

[4] *Fin.* 59 (cf. 43; *CD.* 19, 3); 18.

[5] *Ibid.* III, 33 (= *SVF.* III, 72; cf. *Luc.* 30).

[6] 58, 17; *An. Pr.* 24 b 18. Aristotle himself asserts: περὶ δὲ τὸ συλλογίζεσθαι παντελῶς οὐδὲν εἴχομεν πρότερόν τι λέγειν, ἀλλ᾽ ἢ τριβῇ ζητοῦντες πολὺν χρόνον ἐπονοῦμεν, *Soph. El.* 184 b 1.

telean syllogism,[1] we have no difficulty in finding syllogisms in each of the three figures recognized by Aristotle.[2] Thus the *First Alcibiades*[3] supplies an example of one in the first mood of the first figure (*Barbara*). Here as in Aristotle the major proposition follows the minor,[4] but none of the three propositions is overtly quantified: (πάντα) τὰ δίκαια καλά, (πάντα) τὰ καλὰ ἀγαθά, (πάντα) τὰ δίκαια ἄρα ἀγαθά.[5] The same syllogism is by Sextus Empiricus[6] attributed to "those who belong to the Peripatetic School", meaning doubtless the younger Peripatetics. To illustrate the two other categorical figures, the *Parmenides* is used,[7] and supplies two of the three hypothetical syllogisms.

This type was first explicitly co-ordinated with the categorical by Theophrastus, who evolved three figures.[8] The second and third figures change places—a transposition which our author candidly acknowledges is not in accordance with the general view[9]— and the middle term in the first and the second (i.e. the third Theophrastean) figure is itself a disjunctive proposition. Otherwise the scheme of Theophrastus is faithfully followed. (1) If A is true, then B (viz. neither x nor y nor γ) is true. If B is true, then C is true. If C is true, then D is true. Therefore if A is true, D is true. (2) If A is true, then B (viz. neither x nor y) is true. If C is true, then B is not true (viz. either x or y). Therefore if A is true, C is not true. (3) If A is true, B is true. If A is not true, C is true. (Therefore if C is true, B is not true.)[10] At what date Platonists

[1] Cf. *An. Pr.* 24 a 24 sqq. (connecting *Met.* 04 b 25).

[2] The fourth figure was added by Galen (cf. Prantl, 570), who is not, however, properly speaking its inventor (cf. *UPG.* 563).

[3] Some Platonists are found τὸν Ἀλκιβιάδην διαιροῦντες εἰς τοὺς δέκα συλλογισμοὺς τοὺς ἐν αὐτῷ παραδιδομένους. (*Prol.* Herm. VI, 213.)

[4] As pointed out by Leibnitz, *De Arte Comb.* II, 24.

[5] § 115.   [6] *Hyp.* II, 163.

[7] Cf. E. R. Dodds, *CQ.* XXII, 135.   [8] See Prantl, 380.

[9] κατὰ τὸ δεύτερον ὑ. σχῆμα, ὃ οἱ πλεῖστοι τρίτον φασί, 59, 10–11. Cf. l. 15.

[10] *Ph.* 74–6. The use of δυνάμει and, assuming the text to be complete, the fact that the conclusion is not actually drawn, suggest the writer's consciousness that the choice of this passage might be criticized. The insertion of Plato's διὰ βίου after ἐπιστάμεθα would have removed a certain superficial awkwardness (for μάθησις-ἀνάμνησις cf. 77, 37).

first became interested in the theory of syllogism we cannot say.[1] But we may conjecture that an interest was manifested by Antiochus, and that he used not only the Aristotelean categorical but also the Theophrastean hypothetical syllogism.[2]

The "mixed" hypothetical syllogism (μικτός, the *modus ponens* or *tollens* of later logic) which is now illustrated, and which is subsequently used twice,[3] was the discovery of Theophrastus,[4] from whom it was borrowed by the Stoics.[5] The formula τὸ δὲ ἡγούμενον, τὸ ἄρα λῆγον, is an indication that not Theophrastus but Stoicism exercises influence here. *Topica* 54 and *De Finibus* IV, 55 and 68 show that Antiochus favoured this form of reasoning.

We are now told that the purpose of the *Euthydemus* is to expose fallacies *in dictione* and *extra dictionem*[6]—we have already heard of the use in this dialogue[7] of "eristic" syllogism—and that, in the *Parmenides*[8] and elsewhere, Plato "hinted at the ten categories". Plutarch found them in the *Timaeus*,[9] and orthodox Platonism generally accepted them, or rather subordinated them to its own two categories, καθ' αὐτό and πρός τι. The Peripatetics showed a similar tendency. Andronicus, as we have seen,[10] followed Xenocrates in making καθ' αὐτό and πρός τι his two ultimate categories. Boethus of Sidon found the latter category in the *Sophist* (255 C) and the *Republic* (438 A).[11] Aristo, who left the School of Antiochus to become a Peripatetic, could not determine whether to regard the Universe as falling within the category of τὰ πρός τι,[12] or as being devoid of relation, since nothing is external to it (i.e. as being καθ'

[1] In Plut. 387 hypothetical syllogism seems accepted as part of the Platonic tradition.

[2] Stoicism did not use ὑποθετικόν in the Peripatetic sense (see Prantl, 522).

[3] 63, 33; 64, 11.   [4] Prantl, 385.   [5] *Ibid.* 470.

[6] See p. 9, *supra*. For Ant. *Fin.* IV, 57.

[7] In the σχῆμα Θρασυμάχου called ἀνατρεπτικός (cf. *Prol.* 48, 27).

[8] Of the One we cannot predicate: Essence (141 E), Quantity (150 B), Quality (137 D), Relation (146 B), Place (138 A), Time (141 A), Position (149 A), State (139 B), Activity and Passivity (139 B).

[9] See p. 3, n. 2, *supra* (*Tim.* 35 B).   [10] p. 62.

[11] See Prantl, 542–3.

[12] Prantl gibes at "die Albernheit seines Scholasticismus" (p. 546). Such remarks (see also pp. 83, 613) are themselves inept.

αὐτό). Adrastus explicitly subordinated the Aristotelean categories to those of the Academy.[1] In the *Didaskalikos* it is probable that a similar subordination is intended. For in Chapter IX the two fundamental categories are πρὸς αὐτό and πρός τι, the Idea being ὡς πρὸς αὐτὴν οὐσία and the Sensible World its product and correlate. If the present passage is to be taken seriously, then we must suppose that our writer, like Adrastus and Clement (*supra*, p. 38), following Antiochus, subsumes the ten Aristotelean categories under those of Platonism, by regarding the last nine as πρός τι or συμβεβηκότα.[2]

The remainder of the present chapter (59, 36–60, 34) is devoted to a discussion of the problem of Meaning, the *Cratylus* being for this purpose closely copied. Yet the way in which the discussion begins is reminiscent of Antiochus. Thus the opening phrase ὁ ἐτυμολογικὸς τόπος and the allusion to Plato's skill in defining and dividing (ἡ ὁριστικὴ καὶ διαιρετικὴ πραγματεία) suggest comparison with such Ciceronian passages as *Posterior Academics* 32,[3] and *De Finibus* II, 30.[4]

D. MATHEMATICS

The treatment of Mathematics so closely follows the lines of the *Republic*, that here no question of distinctively Antiochean doctrine arises. How seriously Antiochus studied Mathematics is hard to say. From *De Finibus* v we may infer that he gave Mathematics considerable attention.[5] Yet his pupil Varro, though explicitly recognizing the value of geometry,[6] strangely fails to mention any branch of Mathematics in the *Posterior Academics* 19–34. Elsewhere evidence is forthcoming that Antiochus, in the manner of Plato and the Stoa, insisted on the ethical and religious value of astronomy, and the same view appears in the *Didaskalikos*.[7] On similar grounds our writer eulogizes music,[8] and again the influence of Plato is

---

[1] p. 12, n. 7.   [2] Cf. *Did.* 56, 23.
[3] Cf. (Cic.) *Top.* 35. The words ἐτυμολογία and ἐτυμολογικός are characteristically Stoic (*SVF.* II, p. 9, l. 13, and n. 146).
[4] Cf. I, 22, III, 40.   [5] Cf. v, 9 and 51.
[6] § 6. Democritus would have done better, had he known some geometry (*Fin.* I, 20).
[7] *Fin.* IV, 11; *Did.* 61, 25–6.   [8] *Ibid.* 32–3.

fundamental. Yet again an Antiochean passage may be brought
forward for comparison. How much that we miss in music the
professional musician perceives! As soon as he hears the first note,
he can tell the name of the piece, though we do not even suspect it:
"primo inflatu tibicinis Antiopam esse aiunt, aut Andromacham,
cum id nos ne suspicemur quidem."[1] In this case, of course, the
aim is to prove "quanta vis sit in sensibus". We must not forget,
however, that for Antiochus *mens* and *sensus* mean the same thing.[2]
In both passages the main point is really the same, namely that the
particular sound which our ears perceive suggests to the mind a
conception which enables us to go beyond the sense-perception:
ἀπὸ τῶν ἀκουστῶν μεταβαίνειν ἐπ' ἐκεῖνα, ἃ ἔστιν ἰδεῖν μόνῳ τῷ
τῆς ψυχῆς λογισμῷ.[3] The remainder of the present chapter contains
nothing that adds to what we learn about Mathematics in Plato.

E. METAPHYSICS

In Chapter VIII we enter what is strictly the first department of
theoretical philosophy, τὸ θεολογικόν. The title—περὶ τῶν ἀρχῶν
τε καὶ τῶν θεολογικῶν θεωρημάτων—is an indication that the
subject to be discussed is rather metaphysics, or as Aristotle indifferently terms it πρώτη φιλοσοφία, φιλοσοφία, σοφία, θεολογική,
than "theology" in the narrower sense, which is, however, given
its due place (Chapter X). The Platonic doctrine of Matter (the
term ὕλη is of course not Platonic[4]) is carefully reproduced from
the *Timaeus*, since Matter requires to be considered before the two
other First Causes.[5] Here, even supposing we were able to find
detailed agreement between our writer and Antiochus, we should
not be justified, on that ground alone, in regarding him rather than
Plato as the source. But in fact, despite Theiler's special pleading,[6]
the doctrine set forth in the present chapter differs in more than
one important respect from that which, if correctly reported,

[1] *A. Po.* 20.   [2] *Ibid.* 30.   [3] *Did.* 61, 37 sqq.

[4] Baeumker (114, n. 1) points out that Plato uses ὕλη non-technically
in *Phil.* 54 c. Cf. also *Tim.* 69 A. "(Silvae) nomen dederunt auditores
Platonis, ipse enim nusquam silvae nomen ascripsit", says Chalcidius
in Tim. 308.

[5] Aristotle's Efficient and Final Causes are identified; the Platonic Idea
becomes the Formal Cause.   [6] *VN.* 38–9.

Antiochus foisted on Plato and the Old Academy (*Posterior Academics* 24–9). Theiler argues that Cicero's account of Antiochus's materialism is incorrect.[1] "Cicero hat in diesem Teil bedenklich flüchtig exzerpiert." But if Antiochus had posited *two other* First Principles besides Matter[2] Cicero would scarcely have excerpted his original so hastily as to write: "In eo quod efficeret, vim esse censebant: in eo autem quod efficeretur, materiam quamdam: in utroque tamen utrumque."[3] Whatever be the exact purport of the four last words, they leave no room for the transcendent God of the *Didaskalikos*. Antiochus in fact attempts to show the Old Academics and Peripatetics to have been as uncompromisingly materialistic as their successor Zeno of Citium. "Es bleibt der Platz für ein geistiges und göttliches Prinzip." But surely the Antiochean God is the Stoic πνεῦμα ἔμπυρον, ἀχώριστον τῆς ὕλης,[4] and utterly different from the δημιουργός of Plato,[5] or the πρῶτον κινοῦν ἀκίνητον of Aristotle, or the πρῶτος θεός of our writer.

In the present chapter we are told that Plato calls Matter Space. The statement refers to what Plato writes in *Timaeus* 52. That Plato's Receptacle was really conceived by him to be Space, and not an extended Mass, is the view of Zeller, and the one which modern criticism generally accepts.[6] The statement in the *Didaskalikos*, on this view, is justified. Later, however, as we shall see,

---

[1] "Der Abschnitt enthält nicht die materialistische Lehre, die Strache ...dort findet, und die *jede Brücke* zu den Vorstellungen *bei Seneca* (and the *Didaskalikos*) *unmöglich* machen würde" (italics mine).

[2] Cf. *Did.* 63, 10 sqq.   [3] *A. Po.* 24.

[4] *SVF.* II, 307. Boethus of Sidon (not to be confounded with the Peripatetic of the same name) among the Old Stoics is a striking exception. He denied that the Cosmos is divine or even animate, and placed God in the sphere of fixed stars (*ibid.* p. 265).

[5] For various estimates of Plato's "theology" see Cic. *ND.* I, 30; *DDG.* 567, 27 sqq.; ps.-Justin, *Cohort.* V, 31 E; Jackson, *JP.* 13, 34; Stewart, *PDI.* 59, 113; Constantin Ritter, *Platon* II, 770 sqq.; Taylor, *PMW.* 232, 288, 492.

[6] Cf. Baeumker, 136, etc. (B. denies, p. 156, that Plato's "Matter" is even δυνάμει σῶμα: not so our writer, 63, 7); A. E. Taylor, *ad loc.* Eva Sachs, p. 225, argues that the introduction of Matter is not to be separated from Plato's criticism of the Democritean doctrine of Elements, "und diese wiederum setzt einen Stoff voraus, nicht den blossen Baum". But Plato's Matter begins as Space (cf. *UPG.* 313).

our writer inconsistently declares that "Matter" prior to the beginning of the Universe was moving in disorder: (ὕλην) ἀτάκτως καὶ πλημμελῶς κινουμένην.[1]

If we may trust the *Posterior Academics*, Antiochus strove to retain the Platonic notion of Space as the Receptacle or Substrate. But he tended all the while to regard it as "Matter" in the Aristotelean or Stoic sense: "Subiectam putant omnibus sine ulla specie, atque carentem omni illa qualitate (cf. ὑποκείμενον and ἄμορφόν τε ὑπάρχειν καὶ ἄποιον καὶ ἀνείδεον in the *Didaskalikos*)...materiam quamdam, ex qua omnia expressa atque efficta sint." Doubtless Antiochus intended God or Force (*vis* = *animus   mundi* = *mens* = *sapientia perfecta* = *Deus*)[2] and Space, which are capable of mutual inherence ("in utroque utrumque"), to be distinct from the concrete body which they together produce ("quod ex utroque, id iam corpus...nominabant").[3] But actually his doctrine, as we have it in the *Posterior Academics*, has more in common with Stoic pantheism than with Plato's theory of the Receptacle. Agreement between the Ciceronian passage and the *Didaskalikos* merely shows that they have a common source in Plato, or in Aristotle.[4]

The second of the three ἀρχαί is the Idea, or Formal Cause. The Idea may be defined in five different ways. In relation to God, Man, Matter, and the Sensible World (ὡς πρός τι) it is respectively νόησις, νοητὸν πρῶτον, μέτρον, and παράδειγμα, while regarded *per se* (ὡς πρὸς αὑτήν) it is οὐσία. The first of these definitions is one of considerable interest.[5] Whether or not the view that God thinks the Ideas can be justified by passages in the *Dialogues* (among those who believe that it can are to be ranked Plotinus and his followers in antiquity, and in modern times Lutoslawski, Henry Jackson, and Constantin Ritter[6]), yet that even in the earliest days of Platonism such an interpretation of the Theory of Ideas was offered seems

---

[1] 67, 12 (*Tim.* 30 A).   [2] 29.   [3] 24.
[4] 63, 7 resembles *Gen. Corr.* 329 a 33; *Phys.* 191 a 7–12; Ar. Did. *DDG.* 448.
[5] It is to be observed that the term used is not νόημα but νόησις. Cf. also 64, 27, 37.
[6] *OGPL.* 477 (denied by Frazer, *Diss.* 87). *JP.* 11, 292; cf. 324. *Ke rngedanken plat. Ph.* 321. Lutoslawski (*OGPL.* 15 n., 25 n.) supplies bibliographical information.

quite clear. The Sicilian historian of the fourth century, Alkimos,[1] attributes to Plato the belief that every Idea is a Thought which is eternal and impassive, and therefore an Exemplar which exists in nature: ἔστι δὲ τῶν εἰδῶν ἓν ἕκαστον ἀίδιόν τε καὶ νόημα, καὶ πρὸς τούτοις ἀπαθές· διὸ καί φησιν[2] ἐν τῇ φύσει τὰς ἰδέας ἑστάναι, καθάπερ παραδείγματα.[3] An eternal thought will most naturally imply God as its thinker.[4] We may accordingly presume that the view of the Ideas as thoughts of God was held by some, though not all, members of the Academy who were contemporary with Alkimos. The use of παραδείγματα might even suggest Xenocrates himself, since the Idea was defined by him as παράδειγμα τῶν κατὰ φύσιν αἰώνιον. But though, doubtless, he derived the Ideas as μαθηματικά from the divine νοῦς or μονάς, Xenocrates did not anticipate Plotinus in maintaining ὅτι οὐκ ἔξω τοῦ νοῦ τὰ νοητά.[5] For he regarded the Dyad or World Soul, which he separated from the supreme Monad, as the Number in which the Ideas (μαθηματικά) are contained.[6] Yet, since he called both Monad and Dyad Gods, Xenocrates may be said to have held, in one sense, that the Ideas are contained in God. Of his influence on the later development of the doctrine there can be no doubt.

R. M. Jones has argued that the theory was suggested to the Platonists by the theology of Aristotle.[7] But he is too eager to trace the doctrine straight back to the Old Academy and Aristotle, without paying sufficient attention to the so-called Fifth Academy of Antiochus and his followers Varro and Arius Didymus.[8] According to him it is in the *Didaskalikos* that "the first full statement of the doctrine of the Ideas as the thoughts of God is found".[9] Not to mention Plato himself (e.g. νοῦς ἐνούσας ἰδέας τῷ ὃ ἔστι ζῷον, οἷαί τε ἔνεισι καὶ ὅσαι, καθορᾷ, *Timaeus* 39 E, which Plotinus

[1] So Schwartz in *Pauly-Wiss.* and Susemihl, I, 593.
[2] Probably Plato himself (*Parm.* 132 D).
[3] D. L. III, 13. Field (234) thinks Alkimos derived his whole account straight from the *Dialogues*, and from no other source.
[4] Even though it can be apprehended by the human mind.
[5] *Enn.* v, v.   [6] Fr. 60 H.
[7] *CP.* 21, 317–326.
[8] Eudorus and Arius Didymus he mentions but does not connect with Antiochus, whose name nowhere appears.
[9] p. 322.

assumed to be the very doctrine with which Jones deals[1]), there is extant a passage of Varro, which ought not to be overlooked in the present connexion. Reporting Varro's interpretation of the Samothracian mysteries Saint Augustine writes: "Dicit se ibi multis indiciis collegisse in simulacris aliud significare caelum, aliud terram, aliud exempla rerum, quas Plato appellat ideas; caelum Iovem, terram Iunonem, ideas Minervam vult intellegi; caelum a quo fiat aliquid, terram de qua fiat, exemplum secundum quod fiat."[2] Hirzel declares that, if Varro had been writing in this case from a Stoic or Cynic standpoint, he would not have introduced the Ideas, and that therefore he is following the Old Academy, as he does in Cicero.[3] It would be truer to say that the Ideas are indeed taken over from the Old Academy, but are given a Stoic meaning. Hirzel neglects the *Didaskalikos*, just as Jones neglects Varro. Theiler[4] is apparently the first to point out the parallel: οὐ μόνον ἔκ τινός ἐστι (sc. ὁ κόσμος) γεγονώς, ἀλλὰ καὶ ὑπό τινος,...καὶ πρός τι (viz. the Idea, which is the intellection of God, the Efficient Cause).[5]

Varro's identification of the Ideas with Minerva implies that Antiochus simply adapted them to Stoic theology, perhaps appealing to *Cratylus* 407. Stoicism had its own doctrine of God and His indwelling "Wisdom". Cornutus says that Athene may be regarded as ἡ τοῦ Διὸς σύνεσις, ἡ αὐτὴ οὖσα τῇ ἐν αὐτῷ προνοίᾳ,[6] while Heraclitus the Stoic, after alluding to the birth of the goddess from the head of Zeus, continues: τοῦτον γὰρ ἀπεφηνάμεθα τὸν χῶρον ἰδίως λογισμῶν εἶναι μητέρα.[7] These personifications, however, do not mean the abandonment of pantheism. Regarded as the Universe, the Deity is Zeus. Regarded as the guiding Reason of the Universe, the Deity is Athene. They are one in virtue of their corporeality. Elsewhere is revealed Varro's fundamentally Stoic conception of Minerva,[8] and Saint Augustine in another place criti-

---

[1] Cf. *Enn.* III, ix, 1, II, ix, 6 (where certain Gnostic platonizers are attacked for misinterpreting the Platonic text).

[2] *CD.* 7, 28. [3] Hirzel, III, 501 (n. to 499). [4] *VN.* 18–19.

[5] 63, 36–7. [6] 35, 7 Lang. Cf. *UPG.* 493.

[7] p. 31. This allegorical interpretation is obviously pre-Antiochean. Cf. Diog. Bab. fr. 33; Chrys. *SVF.* II, 908, etc.

[8] *CD.* 7, 16. Following a probably Varronian view, Arnobius (3, 31) declares that Aristotle "Minervam esse Lunam probabilibus argumentis demonstrat".

cizing what is obviously the Varronian belief writes: "Si aetheris partem superiorem Minervam tenere dicunt et hac occasione fingere poetas quod de Iovis capite nata sit, cur non ergo ipsa potius deorum regina deputatur, quod sit Iove superior?" [1] As for orthodox Stoicism, so for Varro, the divine Mind or Fire [2] viewed on a cosmic scale may be called Zeus, while under the aspect of πρόνοια the uppermost part, the "ether", may be referred to as Athene. In the *Posterior Academics* Varro, while not actually using the names Jupiter and Minerva, attributes a similar view to Antiochus.[3] The distinction is less clearly drawn than in the passages already examined. But that it does in fact exist is shown by the contrast which is made between *prudentia* and *necessitas*, i.e. between πρόνοια and εἱμαρμένη. These are both aspects of the Divine Mind. But, whereas in the terrestrial realm εἱμαρμένη (or as it sometimes appears to us τύχη) is omnipotent, the celestial sphere is controlled by πρόνοια.[4] If, then, Antiochus retained the name Idea, it meant to him exactly what πρόνοια meant to the Stoics, and it meant no more. The theory of the Ideas as thoughts of God in the *Didaskalikos* can owe nothing to Stoicism, though it certainly may owe much to Aristotle. Theiler's proposal to connect it with Antiochus [5] cannot therefore be favoured.

In his 65th *Epistle* Seneca, having stated that the Stoics admit only a single cause, namely the efficient, and enumerated the four causes of Aristotle, continues thus: "His quintam Plato adicit exemplar, quam ipse ideam vocat.... Haec exemplaria rerum omnium deus intra se habet numerosque universorum quae agenda sunt et modos mente complexus est: plenus his figuris est, quas Plato ideas appellat, immortales, immutabiles, infatigabiles. Itaque homines quidem pereunt, ipsa autem humanitas ad quam homo effingitur permanet; et hominibus laborantibus intereuntibus illa nihil patitur. Quinque ergo causae sunt, ut Plato dicit, id ex quo, id a quo, id

---

[1] *CD.* 4, 10.
[2] "V. ignem mundi animum facit", Tert. *ad Nat.* 2, 2 (Schmekel, 122, connects the passage with Posidonius). In *CD.* 7, 6: "Dicit Varro deum se arbitrari esse animam mundi, quem Graeci vocant κόσμον, et hunc ipsum mundum esse deum." [3] 29.
[4] The distinction is important in Plotinus, e.g. *Enn.* III, i–iii. (See also Dodds, *Proclus*, 263.) [5] *VN.* 40.

in quo, id ad quod, id propter quod: novissime id quod ex his est."[1]
Schmekel believes this is derived from Posidonius, who, he considers, regarded the active λόγοι of Stoic philosophy as equivalent to the Ideas and to the Numbers of Pythagoreanism,[2] and Schmekel's view is accepted by Norden and Isaak Heinemann. Jones stresses the fact that Seneca is not concerned to blend the Platonic and Aristotelean theory of causes with that of Stoicism, and can find nothing to prove that the interpretation of Platonism which Seneca sets forth is original with Posidonius.[3]

Finally, Theiler rejects Posidonius as the source of either the 58th or the 65th *Letter* of Seneca,[4] and, discovering that on certain points the *Didaskalikos* agrees with them exactly and that the theory of causes exhibited in all three is based on the same bold conflation of Platonic and Aristotelean elements,[5] holds that parts of the doctrine go back to Antiochus and cannot be traced further than him.[6] Now, if the agreement were really as close as Theiler suggests, it might be necessary to postulate the existence of a common source dating from the first century before Christ. But, whereas in Seneca the Platonic Idea is added as a fifth Cause to the four of Aristotle, in the *Didaskalikos* the Efficient and Final Causes are blended together, while the Platonic Idea is not explicitly distinguished from the Formal Cause, the εἶδος or παράδειγμα, of Aristotle, as it is in Seneca.[7] Already in the Old Academy Xenocrates defined the Idea as a παράδειγμα, and Alkimos recognized as conventional the view that the Idea is both a παράδειγμα and a νόημα. Platonists generally, if not unanimously,[8] accepted the three

[1] § 7 sqq. Jones, in quoting the passage, silently omits "plenus h.f.e."
[2] p. 431.
[3] *CP.* 21, 321. Jones does not deny the possibility that Seneca's account *may* be borrowed from Posidonius.
[4] *VN.* 34.   [5] *Ibid.* 16.   [6] *Ibid.* 37.
[7] Theiler (*VN.* 16) connects *Did.* 63, 15 (εἰ δὲ καὶ μὴ εἴη ἔξω τὸ παράδειγμα πάντη πάντως, ἕκαστος ἐν αὐτῷ τὸ παράδειγμα ἴσχων τῶν τεχνιτῶν τὴν τούτου μορφὴν τῇ ὕλῃ περιτίθησιν) and Seneca, *Epp.* 58, 19; 65, 7. But what is important in the *Did.* is the distinction, not between separate Causes (Seneca's *in quo, ad quod*), but between two aspects of the same Cause (παράδειγμα—ἔξω or ἐντός. See also Plot. v, ix, 3).
[8] Cf. D. L. III, 69, etc. (like Theophrastus, *DDG.* 485, followed by Cicero, *Luc.* 118).

74

Causes, God, Matter, and the Idea,[1] and nothing prevents our associating this view with the Old Academy. Seneca, in the 58th *Letter*, actually introduces the characteristically Xenocratean definition of the Idea ("Est eorum quae natura fiunt exemplum aeternum"). But he does not confine himself, as does our writer, to the three principles of the Old Academy, and Theiler's hypothesis fails to explain the discrepancy.

Yet Theiler makes one valuable suggestion. We have mentioned that Schmekel and Norden find Posidonian influence and that R. M. Jones stresses the doxographical character of *Letter* 65. Theiler suggests that Seneca may have had access to a work of Arius Didymus. There are several grounds on which this suggestion may be approved. Arius wrote on Stoicism, Aristotle and Plato. He regarded the Ideas as παραδείγματα and (we may conjecture) placed them in the Mind of God.[2] Himself a Stoic, Arius showed regard for Posidonius, and was also influenced by Antiochus.[3] Not the least important reason for assuming him to be the immediate source is the fact that Seneca (who never mentions Antiochus) in the *Consolation to Marcia* cites a passage from a parallel work by Arius with evident approbation.

Theiler suggests that Arius Didymus "ja nicht schöpferisch in die Formulierung der platonischen Lehre eingegriffen hat".[4] If so, our case is strengthened. For we certainly need to postulate that during the period in which the Old Era drew to a close there was written, under the influence of the Academy of Philo and Antiochus and the Middle Stoicism of Panaetius and Posidonius, a doxographical account, which was freely used by later writers on the history of philosophy.[5] With hardly less certainty we may claim that the doxographer was Arius Didymus. Now, whether we choose

---

[1] Cf. *DDG.* 309; Tim. Locr. 94 c.

[2] R. M. Jones, relying on Euseb. *PE.* 545 B sqq., denies this. But the *argumentum e silentio* is unsafe. Jones himself observes that *Did.* IX contains the doctrine. *Did.* XII is similar to IX, save that the Idea is not once again defined as νόησις θεοῦ. It is natural to conclude that both chapters are derived from Arius, and that the omission in XII has no significance.

[3] V. Arnim, against Strache (*SBWien*, 1926), would rather connect Arius in Stob. II, 117 sqq. directly with Aristotle and Theophrastus. But this is going too far.   [4] *VN.* 37.

[5] For the need, cf. *DDG.* 153; Howald in *Hermes*, 1920.

Posidonius or Antiochus as Seneca's direct source, we have to face the difficulty that Seneca does not display as complete a syncretism as, on either hypothesis, he should. But, if we substitute Arius, the difficulty is removed. We are still able to allow that the eclectics whom Arius is apt to follow may exercise influence here indirectly. But we are not compelled to assume that a synthesis of doctrine is everywhere intended, for Arius is quite capable of placing Stoic and Peripatetic doctrines in juxtaposition without attempting to reconcile them. Moreover, if we assume Arius to be Seneca's immediate source, we may claim for him instead of Antiochus such agreements as can be discovered between Chapter IX of the *Didaskalikos* and the two *Letters*.

We have now to consider the last and in rank the highest of the three ἀρχαί, the transcendent God, who is both Final and Efficient Cause. If we found little trace of Antiochus's influence when we studied the theory of the Idea, we here find absolutely nothing which can possibly be connected with him. Even in the fifth book of *De Finibus*, where Piso expounds the doctrine of the Lyceum and the Old Academy from the Antiochean standpoint, mention is made (as Isaak Heinemann observes[1]) neither of "God" nor of "gods" but only of θειοτέρα τις αἰτία, which is identified with φύσις and conceived in a purely pantheistic sense. The transcendent God of the *Didaskalikos* is certainly not the immanent principle or *anima mundi* of Antiochus and Stoicism.[2] When, towards the end of Chapter X and in Chapter XI, we find the Stoic view of God attacked with the argument (derived from Aristotle) that God cannot be body, as body is a συνδύασμα of matter and form, and that qualities are not bodies, we might even consider this to be a case of that determined opposition which Baeumker believes the later Platonists to have offered to the Stoic materialism which Antiochus unhesitatingly accepted.[3] Yet, despite his stoicizing tendency, Antiochus

---

[1] II, 217.

[2] That, like the Stoics, Antiochus believed the soul to be material, is evident from *A. Po.* 39; *Fin.* IV, 12. 36.

[3] *Op. cit.* 375. Of the opposition to Stoicism we have evidence in Plotinus (IV, vii; VI, i, 26: καὶ ὁ θεὸς δεύτερος αὐτοῖς τῆς ὕλης. καὶ γὰρ σῶμα ἐξ ὕλης ὂν καὶ εἴδους. II, iv, 6; V, iv, 1). With *Did.* 66, 5–6 cf. Galen in *SVF.* II, 116, 16–17.

may, paradoxically enough, have sought to contrast his own dualism[1] with Stoic monistic materialism. The contrast would have been quite improper. For the most orthodox Stoic is inevitably as much (or as little) a dualist as Antiochus himself.[2] Yet it is by no means improbable that the arguments which Carneades had brought against the Stoic σῶμα-doctrine were turned to account by Antiochus,[3] who, in that case, so far from being in the present section of the *Didaskalikos* the object of attack, may even be reckoned its originator.[4]

F. PHYSICS

The subject of physics occupies Chapters XII–XXII, which are homogeneous and seemingly derived from a *Timaeus-Epitome*.[5] That they form a distinct whole may be inferred from the introductory sentence and from the conclusion of Chapter XXII.[6] It is natural enough that a *Timaeus-Epitome* should be thus used. What is more surprising is the arbitrary order in which the topics are discussed.[7] We have observed that the opening portion of Chapter XII is without doubt an abridgement of a passage of the *Epitome Physice* of Arius Didymus. We shall subsequently see other traces of Arian influence in this portion of the *Didaskalikos*. But of Antiochean influence anywhere we can find little trace. Strache[8] makes much of the resemblance between Chapter XII and *Posterior Academics* 28–9. But obviously, as nothing distinctively unplatonic is involved, the similarity may be explained by the circumstance that the *Timaeus* is the common source. The mathematical discussion and the geometrical construction of the elements from triangular

---

[1] *CD.* 19, 3 (of the human microcosm) and *A. Po.* 6. Cf. p. 69, *supra.*
[2] *SVF.* II, 300.
[3] *ND.* III, 30 sqq. is attributed to Carneades by Cicero, and like S. E. *AM.* 145–51 the passage has points of similarity to *Did.* x, xi. Antiochus could regard Carneades with a certain favour (*Tusc.* III, 59; *Luc.* 28; S. E. *AM.* VII, 159). Cf. further *ND.* III, 30–31 with *A. Po.* 27.
[4] Arius Didymus may be the mediator. Cf. *Did.* 66, 21 and *DDG.* 448, 10 and 11 (also Plut. 1085 C–1086 B; Baeumker, 353; Alex. Aph. *An.* 115, 12); *Did.* 66, 24, 30 and *DDG.* 449, 10 sqq.
[5] Perhaps the source of VIII and XXIII as well.
[6] Cf. XVII.　　　　　　　　[7] See *Loci Platonici.*
[8] *Diss.* 88 ("Antiochia haec esse quoniam ostendi", *ibid.* 90).

planes (formed from indivisible minimal lines[1]) are certainly not derived from Antiochus. The *Timaeus* is closely followed, the only point of difference being that, whereas Plato does not specifically mention the dodecahedron,[2] here it is of considerable importance and is constructed (according to a method mentioned in Plutarch also[3]) from pentagons, each of which is itself composed of thirty similar scalene triangles.[4]

In Chapter XIV the doctrine that the Universe is eternal, animate and intelligent, is based on the *Timaeus*[5] and there is no need to introduce—save for the purpose of comparison—*Posterior Academics* 28.[6] The astronomy is likewise derived for the most part from the *Timaeus*. There are, however, some signs of the influence of the *Epinomis* as well.[7] Thus all the seven planets are mentioned by name, the first four (after *Timaeus* 38 C), Moon, Sun, Venus and Mercury, in the supposed order[8] of their proximity to the Earth, but the remaining three, which are unnamed in the *Timaeus*, in the reverse order: Saturn, Jupiter and Mars. Such is the arrangement followed in the *Epinomis*,[9] whereas in a passage of *De Natura Deorum* II (52 sqq.), where Finger detects the influence of Antiochus (comparison with περὶ κόσμου II, however, supports the generally recognized view that the character of the book is Posidonian throughout[10]), the list of names is complete and the enumeration at the same time perfectly consecutive, Saturn the outermost being mentioned first and Venus, Sun and Moon appearing last. More-

---

[1] 65, 32. Cf. Xenocrates, frs. 41 sqq.; Robin, *TPIN.* 229.

[2] Cf. Sachs, 46 (A. E. Taylor, *Tim. Comm.* 377 differs).

[3] 428 A, 1003 D. Cf. Heath, *Gk. Math.* I, 296.

[4] From Plutarch it would appear that Theodorus of Soli favoured this construction. This Theodorus is otherwise unknown. With *Did.* cf. Simpl. *in Phys.* 1165, 29 (Xenocr. fr. 53) and *de Cael.* I, 35, 45.

[5] 30 B.

[6] Stoic philosophy did much to make this doctrine a commonplace (cf. Verg. *Aen.* VI, 724–7; *Georg.* IV, 221).

[7] Theiler's criticism of Taylor's view (*Gnomon*, 1931, 337 sqq.) seems cogent.

[8] Theon Sm. 138 gives the correct order (as Taylor notes, *Tim. Comm.* 193).

[9] 987.

[10] See the introductions to Mayor's edition and Rackham's.

over, the alternative names Φαίνων Φαέθων Πυρόεις[1] and Στίλβων, which are given in *De Natura Deorum* II and in περὶ κόσμου, are omitted in the *Didaskalikos* as they are in the *Epinomis*, while *Epinomis* 987 B (Κρόνου δ' αὐτόν τινες ἐπωνυμίαν φθέγγονται) seems to be re-echoed with the words: Κρόνου τινὲς ἐπονομάζουσιν ἀστέρα. A connexion between the *Didaskalikos* and the *Epinomis* (if we refuse to accept Finger's view of *De Natura Deorum* II, 52) need not exclude the possibility of Antiochean mediation. It is true that in the present chapter nothing is said of the "fifth element", of which Antiochus imagined the stars to be composed. But ether and fire are distinguished in the next chapter,[2] and we may suppose that ether is the stuff of which the sphere of fixed stars consists, the dodecahedron already described, or, as it is now called, ἡ ἄνωθεν δύναμις (compare *vis* in *Posterior Academics* 28).

The subordinate deities or demons mentioned in Chapter XV are of interest as being the givers of dreams and of oracles. This is a view which we find Arius Didymus associating with Stoicism in general.[3] It is specially the view of Posidonius,[4] who contrasted divination by dreams with that which is achieved by artificial methods.[5] The contrast appears in the present passage: ὀνείρατα... καὶ ὅσα κατὰ μαντείαν ὑπὸ θνητῶν τεχνιτεύεται.[6] Whether Antiochus accepted μαντική from Posidonius, or followed Panae-tius in attacking it, cannot be ascertained and is for our purpose not of great importance. For, if we assume that in this part of his work our writer follows an *Epitome* of the *Timaeus* which was written by Arius Didymus, then we may expect to discover occa-sional traces of Posidonian doctrine.

The next point which calls for observation is the recognition of the brain as the centre of the nervous system.[7] Plato lived before

---

[1] Found in Plot. II, iii, 6. None of these is found in Ar. Did. fr. 31 (=*SVF*. II, 527). Celsus mentions a Mithraic order (*CC*. VI, 22); Saturn, Venus, Jupiter, Mercury, Mars, Moon, Sun.

[2] 71, 15. Sachs (65) thinks the "fifth element" was introduced by the Old Academy.

[3] *SVF*. III, 605, 654. Cf. *DDG*. 77.

[4] Cic. *Div*. I, 64.   [5] *Ibid*. 115–16.

[6] The verb, which is the *vox propria* for all actions belonging to τεχνικὸν γένος μαντικῆς (cf. Heinze, *Xen*. 105) is found often in Philo Alex. Cf. for *artificiosa divinatio SVF*. II, 1207 sqq.   [7] 73, 6.

the time of Erasistratus and Herophilus [1] and therefore did not write in the *Timaeus* of "nerves", though he mentioned the absence of "sinews" (νεῦρα) about the head.[2] Posidonius may have recognized the nervous system, but he still upheld the orthodox Stoic view that the heart is the centre of mental activity.[3] When Varro, therefore, writes that it is from the head that the senses and nerves take their beginning ("caput": "quod hinc capiant initium sensus et nervi"[4]) he is not writing from the Posidonian standpoint, and if we take the passage in its context we have no difficulty in concluding that Varro is following Antiochus. Again, when the sense-organs (αἰσθήσεις)[5] are called by our writer the body-guard of the mind's ruling-principle (ἡγεμονικόν) the figure, though favoured by Posidonius,[6] need not be due to him. For without much doubt it was used by Antiochus, if not by Panaetius as well.[7] We may accordingly connect the present passage through Arius Didymus with Antiochus.

When our writer proceeds to distinguish broadly τὸ ἡγεμονικόν from τὸ παθητικόν, we may recall firstly that already in the *Magna Moralia* Plato is said to have divided the soul into a rational and an irrational part,[8] and secondly that the Stoic Mnesarchus, pupil of Panaetius and teacher of Antiochus, reduced the number of parts, which Stoicism generally reckoned as eight,[9] to two, namely τὸ λογικόν and τὸ αἰσθητικόν.[10] Antiochus himself, while insisting that τὸ ἡγεμονικόν ("princeps, pars quae mens nominatur"[11]) and the senses are essentially one,[12] distinguished them as the two aspects of mental activity,[13] but seemingly, although inclined to follow Plato

---

[1] Cf. Jaeger, *Nem. Em.* 51 sqq.   [2] 75 C, 77 E.   [3] Schmekel, 259, 2.

[4] Lact. *Op. Dei* 5 (38, Wilmann, *Fragmenta*). The Stoic-Platonic character of the whole chapter well suits Antiochus. Note also 9 *ad fin.*

[5] "Machinamenta, quibus ad sentiendas et diiudicandas qualitates sensus instructi sunt", Apul. 97, 18. Cf. *Did.* 72, 22.

[6] See Rudberg, 206. (Finger is surely wrong in connecting *ND.* II, 140 with Antiochus instead of Posidonius.)

[7] *De Leg.* I, 26. Plato (*Tim.* 70 B) makes the heart δορυφορικὴ οἴκησις.

[8] 82 a 24.

[9] *SVF.* II, 827. Posidonius, beginning with ἡγεμονικόν and λογικόν, subdivided into twelve parts (Schmekel, 261, 2).

[10] *DDG.* 615, 6 sqq.   [11] *Fin.* V, 36.

[12] *Luc.* 30.   [13] *Fin.* V, 34.

and to assign to the ruling-principle a fixed dwelling-place in the head,[1] could not refuse to admit as possible the view, which is attributed to Xenocrates, that the ruling-principle does not always remain in the same locality.[2]

G. PSYCHOLOGY

In Chapter xvii Psychology is incidental to Physiology. In Chapter xxiii and the two following chapters it is dealt with—not without some repetition[3]—as a separate subject. To this part of the work we may at once proceed.[4] The clash which, it is said, sometimes occurs between τὸ παθητικόν and τὸ λογιστικόν[5] seems to be conceived quite in the manner of Posidonius, who, attacking the traditional psychology of his School, laid emphasis on the fact that feeling is often able to get the better of will and reason, and that a conflict is waged on both sides.[6] Posidonius devoted his criticism especially to Chrysippus and found a warm supporter in Galen,[7] who borrowed not only arguments but also in many cases actual citations of Chrysippus from the περὶ παθῶν of Posidonius.[8] From Galen we learn that the two verses from the *Medea* contained in the present chapter and translated by Chalcidius in his *Commentary* on the *Timaeus*[9] were quoted by Chrysippus, though we are not told for what purpose.[10] Galen himself, probably repeating Posidonius, remarks that he cannot understand how Chrysippus came to quote them, since they are quite incompatible with his own doctrine.

The second quotation which appears in this chapter is from another play of Euripides, the lost *Chrysippus*, and must have be-

---

[1] Assuming that Lact. *Op. Dei* 16 is based on Varro, and hence is Antiochean.

[2] *Ibid.* Cf. Clem. *Strom.* viii, 14, 4.   [3] Admitted in 76, 6.

[4] Perhaps 75, 22 (fuller than *Tim.* 79 c) has some connexion with Antiochus (Clem. *Strom.* viii, 32, 6; S. E. *AM.* viii, 306; Chalc. 236, 16).

[5] 76, 37.   [6] Galen, quoted Schmekel, 258, 1.

[7] In *HP*.   [8] See Schmekel, 259, 2.

[9] "Nec me latet nunc quam cruenta cogitem, / sed vincit ira sanitatem pectoris", 183.

[10] *SVF.* ii, 473. Cf. ii, 1: παρ' ὀλίγον τὴν Εὐριπίδου Μήδειαν ὅλην παρετίθετο κτα.

longed to the passage which is alluded to in *Tusculans* IV, 71: "Atque, ut muliebres amores omittam, quibus maiorem licentiam natura concessit, quis...non intelligit, quid apud Euripidem et loquatur et cupiat Laius?" We have already mentioned[1] that this book probably owes something of its character to the influence of Antiochus. But in Cicero the passion which Laius felt is regarded as of light account. Here the passion is obviously meant to typify the law in the members warring against the law of the mind: "Video meliora proboque: | deteriora sequor." The standpoint appears to be that of Posidonius rather than of Antiochus. We may suppose that Chrysippus quoted both Euripidean passages (perhaps in his θεραπευτικός) and that Posidonius pointed out that he was entitled to use neither, since Euripides maintained the very doctrine which Chrysippus denied. Antiochus may have quoted them too. But for him their meaning would be: "Alii cupiditate, iracundia etiam multi efferuntur; et cum in mala scientes irruunt, tum se optime sibi consulere arbitrantur."[2]

The next chapter is devoted to the proving of the immortality of the soul.[3] All the proofs, as might be expected, are genuinely Platonic. The one which is based on the fact that learning is remembering is of special interest, since the view that knowledge can be acquired inductively alone, by a process of generalizing from particular sense-experiences, is explicitly rejected: εἰ γὰρ ἀπὸ τῶν κατὰ μέρος ἐνενοοῦμεν τὰς κοινότητας, πῶς ἂν τὰ κατὰ μέρος διωδεύσαμεν ἄπειρα ὑπάρχοντα, ἢ πῶς ἀπ' ὀλίγων;[4] This has a somewhat Sceptical ring as we may see from a passage of Sextus Empiricus, who may be reproducing the arguments which were employed against the Antiochean theory of knowledge by Aenesidemus.[5] If the view which our writer expresses owes something to Aenesidemus, that may be due to Arius Didymus. Living somewhat later than Aenesidemus in Alexandria where he had taught,

---

[1] *Supra*, p. 30.
[2] *Fin.* v, 29. Cf. *Top.* 64: "(perturbationes animi) quamquam sunt voluntariae (obiurgatione enim et admonitione deiciuntur) tamen habent tantos motus, ut ea quae voluntaria sunt aut necessaria interdum aut certe ignorata videantur."
[3] ἐπιχείρημα ὅτι ἡ ψυχὴ ἀθάνατος ἡ ἀνθρωπίνη, Codd. in mg.
[4] 78, 3 sqq.   [5] *Hyp.* II, 204 sqq.

Arius could hardly have failed to take into consideration his criticism[1] of Philo of Larissa and Antiochus of Ascalon.

To assume Arius to be the direct source of this chapter is convenient, since just after the rejection of the doctrine which in the *Lucullus* is so strongly emphasized:[2] "Nihil est in intellectu quod non prius fuerit in sensu", there occurs a sentence which has every appearance of being Antiochean, νοοῦμεν ἀπὸ μικρῶν αἰθυγμάτων. So Cicero in *De Finibus* v, 43 uses "scintillulae" ("semina") and in *Tusculans* III, 2 writes that Nature "parvulos nobis dedit igniculos". The Middle Stoics were probably accustomed to refer to the κοιναὶ ἔννοιαι as sparks,[3] the term having for them its literal meaning, whereas in the *Didaskalikos* αἴθυγμα is of course metaphorical. That Antiochus regarded ἔννοιαι in the Stoic sense may be inferred from the fact that for him as for the Stoics soul was ultimately not immaterial but a fiery or firelike substance.[4] Doubtless he called this substance, as did the Stoics, divine, and so may be said to have accepted their doctrine of the divinity of the soulstuff.[5] But that he held the genuine Platonic view[6] that the soul before and after incarnation may dwell as an immaterial entity in an Intelligible World, it is impossible to believe.

The statement that irrational souls are impelled simply by φαντασία and are without general notions or the capacity to combine these scientifically (χρώμεναι οὔτε θεωρήμασι καὶ τῇ τούτων συναγωγῇ οὔτε καθολικαῖς διαλήψεσι) seems to display the in-

---

[1] Phot. *Bibl.* 170 a 14 sqq. Cf. Natorp, *Forsch.* 66, 302. Goedeckemeyer (p. 211) believes that Aenesidemus here alludes to Eudorus and Arius Didymus as well. But, as already remarked, Goedeckemeyer is not justified in regarding Arius as an Academic. Though apparently first and foremost a doxographer, Arius (as von Arnim points out, in *SB Wien*, 1926) was known to antiquity as a Stoic.

[2] Theiler (*VN*. 53) does not take this view: "Es ist hier Cicero (§ 30) sehr flüchtig, und der Ausdruck hat zur Vermutung geführt, es sei Antiochos ein krasser Sensualist gewesen; das ist schon nach der philosophiegeschichtlichen Stellung unwahrscheinlich."

[3] Cf. Schmekel, 396.   [4] *Fin.* IV, 11, 36.

[5] In that sense Cicero, after using the phrase *mortalis deus*, speaks of *divinum animal* in *Fin.* II, 40. Cf. *Tusc.* I, 60 (probably Posidonian).

[6] See, however, Ritter, II, 33, 133. R. is in several respects a modern Antiochus.

fluence of Antiochean terminology.[1] The doctrine of the incarnation of souls (παρεμφυόμεναι ταῖς τῶν ἐμβρύων διαπλαστικαῖς φύσεσι) is directed against the well-known Stoic view that the soul is actualized only at birth by a process of cooling (περίψυξις) of the πνεῦμα.[2] Varro is said by Lactantius to have believed that the soul is air conceived in the mouth, warmed in the lungs, heated in the heart, and diffused into the body.[3] This is obviously the orthodox view of Stoicism, which was doubtless derived by Varro directly from Antiochus.[4] Lactantius, in opposition to Varro's view, declares: "Non enim post partum insinuatur in corpus, ut quibusdam philosophis videtur, sed post conceptum protinus." This and the passage under discussion may be compared with what Galen says in his treatise *Whether the Embryo is Animate*: ἅμα τῇ τοῦ σπέρματος εἰς τὴν μήτραν ἐξακοντίσει συγκατέσπειρεν ὁ τῶν ὅλων δημιουργὸς καὶ τὴν ψυχὴν ἵνα τῷ σώματι καὶ τὴν διοικοῦσαν αὐτῷ δύναμιν ἔχῃ.[5] It is not impossible that Lactantius is arguing from the standpoint of Posidonius.[6] In particular it is important to observe that he compares the relation between the soul and the blood to that between light and oil, the point being that the soul is not present in, but only present to, the blood. So, too, in the πρὸς Γαῦρον[7]—a Neoplatonic and probably Porphyrian treatise wrongly ascribed to Galen—during the course of a criticism of orthodox Stoic and Epicurean theories of sense-perception, these words appear: φυσικὴ γὰρ ἡ ἐμψύχωσις καὶ δι᾽ ὅλου ἡ ἔξαψις κατὰ συμφωνίαν τῶν ἁρμοσθέντων πρὸς τὸ ἐναρμόσαι οἷόν τε, and: οὕτω καὶ ὁ νάφθας ἀφθεὶς ἀφθέντι πυρὶ ἐξάπτεται οὐ διὰ τοῦ μεταξὺ τόπου, ὅταν μηδὲν ἐμποδίζῃ εἰς τὸ καὶ ἄνευ ἀφῆς τὰ ἡρμοσμένα συμπάσχειν ἀλλήλοις. Our writer expresses the relation between soul and body by means of a similar analogy: ἔχει δέ πως οἰκειότητα πρὸς ἄλληλα σῶμα καὶ ψυχὴ ὡς πῦρ καὶ ἄσφαλτος.[8] Whether this and the other two

---

[1] Cf. Clem. *Strom*. VIII, 23, 2 (*SVF*. III, 280, i.e. Ar. Did., and in Cicero, cf. *Fat*. 11; *Ad Att*. XIV, 20, 2).

[2] *SVF*. II, 804 sqq.   [3] *Op. Dei* 17.

[4] So *UPG*. 470.

[5] XIX, 168, K (ἡ φύσις διαπλάττει; *ibid*. 169. Cf. ps.-Alex. *Probl*. II, 73).

[6] Posidonius certainly differed from orthodox Stoicism in holding that the soul enters the body from without. Cf. Schmekel, 249.

[7] 48, 21 Kalbfleisch.   [8] 78, 31. Plainly ψ:σ::π:ἄ.

passages should be traced back to Posidonius is a question which must here be left unanswered.[1] But nothing suggests that any of the three is connected with Antiochus.[2]

The conclusion of the present chapter invites comparison with a passage of Arius Didymus in Stobaeus.[3] Arius professes to report the Aristotelean and Peripatetic view, but in fact, as Wachsmuth and Strache point out, Aristotelean psychology is conflated with that of Plato. Strache, while considering that such confusion is suggestive of Antiochus,[4] is unable to find anything that clearly shows him to have combined Plato's tripartite scheme with the Aristotelean division of the soul into τὸ λογικόν and τὸ ἄλογον.[5] In the *Didaskalikos* the psychology adopted is explicitly tripartite. It is true that a distinction can be drawn in the human soul between that faculty which it shares with the souls of the gods, namely τὸ κριτικόν or τὸ γνωστικόν, and the faculties which after incarnation undergo transformation, namely τὸ ἐπιθυμητικόν (in the souls of gods τὸ οἰκειωτικόν) and τὸ θυμοειδές (in the souls of gods τὸ ὁρμητικόν), and that elsewhere our writer is ready to admit the dichotomy, τὸ λογιστικόν and τὸ παθητικόν. But here, at any rate, he regards the Platonic trichotomy as fundamental, since he maintains that not only the incarnate but also the discarnate soul is subject to the same primary division. Accordingly, despite the use of the terms ὁρμητικόν, παραστατικόν, οἰκειωτικόν,[6] we

[1] A fact which, while proving nothing, need not be overlooked, is that Posidonius wrote about bituminous substances (cf. Jacoby, *FGH.* 2 A, 266).

[2] In *CD.* 19, 3, Varro (doubtless following Antiochus, cf. *ad fin.*) holds that man is the composite soul + body, "sicut duos equos iunctos bigas vocamus", etc.

[3] II, 117.

[4] "Peripateticae huic rationalis animi partitioni adiungitur mirum in modum irrationalis Platonica in partem concupiscentem et irascentem. Quam confusionem quam maxime decere Antiochum nemo non videt", *Diss.* 31.

[5] He cites *Luc.* 124, but this is not helpful.

[6] ὁρμητικόν is not found in Aristotle. It occurs in *DDG.* 457, 2 (Ar. Did.), 438 (647); *SVF.* III, 169 (Ar. Did.); Plut. 1122 B. The Numenian First God (23 Thed.) has τὸ κριτ. and τὸ ὁρμ. Antiochus (S. E. *AM.* VII, 162) doubtless defined πάθος as ἑαυτοῦ τε καὶ τοῦ ἐτέρου **παραστατικόν**. οἰκειωτικόν suggests Stob. II, 118, 12; 143, 11.

need not assume that the present passage contains a characteristically Antiochean doctrine. But we may well believe that it goes back to Arius Didymus.[1]

H. DETERMINISM AND FREEWILL

The source of Chapter XXVI is probably that used by the authors of the two treatises περὶ εἱμαρμένης, of which one is ascribed to Plutarch and the other to Alexander Aphrodisiensis. Antiochus favoured the Stoic theory of causation.[2] At the same time he admitted the cogency of the Carneadean criticism. There is no reason to doubt that Antiochus exercises some influence on the *De Fato* of Cicero,[3] and we may even suspect that the two other treatises on the same theme owe much to him. But an exact investigation of the relation between them cannot be undertaken here.[4] It is only possible to indicate certain parallels between them and the chapter before us. The opening suggests pseudo-Plutarch.[5] The denial of an infinite regression (79, 4 sqq.), which Strache explicitly attributes to Antiochus himself,[6] may be paralleled in the treatise ascribed to Plutarch.[7] The words τὸ ἐφ' ἡμῖν οἰχήσεται καὶ ἔπαινοι καὶ ψόγοι suggest pseudo-Alexander.[8] The contrast between the act which lies freely in a man's power (οὐ κατηνάγκασται τοῦτο) and the result which is fated (τὸ ἑπόμενον τῇ πράξει καθ' εἱμαρμένην συντελεσθήσεται) is reminiscent of a passage in Clement of Alexandria which we have already treated.[9] As in the present chapter the quotation from the *Phoenissae* of Euripides appears in pseudo-Alexander (*SVF.* II, 941)[10] and, with a slight variation, in Maximus Tyrius.[11] It is also translated and discussed by Chalcidius.[12]

The principle of possibility, we are told, is indeterminate and

[1] Perhaps following Eudorus. Cf. Stob. II, 42, 23.

[2] *A. Po.* 28 sqq.

[3] Cf. e.g. § 35 with *Top.* 61 and Clem. *Strom.* VIII, 27, 4 (= *SVF.* II, 347).

[4] See Gercke, in *Rh. M.* 1886, 289, etc.

[5] Ps.-Plut. 570 E. For the Stoic view here criticized cf. *SVF.* II, 998.

[6] *Ant.* 23, 2. Cf. Cic. *Top.* 60; *Fat.* 34; Schmekel, 171.

[7] 569 A. We may also notice the Plotinian criticism of Stoic fatalism, III, i, 7.

[8] *SVF.* II, 984.

[9] p. 40, *supra.* Cf. ps.-Plut. 570.

[10] See also II, 957.

[11] 19, 5.

[12] 153.

leaves room for the freedom of the will. Antiochus, following Diodorus[1] and Aristotle, must have emphasized this, and have anticipated our writer in stating that, once the choice has been made, the law of excluded middle becomes applicable. For, unlike his predecessor Carneades[2] and his successor Aenesidemus,[3] Antiochus denied that any statement—apart from those which refer to particular future events—can fail to be either true or false: "Omne enuntiatum verum aut falsum."[4] Potentiality is distinguished from possibility: (τὸ δυνατὸν) τοῦ δυνάμει, τοῦτ' ἐστὶ τοῦ καθ' ἕξιν καὶ κατ' ἐνέργειαν λεγομένου, διήνεγκε.[5] The conception of potentiality is fundamentally Aristotelean.[6] We may believe that it was important for Antiochus, for we read in Clement of Alexandria (VIII, 13, 7): τὸ δυνάμει... τὸ κατ' ἐνέργειαν... τούτου δὲ τὸ μὲν ἤδη ἐνεργοῦν, τὸ δὲ ἐνεργεῖν μὲν δυνάμενον, ἡσυχάζον δὲ ἢ κοιμώμενον.

I. ETHICS

The third main division of philosophy is reached in Chapter XXVII. The assertion of an esoteric doctrine which Plato communicated to the few whom he permitted to attend his Lecture on the Good is made by other writers.[7] But there is no reason to suppose that this view was taken by Antiochus.[8] The present passage is obviously written under the influence of *Timaeus* 28 c and *Epistle* VII, 341.[9] Our writer next speaks of the way in which all that is called good participates in the Summum Bonum.[10] The admission that there are

[1] *SVF.* II, 284. See Strache, *Ant.* 23, 2.
[2] See Euseb. *PE.* 738 A (Cic. *ND.* I, 70).
[3] Phot. *Bibl.* 212, 170 a 8 (doubtless a criticism directed against Antiochus).
[4] Cic. *Fat.* 10 (Prantl, 450; *SVF.* II, 956–962; ps.-Plut. 574).
[5] A passage corrupted by Hermann. I retain the reading of the MSS.
[6] Plato, *Tht.* 197 B; *Rep.* 477 C; *Soph.* 247–8, may be said to recognize it. Plotinus favours the verbal distinction: ἔχειν and πρόχειρον ἔχειν (I, i, 9, III, viii, 6, VI, ii, 4. 7. 12. Cf. also Praechter, *Hierocl.* 51). For δύναμις as *vis efficiens* cf. "Platonic" *Deff.* 411 C (Plot. v, iii, 15; Dodds, *Procl.* 215).   [7] See Shorey, *What P. Said* 607.
[8] *Fin.* v, 12 only distinguishes the elementary course from the more advanced (in the Lyceum).
[9] (οὐκ) ἀσφαλὲς ἐκφέρειν resembles Cicero's translation of *Tim.* 28 c.
[10] Cf. Ar. Did. Stob. II, 55–6; S. E. *AM.* XI, 70.

other goods besides virtue had been made by Antiochus.[1] Our writer states that these external goods are sometimes called by Plato θνητὰ ἀγαθά, a statement for which there is apparently no justification.[2] The doctrine μόνον εἶναι τὸ καλὸν ἀγαθόν is a Stoic commonplace.[3] We may note in particular that Antipater composed three books to prove against Carneades that, according to Plato, μόνον τὸ καλὸν ἀγαθόν, ὅτι καὶ κατ᾿ αὐτὸν αὐτάρκης ἡ ἀρετὴ πρὸς εὐδαιμονίαν.[4] So too our writer.[5] In the rest of the chapter he closely follows Plato.[6]

Passing by a misapplied text from the *Phaedo* (82 A) and an oft quoted sentence from the *Laws* (715 E)[7] we find the Good described as the source of benefit, a phrase which is obviously commonplace.[8] The definition of εὐδαιμονία[9] is specially associated with Xenocrates, and Arius Didymus finds justification for it in Plato. Strache would as usual make Antiochus the source used not only by Arius but also by the writer of the *Didaskalikos*.[10] Such an assumption is, however, somewhat unnecessary, since the etymological explanation of εὐδαιμονία is of frequent occurrence.[11] The sentence which follows contains a reference to θεωρημάτων παράδοσις. The term

---

[1] *Luc.* 134. Cf. *Fin.* v, 67–8; Varro in *CD.* 19, 3; Stob. II, 55, 7 sqq.

[2] The only verbal parallel which I can discover is τὰ θνητῶν θνητὰ ἀγαθά, Ph. Al. *Qu. D.* I, 152.

[3] Cf. *SVF.* III, 30, 49, 208 (καλόν, καλεῖν).

[4] *SVF.* fr. 56. Cf. Plot. I, iv, 4. [5] 80, 35.

[6] The quotation from *Laws* 631 B is given (with the same variant διττά) by Ar. Did. Stob. II, 54, 12 (cf. also Euseb. *PE.* 589 A).

[7] Attic. Euseb. *PE.* 798 D; Celsus, *CC.* 6, 15; Theon Sm. 100, 14, π. κόσμου 401 b 24 (Apul. 175, 2–3); Ammon. Saccas Phot. *Bibl.* 461 b 12; Clem. *Pr.* 69, 4; Plot. I, viii, 14 (and I, 155, 17; 270, 27).

[8] Plato, *Rep.* 608 E. Cf. π. κόσμου 398 a. Ar. Did. Stob. 52, 22.

[9] 82, 2. [10] *Diss.* 91.

[11] See Heraclitus and Xen. Stob. v, 925 S; Burnet, Introd. to *EN.* I; *Timaeus*, 90 C, *Rep.* 540 C, Xenocr. fr. 81; M. A. 7, 17; Strache, *Diss.* 91 (on Stob. II, 52, 1 sqq.); Posidonius in *SVF.* III, 460. For the demon as "the god within the mind" ("thy spirit which keeps thee", *Ant. Cleop.* II, iii) cf. Shorey, *What P. Said* 536; Arnold, *Rom. Stoic.* 233, n. 101. Cf. also Theon Sm. 14–15 Hiller. See *UPG.* 540. (Plato, *Laws* 803 A, has διδασκαλία καὶ παράδοσις—but not of θεωρήματα of philosophy. See also Lobeck, *Aglaop.* 39.) For προτέλεια cf. *Sym.* 210; Plut. *Qu. Conv.* 8, 2, 1; *DDG.* 608, 11; M. T. 14, 7; Plot. I, vi, 9. (*Phaed.* 67; M. A. III, 12.)

88

θεώρημα, as we have seen, was favoured by Antiochus. We may also notice that Philo of Larissa, as reported by Arius Didymus, compared θεωρήματα and παραγγέλματα περὶ τῆς ὑγιείας.

The definition of virtue which is introduced in Chapter XXIX is not found in the works of Plato himself. Yet it is included among the "Platonic" *Definitions*.[1] Arius Didymus correctly attributes the same definition to Aristotle,[2] and virtue is thus described in *De Finibus* II, 45, an Antiochean passage. The definitions of φρόνησις[3] and σωφροσύνη may be compared with the Antiochean view.[4] The definition of ἀνδρία is the same as in the *Republic* (IV, 429 c–33 c) and was adopted by the Stoic Sphaerus and by Antiochus.[5] The view of justice is fundamentally that which Plato expounds in the *Republic*, but the terms used are more suggestive of Stoicism than of Plato himself, and we may suppose that the actual definition[6] was adopted either wholly or in part by Antiochus.[7] Reason, our writer adds, is the ruler to whom the soul's irrational members must be obedient: ἄρχοντος μὲν τοῦ λογισμοῦ, τῶν δὲ λοιπῶν μερῶν τῆς ψυχῆς κατ' οἰκείαν ἰδιότητα κατεσταλμένων ὑπὸ τοῦ λογισμοῦ καὶ πειθηνίων αὐτῷ γεγενημένων. With this we may compare Cicero, *De Officiis* I, 102. Even if Cicero is following Panaetius there as in the rest of the treatise,[8] yet the bipartite psychology and the use of the term ὁρμή are quite appropriate to Antiochus, and it can easily be supposed that Antiochus closely agreed with the view which is given. We may further observe that Arius Didymus expresses a similar view in language such as our writer uses.[9]

The ἀντακολουθία of the virtues[10] is characteristically Stoic. We

---

[1] 411 c sqq.   [2] Stob. II, 50–1; *Polit.* 23 b 13; *EE.* 12 b 18.
[3] Xen. fr. 76.   [4] *Fin.* v, 67. Cf. *SVF.* III, 262, 266; *EN.* 40 a 25.
[5] *Tusc.* IV, 53 (*SVF.* I, 628).   [6] 82, 32 sqq.
[7] *Fin.* v, 66. Cf. Stob. II, 128, 24–5. Ph. Al. *Op. Mund.* 156 has παντέλεια ἀρετῆς.
[8] Theiler, *VN.* 43, 3, is prepared to make Antiochus the source of *Off.* I, 12 sqq. In the present passage the words "nec vero agere quidquam, cuius non possit caussam probabilem reddere" *may* imply dependence on Philo of Larissa.   [9] Stob. II, 128, 20 sqq.
[10] I.e. the perfect virtues. The "so-called virtues" or "natural talents" are not necessarily inseparable. (So Aspasius, 80, 14: ἀντακολουθοῦσι γὰρ ἔνιαι τῶν ἀρετῶν.) The "chorus of virtues" (*Tusc.* v, 13; Stob. II, 127, 8) is a phrase of Middle Stoicism (Witt, *CQ.* XXIV, 201, 3).

have seen, however, that both Plato and Aristotle adopt a similar view. Antiochus emphasizes the virtues' inseparability[1] and appears to have differed from Stoic philosophers in making the ethical ideal not προκοπὴ εἰς ἀρετήν ("progressio ad virtutem") but προκοπὴ ἐν ἀρετῇ ("cedere et progredi in virtute").[2] This view is emphasized in Chapter xxx, where orthodox Stoicism is also opposed when the vices are declared to vary in their intensity. On this point Antiochus strongly insisted.[3] True to Plato,[4] our writer denies the ethical dualism of Stoic philosophy, holding that the transition from vice to virtue is accomplished gradually. Antiochus was of the same opinion: "Omnes qui virtuti student levantur vitiis, levantur erroribus."[5] The virtues which belong to the affectible part of the soul are now said to derive their perfection from those which are peculiar to the rational part. They acquire their rational character (λόγος) from the strictly rational virtue φρόνησις, and are capable of being trained (ἐξ ἔθους ἐγγινόμεναι καὶ ἀσκήσεως). With this may be compared the following sentence from Arius Didymus's account of Peripatetic ethics: ἦθος δέ ἐστι ποιότης τοῦ ἀλόγου μέρους τῆς ψυχῆς ὑποτακτικῶς ἔχειν ἐθιζομένου τῷ λόγῳ.[6]

During the rest of the chapter (84, 12–30) our writer discusses the doctrine of virtue as a mean.[7] That Antiochus held this doctrine seems unlikely. For Cicero, in criticizing Antiochean eclecticism, calls attention to the incompatibility of Stoic ἀπάθεια with the μετριοπάθεια of the Lyceum and the Old Academy, and declares: "Atrocitas quidem ista tua quo modo in veterem Academiam irruperit, nescio."[8] Unless Cicero is here writing fancifully, Antiochus demanded the complete extirpation of πάθη.[9] According to Strache,

[1] *Fin.* v, 67. ὀρθὸς λόγος is Stoic and Antiochean (*Did.* 83, 5; 56, 13; *Tusc.* iv, 34; *SVF.* iii, 198, 315 sqq.; *UPG.* 544).

[2] *Tusc.* iv, 64, 67. See Strache, *Ant.* 55, 3. So Plutarch wrote the treatise πῶς ἄν τις αἴσθοιτο ἑαυτοῦ προκόπτοντος ἐπ' ἀρετῇ. Cf. also κατὰ προκοπὴν τελειούμενοι, *Exc. ex Theodoto* 15, 1 (and 19, 3).

[3] *Luc.* 133. Cf. *Fin.* iv, 67.

[4] *Ph.* 89 E (yet cf. *Laws* 716).

[5] *Fin.* iv, 65. See also Philo Lar. Stob. ii, 41, 16 sqq.; Philo Alex. fr. 70 (Harris).

[6] Stob. ii, 38, 3. Cf. 117, 1 sqq.

[7] With *Did.* 84, 12 cf. Aspas. 48, 27.   [8] *Luc.* 135.

[9] So Zeller, iii, i, 4, 629; Pohlenz, *Ph. Wo.* 1911, 1500.

however, Antiochus brought Stoic ἀπάθεια and the μετριοπάθεια of the Lyceum and the Old Academy into some kind of unity, and rejected πάθη in the narrower sense of ὁρμαὶ παρὰ φύσιν, but maintained that, if taken to mean any impulse of the irrational faculty, πάθη, as long as they exist in moderation, are natural and proper.[1] Strache's view might be accepted,[2] if Antiochus were not followed by Cicero in the *Third* and *Fourth Tusculans*. There, however, Peripatetic μετριοπάθεια is strongly attacked,[3] and if the relevant passages are derived from Antiochus, then he followed Chrysippus and ranged himself against both Peripatetics and Middle Stoics.[4] Whether Antiochus, however, was always so ready to attack the doctrine of μετριοπάθεια may perhaps be doubted.[5] The doctrine in the present chapter is in any case much more likely to have been derived through Arius Didymus from the Lyceum and the Old Academy, than from Antiochus.

The view expressed in the next chapter that vice is involuntary appears somewhat strange after what has been said in Chapter XXIV. In Cicero's *Topica* the vices are regarded as being, though voluntary, yet due to ignorance. But in *De Finibus* v, 28 the Antiochean view closely agrees with that which we meet in the present passage.[6] It is, however, unnecessary to emphasize the influence of Antiochus.[7] For the doctrine is as old as Socrates, while our writer's phraseology is probably characteristic of Arius Didymus, who, in dealing with the ethical teaching of Stoicism, has the expression ἀπῳκονομεῖτο ἂν τὴν κακίαν,[8] and in describing the views of the Peripatetics

---

[1] *Ant.* 35, 37.

[2] It avails to explain *Fin.* v, 63. Ar. Did. Stob. II, 38, 18–39, 9, is not, as Strache urges, writing eclectically ("trägt rein doxographischer Charakter", Pohlenz, *op. cit.* 1498).

[3] *Tusc.* IV, 38 (see Rabbow, *Ant. Schr.* 163), III, 22.

[4] See Schmekel, 437.

[5] Apart from the admitted difficulty of *Fin.* v, 61 sqq. it is hard to see why, if Antiochus always attacked μετρ., Cicero should write thus: "Cum omnis virtus sit, ut vestra, Brute (an Antiochean, *Ad Att.* XIII, 25, 3), vetus Academia dixit, mediocritas", *Brut.* 149.

[6] Cf. *Fin.* II, 33.

[7] As Strache, *Ant.* 54, 3, is inclined to do.

[8] Stob. II, 105, 18. Cf. also Hierocl. 51 A; Epict. IV, i, 44; Alex. Aph. *An.* 160, 25; Plot. I, iv, 6, v, ix, 1.

states: ἐπεὶ δὲ πολλάκις δι' ἄγνοιαν περὶ τὰς αἱρέσεις καὶ φυγὰς ἠπατώμεθα καὶ τὰ μὲν ἀγαθὰ παρεπέμπομεν, τοῖς κακοῖς δ' ὡς ἀγαθοῖς ἐνετυγχάνομεν, ἀναγκαίως τὴν τῆς ἐπικρίσεως βέβαιον εἴδησιν ἐπεζητήσαμεν.[1] Later in the present chapter[2] we learn that the causes of wrongdoing, ignorance and affection (πάθος), can be removed: ἅπαντα τὰ τοιαῦτα ἔξεστιν ἀποτρίψασθαι. The metaphor goes back to the *Ethics* of Aristotle.[3] But we may well compare *Tusculans* IV, 61: "Omnis eiusmodi perturbatio animi placatione abluatur." The resemblance suggests that in the present chapter the Antiochean attitude towards πάθη is adopted, whereas previously the ideal condition was declared to be μετριοπάθεια, a view which, as we saw, was rejected in *Tusculans* III and IV. If all πάθη are now to be effaced, the statement τὸ μέτριον ἐν τοῖς πάθεσι τὸ βέλτιστόν ἐστιν[4] is no longer applicable. But in fact, though we are not told so here, our writer does not mean to reject *all* πάθη. For he repeats that πάθη, as long as they remain moderate, are necessary. These, however, are τὰ ἥμερα πάθη, ὅσα κατὰ φύσιν ὑπάρχει τῷ ἀνθρώπῳ ἀναγκαῖά τε καὶ οἰκεῖα.[5] But in Chapter XXXI there is nothing to show that the view of πάθη is not the same as that which appears in *Tusculans* III and IV, where μετριοπάθεια is certainly not accepted.

In the next chapter the statement οὐ κρίσεις τὰ πάθη οὐδὲ δόξαι is most naturally connected with Posidonius.[6] That Antiochus followed orthodox Stoicism in opposition to Posidonius is evident from *Tusculans* IV, 65.[7] Later in the chapter it is possible to trace agreement with Antiochus. Thus with the words κακὸν ἐὰν μὲν παρεῖναι ὑπολάβωμεν λυπούμεθα, τὸ δὲ μέλλον φοβούμεθα may be compared *Tusculans* III, 14: "Quarum enim rerum praesentia sumus in aegritudine, easdem impendentes et venientes timemus." With the sentence οὐδὲ γὰρ τὸν τυχόντα ἄν τις διαγένοιτο χρόνον,[8] ἀπογινώσκων ἀπαλλαγὴν ἢ κουφισμὸν τοῦ κακοῦ we may connect *Tusculans* III, 61: "Dolor corporis, cuius est morsus acerrimus, perferetur spe proposita boni." The distinction between ἄγρια and

---

[1] Stob. II, 119, 8 sqq. Cf. *SVF*. III, 389 (Ar. Did.).   [2] 85, 13.
[3] *EN*. 1105 a 2. Cf. Plot. IV, vii, 15: λάβωμεν δὲ ψυχὴν...πάθη... ἀποτριψαμένην.   [4] 84, 27.   [5] 86, 13.
[6] See Schmekel, 263, n.; *SVF*. I, 208, III, 456; Plot. I, i, 9.
[7] Cf. IV, 65, 76, 82, III, 64; *Top*. 64.
[8] The phrase is found in *EN*. 01 a 16 ("for some chance period", Ross).

ἥμερα πάθη is not unlike that which Panaetius drew between ἡδοναὶ παρὰ φύσιν and ἡδοναὶ κατὰ φύσιν.[1] The examples of objectionable πάθη are those which are given in the *Nicomachean Ethics*.[2] In *Tusculans* IV the distinction between the two kinds of πάθη is significantly unrecognized: "misericordia" (ἔλεος) and "pudor" (αἰσχύνη) are grouped together with "aemulatio" (ζῆλος) and "malevolentia laetans malo alieno" (ἐπιχαιρεκακία).[3] But Arius Didymus, as might be expected, introduces it into his account of Aristotelean and Peripatetic Ethics. Our writer, alluding to *Timaeus* 64 E, declares Plato's belief to be that pleasure and pain are non-essential to human life. We feel pain when we move against Nature and pleasure when we return to move in harmony with Nature. Between pleasure and pain there exists a mean state, which is that natural calm in which we spend most of our life. Antiochus esteemed this normal tranquillity and found that Democritus had excellently described its character.[4] Our writer allows a certain accidental value to such pleasures as participate in the Good, but denies that pleasure can have any intrinsic importance. It is purely adventitious, ἐπιγεννηματικὴ τῇ φύσει ὑπάρχουσα καὶ οὐδὲν οὐσιῶδες οὐδὲ προηγούμενον ἔχουσα. For this view authority can be found in the *Philebus*: ἀεὶ γένεσίς ἐστιν, οὐσία δὲ οὐκ ἔστιν τὸ παράπαν ἡδονῆς.[5] The use of ἐπιγεννηματική is, however, unplatonic. Arius Didymus declares that Aristotle regarded pleasure as non-essential, ἐν τῇ ἡδονῇ τὸ ἐπιγεννηματικόν.[6] But the actual phrase cannot be paralleled in the writings of Aristotle.[7] Probably

[1] *SVF.* III, 155.

[2] 07 a 10. Cf. 83 b 18. For ἁ. π. cf. Tim. Locr. 102 E: παθητικᾶς (sc. ψυχᾶς) ἄγρια πάθεά τε καὶ λύσσαι οἰστρώδεες.

[3] § 16. The *aegritudo* and *laetitia* of §14 might seem to resemble the ἡδονή and λύπη which are the ἥμερα πάθη of *Did.* 86, 16. Yet we read in § 35: "Quid autem est non miserius solum, sed foedius etiam et deformius, quam aegritudine quis afflictus, debilitatus, iacens?"

[4] *Fin.* V, 23. Cf. *Fin.* I, 38; the three states (unum gaudere, alterum dolere, tertium nec gaudere nec dolere) of *Tusc.* III, 47; "quies" in *CD.* 19, 1; "pax" *ibid.* 19, 13; Speusippus, *RP.* 288 A, and Hoyer on ἀοχλησία.

[5] 53 C.

[6] Stob. II, 53, 18. What Aristotle really holds (*EN.* 69 b 26) is that ἐπείσακτος ἡδονή is not needed in a βίος ἡδύς.

[7] See also Giambelli, *Riv. Filol.* 92, 473.

ἐπιγεννηματικός (ὄν) was used by Antiochus[1] in the technical sense which it seems to have acquired in the Ethics of the Porch.[2] There is no reason why in the passage before us it should not have been derived from Arius Didymus.

The treatment of friendship in Chapter xxxiii, as already mentioned, is thoroughly Aristotelean.[3] We learn that the name "friendship" may be applied, in an extended sense, to the feeling which parents have for their children, to that between kinsfolk, to that between fellow-citizens, and to that between members of the same society. With this may be compared what Varro following Antiochus ascribes to the Old Academy.[4] The term ἀξιέραστος[5] is used as by Arius Didymus in his account of Stoic ethics.[6] Three kinds of love are distinguished, as by Plato in *Laws* 837, B–D. They are described as ἐρωτικὴ ἀστεία, φαύλη, μέση, the use of ἀστεία being probably due to the influence of Stoicism.[7]

The remainder of the treatise can be dealt with briefly. Obviously the *Republic* is the source mainly followed in Chapter xxxiv.[8] Political virtue is defined at the end of the chapter as ethical virtue is defined by Arius Didymus: κοινὴν δοξαστικῆς καὶ ἠθικῆς ἕξιν θεωρητικὴν καὶ προαιρετικὴν καὶ πρακτικὴν τῶν ἐν ταῖς πράξεσι καλῶν.[9] The character of the sophist in the next chapter is portrayed as by Plato. Arius Didymus attributes a similar view to Stoicism.[10] Finally, the term συνέμφασις (89, 19) is apparently technical in Stoic philosophy and may have been adopted by Antiochus.[11]

---

[1] Cf. *Fin.* III, 32 (= *SVF.* III, 504).

[2] Cf. D. L. VII, 86. Cf. also Ph. Al. *Quod Det.* 124: τὸ χαίρειν ἐπιγέννημα σοφίας; Oc. Luc. I, 8.

[3] For Aristotle's debt to Plato cf. W. Ziebis, *Begriffe der* φιλία *bei Plato*, 56.

[4] *CD.* 19, 3. [5] 87, 28. 36.

[6] *SVF.* III, 717. Cf. 719, 650 (D. L. VI, 105; *Tht. Komm.* xxxii, 8, 27). For βοσκηματώδης (*Did.* 87, 25) cf. Ar. Did. Stob. II, 52, 15; Cic. *Off.* I, 105; Oc. Luc. 4, 14; βοσκημάτων βίος in *EN.* 95 b 20 (after Plato, *Rep.* 586 A).

[7] *SVF.* III, 613. See Purser in *Hermath.* 17, 54. Plot. IV, iii, 32 has τὰ ἀστεῖα τῶν παθῶν τῇ σπουδαίᾳ (ψυχῇ).

[8] Cf. 88, 30 and *Prol.* Herm. VI, 220.

[9] Stob. II, 145, 11 sqq.; *EN.* 40 a. [10] *SVF.* III, 611, 686.

[11] S. E. *AM.* VII, 239 (partly given *SVF.* III, 399).

94

vii

ANTIOCHUS, ARIUS DIDYMUS, AND MIDDLE PLATONISM

From the preceding inquiry the following points emerge. In many places our writer expresses views which agree with those which are known to belong to Antiochus or are usually attributed to him. Sometimes he closely follows the Old Academy. Throughout the work he exhibits many points of agreement with Arius Didymus, and without doubt in at least one place abridges a passage from his *Epitome*. We know that Arius was a doxographer who besides reporting the doctrines of Zeno and Chrysippus, of Panaetius and Posidonius, wrote on Plato and Aristotle and was attracted by Academic writers of his period, Eudorus and Philo of Larissa, and we need feel no doubt that he was also strongly influenced by Antiochus of Ascalon, though it is unnecessary to assume with Strache that Arius followed him slavishly.

Strache, while unwilling to believe that our writer actually excerpts the *Epitome* of Arius Didymus, admits that the views attributed to Plato by Arius in that work may play a part in the *Didaskalikos*.[1] Strache arrives at this conclusion after having assumed that every view in the *Didaskalikos* which can be paralleled in Cicero or in the remains of Arius is purely Antiochean. But neither Arius[2] nor our writer follows Antiochus unswervingly, and though the latter is doubtless often important, there is no reason why every agreement between the *Didaskalikos* and the remains of Arius should be explained *ipso facto* as due to Antiochus. We have discovered Posidonian doctrine in more than one place. This is most naturally explained by assuming that the writer of the *Didaskalikos* follows Posidonius indirectly. If both Antiochus and Posidonius exercise

---

[1] "In Platonis scripta introductionem quodammodo adhiberi posse ad Arii de Platone placita recuperanda mihi persuasum est", *Diss.* 100.

[2] Cf. *DDG.* 72: "At est ubi cum Antiocho pugnent" (the views of Arius).

indirect influence, and if our writer is using a single doxographical source, then the probability is that the source is Arius Didymus, whose account of Plato would naturally be coloured by the views not only of Antiochus but of Posidonius also.

It is important not to mistake the character of the *Epitome* of Arius Didymus. It was written by a Stoic and in it were described the views of Stoics, of Aristotle and the Peripatetics, and of Plato.[1] A doxographer is almost bound to have some familiarity with those writers whose views he claims to report. We may be quite sure that Arius (as also the writer of the *Didaskalikos*) read Plato and Aristotle[2] for himself. But at the same time Arius dealt with them freely and in the manner of Antiochus and the Middle Stoics. To take but a single example, he declared the Aristotelean view to be that matter is σωματικὴ διὰ τὸ πάσαις ὥσπερ ἐκμαγεῖον ὑπόκεισθαι ταῖς ποιότησιν.[3] Now Aristotle had refused to accept Plato's ἐκμαγεῖον.[4] This example is sufficient to disprove von Arnim's assertion, that the aim of Arius Didymus, in accordance with the classicism of the Augustan Age, can only have been to present to his contemporaries the chief systems of Greek philosophy in their pure and unmixed form.[5] Admittedly during this period there was a revival of interest in the original works of Plato and Aristotle and of their immediate successors. But philosophers were really much more eclectic than von Arnim is prepared to allow, and Arius is no exception. He may have left differences unreconciled[6] which Antiochus must have sought to overcome. But he also made good use of the Antiochean method, which considerably simplified the history of philosophy.[7]

Hippolytus gives an account of Plato's doctrines[8] which is important for our purpose. Here we read of the three ἀρχαί, God,

---

[1] Cf. *DDG*. 70 sqq.

[2] Strache's opinion that Arius would not have read Aristotle's *Categories* (*Diss.* 57) is entirely without basis.

[3] *DDG*. 448, 9. [4] Cf. *Met.* 988 a 1.

[5] *SBWien*, 1926; *Ar. Did. Abriss* 12.

[6] See Pohlenz, *Ph. Wo.* 1911, 1500.

[7] Kroll, *NJ*. 1903, 686, observes that Antiochus "gehörte zu den auch heute nicht ausgestorbenen Leuten, welche das Studium der Philosophie möglichst leicht machen wollten".

[8] *DDG*. 567.

Matter, and Idea, the last being described as the thought of God. Matter is coeval[1] with God (σύγχρονον τῷ θεῷ)[2] and thus the Universe is uncreated (ἀγένητον τὸν κόσμον). The text from the *Laws* (715 E) is quoted as in the *Didaskalikos* (81, 31). We learn of the divergent opinions among Platonists respecting metensomatosis. As in the *Didaskalikos* external "goods" are said to be capable of being turned to a good or a bad use[3] and virtues are called both ἀκρότητες and μεσότητες. The phrase ὅσιός τε καὶ δίκαιος μετὰ φρονήσεως (569, 15) suggests comparison with *Didaskalikos* 81, 21. The virtues but not the vices are characterized by their ἀντακολουθία. Plato, we are informed, εἱμαρμένην φησὶν εἶναι, οὐ μὴν πάντα καθ᾽ εἱμαρμένην γίνεσθαι.[4] The description of the involuntariness of vice is reminiscent of Chapter XXXI of the *Didaskalikos*: ἀκούσια δέ φησιν εἶναι τὰ ἁμαρτήματα· εἰς γὰρ τὸ κάλλιστον τῶν ἐν ἡμῖν, ὅπερ ἐστὶν ἡ ψυχή, οὐκ ἄν τινα τὸ κακὸν παραδέξασθαι, τοῦτ᾽ ἐστι τὴν ἀδικίαν· κατὰ ἄγνοιαν δὲ καὶ σφάλμα τοῦ ἀγαθοῦ, οἰομένους καλόν τι ποιεῖν, ἐπὶ τὸ κακὸν ἔρχεσθαι. Punishment has a remedial value.[5] Evil is merely a byproduct of good (κατ᾽ ἐναντίωσιν καὶ παρακολούθησιν τοῦ ἀγαθοῦ ἢ καθ᾽ ὑπερβολὴν ἢ κατὰ μείωσιν).[6] The account of Aristotle which follows is closely connected with that of Plato.[7] We must therefore observe further that the ten categories are classified as Substance and Accidents (compare p. 66 above) and that Aristotle is made to hold a view which we may suspect to be Antiochean, that the soul at death vanishes (ἐναφανίζεσθαι) in the Fifth Element.

That this doxographical account of Plato and Aristotle is derived from a work of Arius Didymus is maintained with much plausi-

---

[1] ἰσόχρονος καὶ ἡλικιῶτις, "Justin", *Cohort.* 23.
[2] 567, 18. Cf. l. 15 with *Did.* x *ad init.*
[3] 569, 3. Cf. *Did.* 81, 12.
[4] 568, 19; *Did.* 79, 1.
[5] Cf. *Did.* 85, 10. Aspas. (76, 33, on *EN.* 13 b 23) argues: εἰ ἀκούσιον ἦν τὸ ἀδικεῖν, οὐκ ἂν ἐκόλαζον οἱ νομοθέται τοὺς τὰ κακὰ δρῶντας. κολάζουσι δέ. οὐκ ἄρα ἀκούσιον.
[6] Cf. Apul. 95, 16 (after *Rep.* 379): "nec ullius mali causa deo poterit adscribi."
[7] "Sicher verwandt", Howald, *Herm.* 1920, 74.

bility by Howald.[1] Arguing that it is an "elender Extrakt" from a handbook composed by Arius on the history of philosophy, Howald suggests that this is also the source which is followed in the *Didaskalikos* and in the *De Platone* of Apuleius. The *Didaskalikos* is closely copied from the original, but the *De Platone* is a summary written with some regard for style.[2] Howald distinguishes this handbook as "A" from the ἐπιτομή of which fragments survive and is inclined to identify it with the περὶ αἱρέσεων, mentioned as the title of a work of Arius by Stobaeus (II, 6, 13, Wachsmuth).[3]

Sinko first showed by a detailed comparison that the *Didaskalikos* and the *De Platone* agree to a remarkable extent.[4] The explanation which he favours—though he is not entirely consistent[5]—is, that the common source which the two treatises presuppose is a work of the second-century Platonist Gaius. The importance of Gaius will be indicated subsequently in connexion with the authorship of the *Didaskalikos*. At present we need consider only the hypothesis which is made by Howald. In order that we may test it, we must study the *De Platone* in the light of the knowledge acquired during the course of the preceding investigation.

The first four chapters are biographical. The account of Plato's life, though brief, is similar to that which is given in the opening part of the third book of Diogenes Laertius,[6] and to other biographies of Plato which have come down to us.[7] When Apuleius commences to deal with Plato's philosophy, he mentions the three ἀρχαί which we have encountered in the *Didaskalikos* and in the *Philosophoumena*,[8] God being considered before Matter and the

---

[1] Howald, *Herm.* 1920, 75. The provenance of the ἅμαξα-view of the Universe is uncertain, but we may perhaps attribute it to Antiochus (cf. also "navem, si adeo saepe refecta esset, ut nulla tabula eadem permaneret quae non nova fuisset, nihilo minus eandem navem esse existimari..."; Sokolowski, *Phil. Pr. Recht.* 505; and Plut. *Thes.* 23).

[2] Purser (*Hermath.* 17) finds it a most dreary treatise.

[3] See however *DDG.* 78–9.   [4] *Diss. phil. cl. Cracov.* 1905, 129 sqq.

[5] E.g. p. 140 (on Apul. 91, 12; *Did.* 69, 27).   [6] To about Ch. 46.

[7] See Howald, *Philol.* 1917, 126. Sinko, p. 177, would derive all from Gaius.

[8] Sinko's emendation of 86, 10–12, which Thomas mentions but does not adopt, is the only way of avoiding "formas...informes", which makes nonsense.

Ideas. The divine attributes ἀπερίμετρος, ἀόρατος, ἀδάμαστος, "innominabilis" (i.e. ἀκατονόμαστος[1]) cannot be paralleled in the *Didaskalikos*. But "incorporeus", "unus", "nihil indigens", "indictus" naturally suggest ἀσώματος, ἁπλοῦς, ἀπροσδεής, ἄρρητος.[2] The quotation from the *Timaeus* which follows, despite Apuleius's confident declaration "Platonis haec verba sunt", is inexact, and either written from memory or (as is more probable) borrowed at second hand:

| (*Timaeus* 28 c) τόν...ποιητὴν καὶ πατέρα τοῦδε τοῦ παντὸς εὑρεῖν τε ἔργον καὶ εὑρόντα εἰς πάντας ἀδύνατον λέγειν. | (Apuleius 87, 1) θεὸν εὑρεῖν τε ἔργον εὑρόντα τε εἰς πολλοὺς ἐκφέρειν ἀδύνατον. |

As we have seen, ἐκφέρειν is also substituted for λέγειν in the *Didaskalikos* (79, 33). Probably the description of matter as "inprocreabilis, incorrupta" is a translation of ὕλη ἀγένητος καὶ ἄφθαρτος,[3] a phrase which does not, however, occur in the *Didaskalikos*. Another point of difference is the use of "infinibilis" (i.e. ἄπειρος). Otherwise the account closely resembles that which is given in *Didaskalikos* VIII and XII. Of interest are the words "corpora propter insignem evidentiam sui simili iudicio cognosci". That this view goes back ultimately to Antiochus may be regarded as certain. It does not appear in the *Didaskalikos* and is not easily reconciled with what Apuleius himself writes later in this same chapter. Apuleius now considers the Ideas, and this passage, like the opening of *Didaskalikos* XII, is certainly derived from Arius Didymus.[4]

In the *Didaskalikos*, as we saw, ἡ νοητὴ οὐσία is contrasted with ἡ πλανωμένη τε καὶ ῥευστή (52, 9). So too Apuleius: "οὐσίας, quas essentias dicimus, duas esse ait." Of these essences the one is intelligible, the other opinable.[5] "Sensibilia" are in flux and Apuleius appears to be translating freely what in the original Greek must have been identical with or closely similar to *Didaskalikos* 54, 25 sqq.:

[1] Used by Ph. Al. and Celsus *CC*. 7, 42. Cornutus (38, 14) uses ἀδάμαστος of Athene and perhaps Varro translates the same word by "invictus" (cf. *CD*. 7, 11).

[2] 66, 1. 6, 64, 28.

[3] But ζῷον ἀγένητον καὶ ἄφθαρτον, 67, 2 (Ar. Did.).

[4] *PE*. 545 B–C.

[5] 88, 4–9. Compare also 92, 10 sqq.

"intellegendi substantia quoniam constanti nititur robore, etiam quae de ea disputantur, ratione stabili et fide plena sunt (ὁ μὲν ἐπιστημονικὸς (sc. λόγος) τὸ βέβαιον ἔχει καὶ μόνιμον, ἅτε περὶ τῶν βεβαίων καὶ μονίμων ὑπάρχων); at eius, quae veluti umbra et imago est superioris, rationes quoque et verba (so he expands λόγος) quae de ea disputantur inconstanti sunt disciplina¹ (ὁ δὲ πιθανὸς καὶ δοξαστικὸς πολὺ τὸ εἰκὸς διὰ τὸ μὴ περὶ τὰ μόνιμα εἶναι)."²

In Chapter XII Apuleius turns to Plato's theodicy. Plato, we learn, "ita definit: providentiam esse divinam sententiam, conservatricem prosperitatis eius cuius causa tale suscepit officium; divinam legem esse fatum, per quod inevitabiles cogitationes dei atque incepta conplentur. Unde si quid providentia geritur, id agitur et fato, et quod fato terminatur, providentia debet susceptum videri."³ In this passage πρόνοια is identifiable with God's νοήματα. Should God be termed Zeus, Providence must be personified as Athene.⁴ Apuleius does not, however, express the relation thus, for like the writer of the *Didaskalikos* he believes the Platonic theology to differ from Stoic pantheism, because the supreme God ("summus exsuperantissimusque deorum omnium") is not organic with the Universe of which He is the Creator. Accordingly Providence is declared to reside in the transcendent God. Fate and Fortune are described in the manner of Antiochus.⁵ The words "nec sane omnia referenda esse ad vim fati puta[n]t, sed esse aliquid in nobis" may be compared with οὐ πάντα καθειμάρθαι and ἀδέσποτον ἡ ψυχή of *Didaskalikos* XXVI.⁶

In the second book of the *De Platone*, which is devoted to Ethics,⁷

¹ "Belong to a branch of study quite indeterminate", suggests Purser.
² Apuleius (88, 8–9) writes: "Sicut superior (sc. essentia) vere esse memoratur, hanc non esse vere possumus dicere." While in the *Didaskalikos* ἡ πλανωμένη τε καὶ ῥευστὴ οὐσία is not explicitly identified with τὸ μὴ ὄν, such a doctrine is probably implied in Chapter XXXV (ἔστι δὲ τὸ μὴ ὄν...μετὰ συνεμφάσεως τῆς πρὸς ἕτερον, ὅπερ τῷ πρώτῳ ὄντι παρέπεται).
³ Plato πρῶτος ἐν φιλοσοφίᾳ...ὠνόμασε...θεοῦ πρόνοιαν, asserts D. L. III, 24. Cf. also Theophr. fr. 20, *DDG*.
⁴ See p. 72, *supra*. Plato, *Crat.* 407 A–B; Chalc. 176; *Exc. ex Theodoto* 69–74.   ⁵ *A. Po.* 29.   ⁶ See p. 86, *supra*.
⁷ The περὶ ἑρμηνείας, which there is no good reason to regard as spurious (cf. *UPG.* 545), completes the trilogy.

goods are divided into the divine and the human. Of the human, those which belong to the soul (i.e. the four cardinal virtues) as participating by nature in the Good may be considered divine, but goods of the body and those which are external differ, inasmuch as they do not necessarily participate in the Good.[1] Apuleius adds: "Et illum quidem qui natura inbutus est ad sequendum bonum non modo sibimet ipsi natum putat sed omnibus etiam hominibus."[2] With this may be compared the Antiochean view in *De Finibus* v, 65.[3] The expression "semina quae debeant emicare" used in Chapter III is obviously parallel to αἰθύγματα in the *Didaskalikos*.[4] Apuleius, however, supposes that the seed not only of good but of evil also is inborn in the soul, a doctrine which does not appear to have been held by Antiochus,[5] and which is not mentioned in the *Didaskalikos*. Yet "hominem ab stirpe ipsa neque absolute malum nec bonum nasci" agrees with οὐδὲ πάντας ἀνθρώπους ἢ σπουδαίους εἶναι ἢ φαύλους.[6]

In Chapter V virtue is defined as in the *Didaskalikos*.[7] The virtues may be regarded either as means or as extremes: "Et medietates (μεσότητας) easdemque virtutes ac summitates (ἀκρότητας) vocat." Subsequently Apuleius shows agreement with *Didaskalikos* XXIX, except that he gives a fuller account of justice, which is influenced by Aristotle.[8]

The remainder of the book, except in such chapters as VIII and XXV where the range is wider, in most respects exhibits close correspondence with the *Didaskalikos*. Certain Stoic features, however, which are absent from the latter, deserve mention. Thus Apuleius insists that for the irremediably evil man death is a blessing.[9] Con-

---

[1] II, i. ii. Cf. *Did.* XXVII.   [2] 105, 6 sqq.

[3] Cf. also *Fin.* II, 45; *CD.* 19, 3 (the basis, as we perceive from *Fin.* II, 45, is Plat. *Ep.* IX: ἕκαστος ἡμῶν οὐχ αὑτῷ μόνον γέγονεν, ἀλλὰ τῆς γενέσεως ἡμῶν τὸ μέν τι ἡ πατρὶς μερίζεται κτα.).

[4] See p. 83, *supra*.

[5] In *Tusc.* III, 2: "paene cum lacte nutricis errorem suxisse" (videmur).

[6] Did. 83, 29.   [7] See p. 89, *supra*.

[8] 110, 8 is compared by Thomas with *EN.* 30 b 30. The resemblance is not very close.

[9] 120, 20. Thomas compares *Polit.* 308 E–9 A. He might well have added *Gorg.* 512 A–B. Plutarch thinks Chrysippus approves of Antisthenes's δεῖν κτᾶσθαι νοῦν ἢ βρόχον (*SVF.* III, 167. But cf. 760).

version to perfect virtue is sudden, as it is for the Stoic Sage.[1] Other details in the picture of the Sage suggest a Stoic original. The Sage alone is rich.[2] His life is filled with praise and renown. More important still, the Sage will if the need arises take his own life.[3] Varro, appealing to the Peripatetics and the Old Academics, expresses a similar view,[4] as does Cicero in De Finibus III, 60, and Arius Didymus attributes it to the Peripatetics.[5] Plato himself, however, did not countenance suicide.[6]

It is impossible to doubt that the Didaskalikos, the account of Plato in the Philosophoumena, and the De Platone, are intimately related.[7] If we consider only those writers whose work has not been entirely lost, the case for assuming an Arian work as the source of all three is very strong. But whether we ought to follow Howald in postulating "A" rather than the Epitome is open to question. Points of agreement with the Epitome have been found throughout the Didaskalikos. According to our conjecture, that part of the latter treatise which deals with Plato's physical doctrines (Chapters XII–XXII) is derived from Arius's Epitome. Here at any rate there is no need to assume dependence on "A". The Epitome would naturally contain an account of what Plato wrote in the Timaeus.

It is fairly obvious that the writer of the Didaskalikos is not excerpting the Timaeus itself.[8] Significant is the fact that the order in which the five senses are discussed (Chapters XVIII, XIX) and which is exactly the reverse of the Platonic is the arrangement recognized by Arius Didymus.[9] When, however, we turn to the

---

[1] SVF. III, 539. Plato, Ep. 341 C, ought not to be forgotten.

[2] 124, 5. Cf. SVF. III, 593 (Ar. Did.); Did. 81, 13 sqq.

[3] 127, 14.   [4] CD. 19, 4.

[5] Stob. II, 126, 5 sqq. Strache (Diss. 37) rightly protests against Wachsmuth's alteration of καὶ το κακῶς. Cf. also SVF. III, 758 (Ar. Did.).

[6] Ph. 62 B. Plotinus allows it in exceptional cases, e.g. if a man knows that he is losing his reason (I, ix). Cf. also I, iv, 16.

[7] Nothing in D. L. III (a "scissors-and-paste compilation", as Field, 234, terms it) is very closely connected with these three accounts of Plato, except that (as already mentioned) the biographical section resembles De Plat. I, i–iv. The placita proper (67–79) may owe something to Posidonius.

[8] Thus in 68, 19 we read πρὸς and in 68, 34 εἰς τὸ πᾶν. Plato wrote, Tim. 55 C, ἐπὶ τὸ πᾶν. σφιγγομένη 71, 25 replaces εἰλλομένη (or ἰλλ.) of Tim. 40 B.   [9] DDG. 456, 1.

De Platone we have to admit that the order in which Apuleius treats the topics derived from the *Timaeus* differs not only from that of Plato himself but also from that which is adhered to in the *Didaskalikos*.[1] Sinko even maintains that Apuleius used the *Timaeus* side by side with a doxographical work.[2] But that this should have been the case does not seem very probable, for Apuleius could write concerning Plato's view of God: "*ut ait ipse*, ἀόρατον, ἀδάμαστον..." and confidently assert "Platonis haec verba sunt" in the very act of misquoting *Timaeus* 28 c. It appears on the whole best to assume that Apuleius followed Arius Didymus's *Epitome* in Book I as in Book II of the *De Platone*, but that he took considerable liberties with his original.

At this stage we have reached the following conclusions. Firstly, the philosophical structure of the *Didaskalikos* is mainly dependent on the eclectic system of Antiochus of Ascalon. Secondly, the writer is not directly indebted to Antiochus but rather to Arius Didymus, who in his doxographical account of Plato incorporated much Antiochean doctrine and sometimes practised an eclecticism of his own, introducing from Aristotle and the Old Academy elements which Antiochus himself had not employed. Thirdly, the *Didaskalikos* is intimately connected with the account of Plato in the *Philosophoumena* of Hippolytus and with the *De Platone* of Apuleius. This at once leads us to the question of the authorship.

[1] See Appendix.   [2] p. 177.

viii

THE WRITER

In the MSS. of the *Didaskalikos*, whenever an ascription appears, the name given is Alkinoos. Now there are just two references to an Alkinoos whom we could possibly identify with the author of the work before us. Philostratus, writing in the second or third century of our Era, says of a certain sophist named Marcus: διδάσκων γὰρ περὶ τῆς τῶν σοφιστῶν τέχνης...παράδειγμα τοῦ λόγου τὴν Ἶριν ἐποιήσατο...ὁ τὴν Ἶριν ἰδὼν ὡς ἓν χρῶμα οὐκ εἶδεν, ὡς θαυμάσαι, ὁ δὲ ὅσα χρώματα, μᾶλλον ἐθαύμασεν.[1] οἱ δὲ τὴν διάλεξιν ταύτην Ἀλκινόῳ τῷ Στωικῷ ἀνατιθέντες διαμαρτάνουσι μὲν ἰδέας λόγου, διαμαρτάνουσι δὲ ἀληθείας.[2] The only other reference to an Alkinoos whom we might connect with the *Didaskalikos* occurs in Photius. Here we are informed that the author of the treatise περὶ τῆς τοῦ παντὸς οὐσίας refutes καὶ περὶ ψυχῆς καὶ ὕλης καὶ ἀναστάσεως Ἀλκίνοον ἀλόγως τε καὶ ψευδῶς εἰπόντα.[3]

It will be convenient to consider the latter passage first. The author of the treatise mentioned is Hippolytus[4] and allusion is doubtless made to an extant passage: ἐκ τοῦ πρὸς Ἕλληνας λόγου τοῦ ἐπιγεγραμμένου κατὰ Πλάτωνος περὶ τῆς τοῦ παντὸς αἰτίας.[5] But nowhere in it does the name Ἀλκίνοος occur. We may assume that Photius had this passage in mind and explain the statement which he makes as follows. He would have read the *Didaskalikos*, which by his day was ascribed to "Alkinoos",[6] and have disliked, as a Christian, those passages (e.g. 72, 12; 78, 28) in which the dogma of metensomatosis is affirmed. On turning to the treatise of Hippolytus he would have found the same dogma attacked. Thus

---

[1] Clearly a reference to *Theaet.* 155 D. [2] p. 40, 23.
[3] *Bibl.* 48, 11 b 19. [4] Cf. *Dict. Christ. Biog.* III, 96, 100.
[5] *Hippol. frs.* ed. Lagarde, 1, 68 sqq.
[6] Photius wrote somewhat earlier than A.D. 925, the date of the production of Vindob. 314, the oldest of our *Did.* MSS. But the "Alkinoos"-ascription is certainly older.

what Photius means to say is that, since Plato is refuted, the writer of the *Didaskalikos* is refuted also, and there is no question of an attack upon "Alkinoos" by Hippolytus himself. The possibility of such an explanation was apparently not considered by Freudenthal, who denied that Photius alludes to the writer of the *Didaskalikos*, since nowhere in this work is there any mention of the Christian belief in the Resurrection.[1] If, however, we suppose that Photius is giving his own impression and that his statement is not to be taken *au pied de la lettre*, the words καὶ ἀναστάσεως no longer present difficulty.[2]

In the passage quoted from Philostratus we observe that the Alkinoos alluded to is a Stoic. It may readily be granted that when Stoicism though a declining force was not yet defunct, and when a Stoic could be a Platonist without appearing to be inconsistent,[3] treatises on Plato's philosophy could be written by those who professed allegiance to the Porch. Arius Didymus, as we know, was a Stoic, and it is his account of Plato, according to our view, on which the *Didaskalikos* is based. Yet it appears almost inconceivable that the *Didaskalikos* should be the work of a Stoic. The theology of Chapter x is quite without parallel in Stoic authors. The words τοῖς πλείστοις τῶν ἀπὸ Πλάτωνος ἀρέσκει (63, 22) suggest that the writer is himself a Platonist. Plato is the only philosopher whose views he professes to report. The essential fabric is Platonic;[4] as to the resemblance, or according to Philostratus lack of resemblance, between the Stoic Alkinoos and the sophist Marcus, nothing in the *Didaskalikos* is comparable with the example chosen, which, therefore, is of no use for our purpose.

Having dealt with the references to Alkinoos in Philostratus and

---

[1] Frl. 276–7.   [2] See also Fabricius, V3, 523.

[3] "Trypho the Stoic and Platonist" is mentioned by Porphyry (*Vit. Plot.* 17) without any trace of surprise at such divided allegiance. Marcus Aurelius, who is very sensitive to doctrines belonging to other Schools, is largely influenced by Plato. He cites *Rep.* 486 A (VII, 35); *Apol.* 28 B (VII, 45); *Gorg.* 512 D (VII, 46) (*Theaet.* 173 E, II, 13). Geffcken, *Unterg.* 32, explains the decline of Stoicism after the death of Marcus Aurelius: "In der Hauptsache hat die Stoa vielmehr durch die Aufsaugung ihrer Lehren durch andere Systeme ihr Ende gefunden." But even in Plotinus's day Stoicism was not "dead".

[4] Cf. Frl. 277.

Photius,[1] we may now compare the two following versions of a passage in a catalogue of the names of the more important ancient philosophers:

ἐν δὲ φιλοσοφίᾳ διέπρεψαν Πλά-   ἐν δὲ φιλοσοφίᾳ διέπρεψαν...
των καὶ Ἀριστοτέλης...ὧν τὸν   χρησιμότεροι δὲ Γάϊος, Ἀλκῖνος
μὲν Πλάτωνα ὑπομνηματίζουσι   (sic cod.).[3]
πλεῖστοι· χρησιμώτεροι δὲ Γάϊος
Ἀλβῖνος....[2]

There is not the slightest doubt that Ἀλκῖνος is a mistake for Ἀλβῖνος.[4] Proclus twice mentions Albinus and Gaius together.[5] Moreover, as we know from the Pinax in Codex Parisinus Graecus 1962, Albinus edited the lectures of Gaius on the doctrines of Plato. Finally, the *Introduction* which he himself wrote to the *Dialogues* of Plato is still in existence.

Now, if Ἀλβῖνος is corrupted into Ἀλκῖνος, we are quite justified in raising the question whether the Ἀλκίνοος which appears in the MSS. of the *Didaskalikos* may not also be a corruption of the same name. For Albinus was clearly a Platonist of some importance, and it is equally certain that his name could be corrupted in more ways than one:

Ἀλβίνου τῶν Γαΐου σχολῶν ὑπο-   (usi sumus, says Priscian) Lavini
τυπώσεων Πλατωνικῶν δογ-   quoque ex Gaii scholis exem-
μάτων.[6]   plaribus Platonicorum dogma-
   tum.[7]

On examining all the references which are made to the views of Albinus, we find nothing which contradicts the teaching of the *Didaskalikos* and a large measure of agreement which cannot be explained as due to accident. Writing at the beginning of the third century, Tertullian declares that Albinus regards as divine the

---

[1] It is hardly necessary to point out that the expression "Apology of Alkinoos" in Aelius Aristides I, 536 and III, 598 may be paralleled in Plato, *Rep.* 614 B.

[2] Given by Diels, *Tht. Komm.* xxvi (after Kröhnert, *Canones* 11).

[3] Cramer, *Anec. Gr.*² IV, 196.

[4] Cramer himself emends to Ἀλβῖνος.

[5] *In Rep.* II, 96 Kroll. *In Tim.* I, 340 Diehl. Cf. also *Did.* 78, 20.

[6] Pinax in Paris. Graec. 1962, fol. 146 v.   [7] Prisc. 553 b 32.

saying about the reciprocal migration of souls.[1] From Tertullian
we learn also that Albinus carefully distinguished two kinds of
opposites[2] (cf. *Did.* 77, 30). Iamblichus thus reports the reasons
given by Plotinus and Albinus for the descent of the soul: καὶ οὗτοι
μὲν προϋποκειμένων τῶν ἀτάκτων καὶ πλημμελῶν κινημάτων (*Did.*
67, 12) ἐπεισιέναι φασὶν ὕστερα τὰ κατακοσμοῦντα αὐτὰ (*Did.* 69,
30) καὶ διατάττοντα καὶ τὴν συμφωνίαν ἀπ' ἀμφοτέρων οὕτως
συνυφαίνουσι, κατὰ μὲν Πλωτῖνον τῆς πρώτης ἑτερότητος[3]...κατ'
Ἀλβῖνον δὲ τῆς τοῦ αὐτεξουσίου διημαρτημένης κρίσεως αἰτίας
γιγνομένης τῶν καταγωγῶν ἐνεργημάτων.[4] Proclus mentions the
view of Albinus that the irrational soul is mortal.[5] But the most
convincing proof that Albinus is the author of the *Didaskalikos* is
supplied by Proclus in discussing the sense in which the Universe
may be said to have been begotten: καὶ ὅ γε Πλατωνικὸς Ἀλβῖνος
ἀξιοῖ κατὰ Πλάτωνα τὸν κόσμον ἀγένητον ὄντα γενέσεως ἀρχὴν
ἔχειν...ἵν' ᾖ καὶ ἀεὶ ὢν καὶ γενητός, οὐχ οὕτως ὢν γενητὸς ὡς
κατὰ χρόνον (*Did.* 69, 27) ἀλλ' ὡς λόγον ἔχων γενέσεως διὰ τὴν
ἐκ πλειόνων καὶ ἀνομοίων σύνθεσιν, ἣν ἀναγκαῖον εἰς ἄλλην αἰτίαν
αὐτοῦ τὴν ὑπόστασιν ἀναπέμπειν πρεσβυτέραν (*Did.* 69, 29).[6]

All that is known of the life of Albinus is soon told. Galen,
having attended at Pergamum the lectures of a "pupil of Gaius",[7]
went from there to Smyrna in order to come in contact with "the
Platonist Albinus". This took place in the year 151/2. Doubtless,
like the nameless Platonist, Albinus was a pupil of Gaius, whose
lectures on Plato he is known to have edited. Gaius himself must
have been a Platonist of some importance, for we find that his
Commentaries (ὑπομνήματα) were read in the School of Plotinus,[8]
while we have seen that Proclus includes him among the κορυφαῖοι.[9]
But in what sense Albinus was his follower is purely a matter of
speculation. It is possible to suppose that Gaius founded a School

---

[1] *An.* 28.   [2] *Ibid.* 29.   [3] Cf. *Enn.* v, i, 1.
[4] Stob. I, 375 w. Freudenthal compares *Did.* 78, 30. See also *Tht.
Komm.* xxix.
[5] *In Tim.* III, 311.   [6] *Ibid.* I, 219, 2.
[7] v, 41 K. Galen had just turned fourteen. The date is therefore 144.
[8] *Vit. Plot.* p. 14, 3 Müll.
[9] But since the Neopythagorean Numenius is included as well, the term
should not be pressed too far.

in Smyrna, to which Theon (i.e. the author of the Mathematical Introduction to Plato), Albinus, and the unknown author of the *Commentary* on the *Theaetetus*, all belonged.[1] We might then regard Albinus as Gaius's successor. On the other hand, according to the testimony of Galen, at about the time when Albinus was active in Smyrna there was teaching in Pergamum another pupil of Gaius,[2] whence we might infer that the latter city was the real centre and that Albinus was not actually head of the school established by Gaius.

Freudenthal, although not the first to reject "Alkinoos",[3] was the first to argue from a detailed comparison between the *Prologos* and the *Didaskalikos* that these works were written by a single author, necessarily Albinus.[4] Yet the name "Alkinoos" continues to be used, even in the new edition of *Liddell and Scott*.[5] Schissel and Howald attempt to discredit Freudenthal, but both fail to produce any convincing argument on the other side. Howald indeed asserts that, as the *Prologos* is closely connected with Book III of Diogenes Laertius and the *Didaskalikos* is not, therefore the latter requires a separate author.[6] But he is only able to make this pronouncement by refusing to attach significance to a number of agreements between the *Prologos* and the *Didaskalikos* which, taken all together, point to a single writer.[7]

All the evidence, in fact, from the *Prologos*—and despite the small compass of the work almost every sentence yields some-

[1] The case of Apuleius is different. Cf. *UPG.* 546.

[2] For it is fairly obvious that this was not Albinus himself.

[3] See Ruhnken, *De Longino* § 7. "Albinus philosophus Platonicus, qui vulgo male Alcinous appellatur." Fabric. (Harles), III, 159 (with which V, 524 is inconsistent).

[4] Gesner (*Biblioth.* 32) suggested that the author of both was *Alcinous*.

[5] So, too, Shorey, *CP.* 3, 97; R. M. Jones, *CP.* 13, 195; 21, 109, 322. "Alcinous", *Enc. Brit.* (an unreliable article). Mutschmann, *Div. Arist.* pref. 3, has "Alcinous", but later, p. 16, "Albinus".

[6] *Hermes*, 1920, 75, n. 1. Schissel (*Marinos*, 107) believes in Alcinous, of whose existence, he maintains, "manche Zeugnisse vorhanden sind".

[7] Cf. e.g. *Prol.* 51, 7 and *Did.* 53, 26; 56, 27; 59, 37; *Prol.* 51, 1 and *Did.* 53, 32 sqq.; *Did.* 55, 15 (after *Soph.* 263, etc.) and *Prol.* 47, 21 (the terms are characteristically Stoic. There is a much wider use of λόγος in a fragment of Thrasyllus (whom Albinus names, *Prol.* 49, 13) preserved by Porphyry, *on Harm. Ptol.* 12, 21, Düring); 56, 21 and 47, 5; 58, 15 and 51, 8; 48, 25; 82, 7 and 49, 34.

thing—goes to support the view that the Platonist who wrote it was the writer of the *Didaskalikos* besides, and that the name Ἀλκίνοος in the MSS. of the latter is a corruption of Ἀλβῖνος. This false form may be supposed to have crept in during the earliest period of minuscule writing, at about the beginning of the ninth century. An earlier date is unlikely owing to the circumstance that, whereas B and K in minuscule of this period (e.g. in Cod. Vind. 314) are easily confused,[1] such confusion is practically impossible in majuscule.[2] We have already observed an example of αλβινος corrupted to αλκινος,[3] and, once this false form had gained admittance into a MS. of the *Didaskalikos*, the next scribe would naturally "correct" it to αλκινοος, the name which must have stood in the Archetype from which all our MSS. are descended.[4]

A possible objection which might be raised against attributing the *Didaskalikos* to Albinus is that the latter in the *Prologos* appears to possess considerable first-hand knowledge of the Platonic writings, whereas the writer of the *Didaskalikos* seems if not entirely at any rate generally dependent on a doxographical source. But it does not appear that Albinus in the *Prologos* quoted directly from Plato:[5]

(*Prol.* 47, 9 sqq.) περὶ παντός, ὦ παῖ, μία ἀρχὴ τοῖς μέλλουσι καλῶς βουλεύεσθαι, εἰδέναι περὶ οὗ ἂν ἡ βουλὴ ᾖ, ἢ παρὰ τοῦτο ἁμαρτάνειν κτα.	(*Phdr.* 237 c) περὶ παντός, ὦ παῖ, μία ἀρχὴ τοῖς μέλλουσι καλῶς βουλεύεσθαι, εἰδέναι δεῖ περὶ οὗ ἂν ᾖ ἡ βουλή, ἢ παντὸς ἁμαρτάνειν κτα.
(*Prol.* 50, 19) οὐδὲ γὰρ οἱ ἰατροὶ νενομίκασι, πρότερον τῆς προσφερομένης τροφῆς ἀπολαῦσαι τὸ σῶμα δύνασθαι, εἰ μὴ τὰ ἐμποδίζοντα ἐν τούτῳ τις ἐκβάλοι.	(*Soph.* 230 c) οἱ περὶ τὰ σώματα ἰατροὶ νενομίκασι μὴ πρότερον ἂν τῆς προσφερομένης τροφῆς ἀπολαύειν δύνασθαι σῶμα, πρὶν ἂν τὰ ἐμποδίζοντα ἐν αὐτῷ τις ἐκβάλῃ.

[1] E.g. ℳαι ℳϐιαι α (*Did.* 62, 18, fol. 3 recto in O).
[2] So Diels, *Tht. Komm.* xxviii, 2.   [3] p. 106.
[4] This, as Freudenthal pointed out, is established by the existence of a lacuna in all the MSS. at 69, 14–15.
[5] Freudenthal's theory that the *Prologos* as we have it is an unsatisfactory epitome of what Albinus actually wrote (256 sqq.) cannot be proved, and the difficulties in Ch. III are better treated by Schissel (*Hermes*, 1931) than by Freudenthal.

Again, after having discussed the first part of the definition of the dialogue:[1] λόγος ἐξ ἐρωτήσεως καὶ ἀποκρίσεως συγκείμενος περί τινος τῶν πολιτικῶν καὶ φιλοσόφων πραγμάτων, μετὰ τῆς πρεπούσης ἠθοποιΐας[2] τῶν παραλαμβανομένων προσώπων..., Albinus proceeds: ἐπὶ τούτοις φησὶ καὶ τῆς κατὰ τὴν λέξιν κατασκευῆς. The effect of this is to make Plato the author of the whole definition. Since Albinus was a Platonist of some importance, we may credit him with having read Plato for himself. Yet, in these two handbooks, he shows himself less a follower of Plato than of tradition.

Freudenthal describes each work as a mosaic made up of Platonic words and sentences.[3] In the *Didaskalikos* it seems obvious that the pattern is frequently repeated which had been composed by Arius Didymus and which of course contained a large amount of unplatonic material. That Albinus was capable of ornamenting his original is proved by the circumstance that, whereas Arius wrote συχνὰς εἰκόνας ἑνὸς ἀνδρός and κατὰ πρόνοιαν, the corresponding phrases in the *Didaskalikos* are ἑνὸς ἀνδρὸς εἰκόνες μυρίαι ἐπὶ μυρίαις and κατὰ θαυμασιωτάτην πρόνοιαν.[4] These attempts to embellish the style of the passage are not without significance. In the *Prologos* high tribute is paid to the literary qualities of the Platonic dialogues: τὸ Ἀττικόν, τὸ εὔχαρι, τὸ ἀπέριττον, τὸ ἀνενδεές.[5] Hence we may infer that Albinus endeavoured to reproduce these qualities in his own writing and, in copying out passages of Arius, introduced what he took to be appropriate changes in diction, as in these two examples.[6]

Nevertheless the *Didaskalikos*, as befits an elementary textbook, is written on the whole in a plain and unaffected style. In contrast

---

[1] Cf. D. L. III, 48.

[2] ἦθους ἐμποίησις, Ar. Did. Stob. II, 39, 10 (cf. Clem. *Paed.* I, 2, 1, connected with Posidonius in Sen. *Ep.* 95, 65, who uses ἠθολογία. Kroll, *Rh. Mus.* 1903, 568 suggests that Posidonius may have taught Antiochus to use the word ἠθολ.).

[3] "Beide zeigen einen aus platonischen Worten und Sätzen zusammengewürfelten Musivstil" (Frl. 296).

[4] 67, 4. 10.

[5] 48, 12. Cf. Cic. *Or.* 75 sqq. (on Attic style). Tert. *An.* 6 writes: "mulsa aqua de eloquio Platonis".

[6] Arius himself admired Plato's style, citing *Laws* 631 B–D: καὶ διὰ τὸ κάλλος τῆς φράσεως καὶ διὰ τὴν σαφήνειαν (Stob. II, 54, 10).

with a Plutarch or a Maximus Tyrius, Albinus avoids all exuberance. The *Didaskalikos* suggests that he was better as a lecturer than as an author, and Diels rightly speaks of "die schlichte und durch keine Kunst gehobene Gelehrtensprache".[1] The atmosphere of the lecture-room is preserved by the use of connexions like ἑπομένως and ἀκολούθως[2] or the verbal adjective in -έον, which has the convenience of indicating where a fresh topic begins.[3] The elementary character of the treatise is made clear by such phrases as ἐπὶ κεφαλαίων and ἐπὶ τοσοῦτον ὑπογεγράφθω.[4]

Lastly, we must examine the view advanced by Freudenthal and accepted by Zeller-Nestle and Überweg-Praechter,[5] that the work has not come down to us in its original form. Freudenthal argues that the work must have been edited by some later Platonist.[6] To the hand of this hypothetical and anonymous reviser he attributes the epilogue (Chapter xxxvi) and also a whole section of Chapter x (65, 14–30).[7] These are not the only signs of "ein täppischer Bearbeiter". Certain subjects, he holds, are treated at excessive length. Others receive scanty attention. Mathematics and logic are taken out of their proper order. The scheme given in Chapter iii is not completely adhered to in the sequel. Some statements are brief to the point of obscurity. For example, no one who was not well versed in the writings of Aristotle and the Stoics would understand what was meant by τοῦτο ἔσται ἢ ἀληθὲς ἢ ψεῦδος or by ἄμεσα ἐναντία.[8] The presence of certain glosses betrays the hand of the reviser: 59, 37–60, 2 (ἁπλῶς δὲ—διαλεκτικῆς); 81, 37–82, 2 (ὅθεν–εὐεξίαν); 87, 29–32 (ὅθεν–ἀνάπαλιν). Moreover, the sequence in Chapter x has been seriously disturbed by "eine fortlaufende Reihe von Anstössen der lästigsten Art".[9] Thus

---

[1] *Tht. Komm.* xxxiii.

[2] Cf. 62, 21; 69, 36; 73, 28; 74, 5; 78, 27; 81, 6, 35; 84, 10, 26. Strache cf. *Fin.* iii, 20. 50, 55.

[3] 54, 6; 60, 36; 62, 22; 64, 6; 66, 34; 76, 5; 79, 31; 85, 21.

[4] 61, 9; 79, 30; 60, 35.

[5] Z–N, iii, a, 835; *UPG.* 541.   [6] Frl. 301.

[7] Frl. 318: "unterbricht in störendster Weise den Zusammenhang." Hence he suggests that the original connexion may have been (κινεῖται): καὶ γὰρ ἀμερῆ δεῖ αὐτὸν εἶναι· οὐδὲν δὲ οὔτε κινεῖ οὔτε κινεῖται, ᾧ μέρη μή ἐστιν. ἀμερῆ τε κτα.

[8] *Ibid.* 301.   [9] *Ibid.* 302.

ἄρρητος comes between positive attributes and so is misplaced. The abstract nouns θειότης, οὐσιότης, ἀλήθεια, συμμετρία (64, 30) are inappropriate after a series of adjectives and before ἀγαθόν. θειότης and οὐσιότης are the very words which require elucidation.[1] Yet these are left unexplained, whereas others like καλόν and πατήρ are introduced without warning and their meaning carefully explained. For none of these blemishes should we hold Albinus himself responsible. The *Didaskalikos* has undergone a general revision, which has been greatly to its detriment.

We have already indicated that the view which Freudenthal takes of the final chapter is quite unjustified. To talk of "Worte, die vielmehr der Bemerkung eines byzantinischen Gelehrten als dem Geständnisse eines hochangesehenen Schulhauptes aus dem zweiten nachchristlichen Jahrhunderte gleichen"[2] is completely to ignore the method of composition and the fundamental character of the *Didaskalikos*, and to make Albinus a more important Platonist than actually he was. In the *Didaskalikos* Albinus is content to follow tradition, and this explains the apology with which he concludes his account. Even assuming that his importance as a teacher of Platonism was great, yet in this treatise he writes without the slightest desire to be thought an original thinker. If we assume Albinus's general dependence on Arius, the difficulties which Freudenthal raises at once disappear. For then Albinus is himself the redactor of an account of Plato written by a doxographer whom we know to have been unsystematic,[3] and the hypothesis that the *Didaskalikos* underwent revision[4] and mutilation at the hands of a Byzantine scholar may be dismissed altogether.

The disproportionate treatment of certain subjects, the inadequate discussion or complete omission of others, and the failure to adhere to the order originally proposed, mean that Albinus reproduced some parts of his original with great fidelity, while he neglected others, and rearranged certain topics to improve the structure,

---

[1] Frl. 318. [2] *Ibid.* 302.

[3] Cf. Theiler, *VN.* 36: "Wiederholungen, Mangel an Ausgeglichenheit."

[4] The text has, however, undergone corruption, both usual and unusual. Freudenthal says nothing of those MSS. of transposition which I classify as ψ.

which, owing to his choice of material, could not be built up in complete accordance with the preliminary design. So, in the final chapter, the genuineness of which is incontestable, we may presume that it is precisely to those passages which Freudenthal finds so puzzling that Albinus alludes, when he mentions τὰ σποράδην καὶ ἀτάκτως εἰρημένα, and that he would not deny that some remarks would gain by expansion and that Chapter x is in some respects unsatisfactory. But, when Freudenthal alleges that a number of passages foreign to the original treatise have been incorporated in it, he is altogether hypercritical and the examples which he chooses are unconvincing. The style of 65, 14–30 agrees with that of the whole treatise,[1] while the description of the three ways of apprehending God ("viae negationis, causalitatis, eminentiae") harmonizes perfectly with the rest of the chapter. The proposal to reject 59, 37–60, 2 cannot be accepted, for the juxtaposition of ἐν τῷ Κρατύλῳ διεξέρχεται and τὰ δὲ ἐν τῷ Κρατύλῳ would be intolerable (even in the *Didaskalikos*). Nor can 81, 37–82, 2 be a gloss, for Apuleius has a similar passage.[2] Finally, to regard 87, 29–32 as spurious, because the words (Ἔρωτα) μηδέποτε ἐν γηίνῳ σώματι γεγενημένον may be directed from the Christian standpoint "gegen heidnische Vorstellungen von körperlichen Erscheinungen der Götter",[3] is sheerly fantastic.

[1] ἐνοήσαμεν...νοήσαντες and ὃν ἔχει λόγον...τοῦτον ἔχει τὸν λόγον are typical.

[2] "Ad ornamentum quidem genialis loci, (id) est virtutis", etc. 126, 20 ("quid sit, incertum est", Thomas).

[3] Frl. 302, n.

ix

ALBINUS AS A MIDDLE PLATONIST

In the history of ancient thought the second century of the Christian Era is an age in which the chief attraction is the Platonic philosophy. Besides Platonists proper, such as Theon of Smyrna, Albinus, Calvisius Taurus, Atticus, Celsus, Maximus of Tyre, and Severus, mention may be made in this connexion of Nicomachus and Numenius among the Neopythagoreans, the Hermetists and Gnostics, Aspasius and Adrastus among the Peripatetics, Marcus Aurelius among the Stoics, and Pantaenus and Clement among the members of the Christian Catechetical School at Alexandria. It is certainly true that the revival of dogmatic Platonism had begun two centuries earlier, but its influence hardly becomes predominant till this date. Epicureanism is by now practically defunct,[1] Scepticism no longer enjoys the vogue it once possessed,[2] Stoicism is unable to satisfy men's religious longings and despairs of itself, the Neopythagoreans and the Peripatetics[3] show a marked inclination to adopt Platonic doctrines, and Platonism itself has readily absorbed the teaching of other Schools. Some of its adherents may differ in their estimate of Aristotle and Stoicism. An Atticus may launch a violent attack on the former and ally himself with the latter. A Favorinus may consider the Peripatetic position to be the most satisfactory[4] and assail Stoic epistemology. But the eclectic character of Middle Platonism persists, though admittedly there is a general lack of systematization.[5]

[1] The last important Epicureans were Diogenes of Oenoanda and Diogenianus. Plotinus attacks the doctrines of the School (III, i, 3, IV, vii, 3), but in his day it had ceased to exist.

[2] Sextus Empiricus (about the middle of the second century) appeals much to earlier Sceptics. By his time Scepticism seems to have passed its prime.

[3] In contrast with the Platonists, they are more conservative. Cf. *UPG.* 527, 559.

[4] *UPG.* 547 (where he is treated as a Middle Platonist).

[5] Cf. *ibid.* 529.

If we are to speak of a Platonic School, we must not interpret the words in too narrow a sense. Calvisius Taurus is known to have been scholarch of the Athenian Academy in the time of Hadrian and Antoninus Pius, and Atticus seems to have succeeded him in the office. To the Academy, doubtless, belonged Lucius and Nicostratus.[1] But of the other Platonists of the second century, Theon and Albinus are associated with Smyrna, some, like Nigrinus and Maximus, engaged in philosophy at Rome, while Celsus probably and Ammonius Saccas certainly belonged to Alexandria.

It is probable that in the Academy itself there was a special hostility towards Aristotle. Taurus wrote on the difference between his doctrines and those of Plato, while Atticus, like Lucius and Nicostratus,[2] brought objections against his categories and otherwise attacked him severely. Already Plutarch, although apparently willing like the *Theaetetus*-Commentator to make use of the *Topica* and to accept Aristotle's categories,[3] had written of the Old Peripatetics, ὑπεναντιώμενοι τῷ Πλάτωνι καὶ μαχόμενοι διατελοῦσι,[4] had called attention to Aristotle as the critic of the Ideal Theory, πανταχοῦ κινῶν καὶ πᾶσαν ἐπάγων ἀπορίαν,[5] and had declared that the *Metaphysics* is of no practical value.[6] Yet he is not as systematic a critic of Aristotle as Atticus.

When we turn to the *Didaskalikos*, the works of Maximus,[7] or the *Theaetetus-Commentary*, we find almost no such hostility to Peripateticism. Severus comes much under its influence.[8] More important still, we learn that Ammonius Saccas was profoundly dissatisfied with the futile quarrels between Platonists and Peripatetics and that εἶδε καλῶς τὰ ἑκατέρου καὶ συνήγαγεν εἰς ἕνα καὶ τὸν αὐτὸν νοῦν, καὶ ἀστασίαστον τὴν φιλοσοφίαν παραδέδωκε πᾶσι

[1] Praechter shows Zeller mistaken in regarding Nicostratus as a Stoic.
[2] Cf. Simpl. *Cat.* 30, 16.
[3] According to the Lamprias-Catalogue, he wrote a work in eight books on the *Topica* and a tract on the ten categories (see Volkmann, 20 sqq.).
[4] *Adv. Colot.* 1115.   [5] Cf. Volkmann, 17.
[6] *Vit. Alex.* 7.
[7] In 33, 5 Maximus shows himself in agreement with Antiochus regarding Aristotle and the Old Academy.
[8] Cf. Simpl. *Cat.* 76, 13 sqq. (against Nicostratus's view).

τοῖς αὐτοῦ γνωρίμοις.[1] It may be suspected that Ammonius was especially opposed to that type of Platonism represented by Atticus, and that the New Platonism which he developed at Alexandria was an answer to the reformed orthodoxy which characterized the Academy of his day.

The two Middle Platonists with whom Albinus has most in common are Maximus of Tyre and the *Theaetetus*-Commentator. The resemblances to Maximus are especially noticeable when Albinus is dealing with theology (*Didaskalikos* x) and with the immortality of the soul (*Didaskalikos* xxv). But he differs both from Maximus and from Plutarch, Numenius, and Plotinus, in betraying hardly any sign of religious ecstasy.[2] The parallels between the *Didaskalikos* and the *Theaetetus-Commentary* occur in the departments of logic and ethics. We may almost suppose, as Diels suggests, that the main pedagogical purpose of the *Commentary* is to familiarize the novice with the syllogistic method of Aristotelean logic. The Commentator in one place goes out of his way to introduce a quotation from the *Topica* (127 a 12–19),[3] and it is otherwise quite obvious that, in agreement with Albinus but in complete contrast with Lucius, Nicostratus, and Atticus, he holds the logic of Aristotle in high esteem. Nor does he scruple to name Aristotle, whereas Albinus makes Plato the father of logic.[4] Again, whereas Albinus never mentions the Stoics, the Commentator makes three references to them, each of which is hostile.[5] Furthermore, the criterion of knowledge for Albinus is λόγος. The Commentator, however, writing on *Theaetetus* 151 D, takes a different view,[6] if what is said is meant to be regarded as the Platonic as well as the Socratic view. And as he has already made Socrates's words at 150 C the basis of a deduction about Plato,[7] we may suspect that here too he considers that the Socratic view of Knowledge as ὃ φαίνεται αὐτῷ is the

[1] Hier. Phot. *Bibl.* 461 a 36. Porphyry wrote περὶ τοῦ μίαν εἶναι τὴν Πλάτωνος καὶ 'Αριστοτέλους αἵρεσιν. The attitude reported by August. *CD.* 8, 12, is different.

[2] Cf. *UPG.* 545.   [3] 24, 25.

[4] Cf. Praechter, *Hermes*, 1922, 514.

[5] 6, 35 sqq.; 11, 23; 70, 18. Praechter (*Hermes*, 1916, 525) believes that the attack is aimed not directly at Stoicism but at a stoicizing Platonism.

[6] 61.

[7] 55, 8: τὸν Πλάτωνα ἔχειν δόγματα καὶ ἀποφαίνεσθαι πεποιθότως.

genuinely Platonic standpoint. We know that Albinus, following Gaius, believed that Plato δογματίζει διχῶς, ἢ ἐπιστημονικῶς ἢ εἰκοτολογικῶς.[1] But we are nowhere told that he regarded the Platonic view of knowledge as being what the Commentator apparently imagined it to be.[2]

The coincidences between the *Didaskalikos* and the *Commentary* in the sphere of ethics have been pointed out by Diels[3] and Praechter.[4] The latter scholar believes that it is possible to reconstruct the οἰκείωσις-theory held by Gaius from a passage of the *Commentary*.[5] Praechter concludes that Gaius, while accepting the main lines of the Stoic (and Antiochean) οἰκείωσις-theory, denied that it was as widely applicable as Stoicism had assumed, and maintained that justice and virtue in general are due, not to the fact that the original egoism of οἰκείωσις develops into altruism, but to an inward assimilation to God, or, as the Commentator states, οὐκ ἀπὸ τῆς οἰκειώσεως εἰσάγει ὁ Πλάτων τὴν δικαιοσύνην, ἀλλὰ ἀπὸ τῆς πρὸς τὸν θεὸν ὁμοιότητος.[6] Praechter here assumes that agreement between the Commentator and Albinus (τέλος ἐξέθετο ὁμοίωσιν θεῷ κατὰ τὸ δυνατόν[7]) means that Gaius is the common source. While that possibility is not to be denied, we should not overlook the circumstance that Arius Didymus (as Diels points out) already emphasized this particular Platonic doctrine: Σωκράτης, Πλάτων ταὐτὰ τῷ Πυθαγόρᾳ τέλος ὁμοίωσιν θεῷ. σαφέστερον δ' αὐτὸ διήρθρωσε Πλάτων προσθεὶς τὸ κατὰ τὸ δυνατόν.[8] So, too, when the Commentator declares τοῦ σπουδαίου ἐστὶν τὸ γνῶναι τὸν ἀξιέραστον, he agrees not only with Albinus[9] but with Arius also.[10] All three, moreover, in agreement with the view of Antiochus, distinguish the perfect and the imperfect virtues.[11] Thus we see that

[1] Procl. *Tim.* I, 340. (Proclus thinks Albinus and Gaius relied on *Tim.* 29 B.)

[2] It is worth noticing that even Plutarch is able to write: ἑαυτοὺς τὸ ἄγαν τῆς πίστεως ἀφαιρῶμεν (431 A).

[3] xxxi.   [4] *Hermes*, 1916, 511 sqq.

[5] 5, 24 sqq.   [6] 7, 14 sqq.

[7] Praechter (*UPG.* 541); also cf. *Prol.* 151, 3; *Did.* 53, 6.

[8] Stob. II, 49, 8 (cited by Diels, xxxi).

[9] *Did.* 87, 35.   [10] Stob. II, 65, 20.

[11] All three speak of εὐφύεια as being imperfect virtues (see Diels, *Tht. Komm.* xxxii).

the Commentator sometimes shows himself in harmony both with Albinus and with Arius.[1]

Everything that Gaius wrote has been lost and it is surely unwise to magnify his importance at the expense of Arius. There is possibly some justification for classifying certain writings of second-century Platonism, the *Didaskalikos* and the *Prologos*, the *De Platone* of Apuleius, some of the treatises of Maximus, and the *Theaetetus-Commentary*, as products of the "Gaiusgruppe".[2] But the fact has still to be borne in mind that (with a single exception[3]) we are quite ignorant about the doctrines which Gaius himself professed. With Arius Didymus the case is very different. The amount of material on which we may base our judgments about him is considerable. We can establish that Albinus, the Commentator, and Arius agree more than once. That in these cases Gaius may exercise influence is not to be denied. But it must at the same time be admitted that Arius alone would suffice as the source.

We can see from the exegesis of *Theaetetus* 152 D that the Commentator agrees with Albinus in discovering the Aristotelean categories in Plato.[4] In contrast with Nicostratus and his predecessor Lucius, who both wrote against the *Categories* of Aristotle σχεδόν τι πρὸς πάντα τὰ εἰρημένα κατὰ τὸ βιβλίον ἐνστάσεις κομίζειν φιλο-τιμούμενοι,[5] the *Theaetetus*-Commentator and Albinus, doubtless following the example of Antiochus, accepted the Aristotelean doctrine in its entirety. Thus Praechter is probably right in saying that two lines were taken by the Platonic School in the first centuries after Christ with regard to the categories of Aristotle.[6] The positive line started with the eclecticism of Antiochus and was followed by Albinus, the *Theaetetus*-Commentator Ammonius Saccas, Longinus and Porphyry. The negative began with the sceptical New Academy, and can be traced via Lucius, Nicostratus and Atticus to Plotinus.

---

[1] If Diels's conjectural restoration of *Tht. Komm.* 69, 37–8 is accepted: (ἡ οὐσία) οὔ(τ') α(ὐ)ξ(άνεται οὔτε) μ(ει)οῦται... the resemblance to Arius Didymus (reporting Posidonius's view, *DDG.* 462, 27) is strikingly close (τὴν γὰρ οὐσίαν οὔτ' αὔξεσθαι οὔτε μειοῦσθαι κατὰ πρόσθεσιν ἢ ἀφαίρεσιν).

[2] So Theiler, *VN.* 3 *et passim*. Yet Theiler has to confess, "Wenig Wert hat für uns der anonyme Theaetetkommentar".

[3] Procl. *Tim.* I, 340.

[4] 68, 10 sqq. See also Praechter, *Hermes*, 1922, 514.

[5] Simplicius, cited by Prantl, 618, 2. [6] *Hermes*, 1922, 517.

The only difficulty about this theory is that there is no obvious connexion between Alexandria in the first century before Christ and the Athenian Academy of the second century after Christ. It is impossible to suggest either Arius Didymus, Favorinus, or Plutarch as a mediator. For Arius Didymus, while certainly quoting from a doxographical work of Eudorus, does not follow him in criticizing Aristotle's categories.[1] Favorinus is known to have been attracted by Aristotle. Plutarch appears to have emphasized the unity of the Academy in a work entitled περὶ τοῦ μίαν εἶναι τὴν ἀπὸ Πλάτωνος ᾿Ακαδημίαν.[2] Yet Plutarch, as we have seen, is quite ready to believe that the categories explicitly formulated by Aristotle were implicitly recognized by Plato.[3]

Nevertheless, despite the absence of any clear historical link, the fact can hardly be doubted that Nicostratus and Eudorus brought the same objections against the categories.[4] The latter doubtless anticipated Nicostratus and Plotinus in rejecting Aristotle's οὐσία, on the ground that Sensible and Intelligible Reality cannot properly be subsumed under a single genus.[5] Both Eudorus and Nicostratus had the same criticisms to make of the categories of Relation and Quality,[6] and appear to have carried out a systematic attack, bringing forward a variety of ἐνστάσεις and ἀπορίαι.[7] The same hostility was displayed by Atticus, and it is possible that Taurus, in the treatise which (according to Suidas) was written περὶ τῆς τῶν δογμάτων διαφορᾶς Πλάτωνος καὶ ᾿Αριστοτέλους, and which was entitled περὶ σωμάτων καὶ ἀσωμάτων, argued, like Nicostratus, that Sensibles and Intelligibles do not constitute a single genus.[8]

On the question of the creation of the Universe, the Platonists of the second century were divided. That Plato in the *Timaeus* teaches that the Universe was created at a certain point in time by the

[1] Cf. Stob. II, 137, 8–12.

[2] No. 63 in the Lamprias-Catalogue. We have seen that the same point of view is held by the *Tht.* Commentator (55). Philo of Larissa emphasized the continuity of the Academic tradition.   [3] *An. Pr.* 1023 E–F.

[4] The Stoics Athenodorus and Cornutus show a similar spirit (cf. Praechter, *loc. cit.* 508).

[5] Theiler (*VN.* 6 sqq.) would trace this distinction back to Antiochus.

[6] See Prantl, 540, 619; Praechter, *loc. cit.* 511.

[7] See Praechter, *loc. cit.* 496 sqq.

[8] This possibility is suggested by Praechter, *loc. cit.* 511.

Demiurge out of a mass which was moving primordially in chaos, was the belief of Atticus, as it had been of Plutarch. Atticus, however, like Plutarch, appears to feel that this purely literal interpretation of the *Timaeus* may incur criticism from orthodox Platonism.¹ The allegorical interpretation of Plato's cosmogonical account was doubtless adopted by Eudorus, as by Xenocrates, Antiochus, and at any rate some Neopythagoreans,² while in the second century of the Christian Era the same line is taken by Taurus, the peripateticizing Severus,³ and doubtless other Platonists as well.⁴ We have seen that in *Didaskalikos* xii Albinus regards matter as ἀτάκτως καὶ πλημμελῶς κινουμένη πρὸ τῆς οὐρανοῦ γενέσεως, but that later he says of the Universe, ἀεὶ ἐν γενέσει ἐστί. To Albinus there must have appeared to be no inconsistency, and in fact, according to the testimony of Proclus in a passage which we have already examined,⁵ he expressly attributed to Plato the doctrine: τὸν κόσμον ἀγένητον ὄντα γενέσεως ἔχειν ἀρχήν. In the *Didaskalikos*, however, after the literal interpretation of *Timaeus* 30 A in Chapters xii and xiii, the reader is hardly prepared for the statement: οὐχ οὕτως ἀκουστέον αὐτοῦ, ὡς ὄντος ποτὲ χρόνου, ἐν ᾧ οὐκ ἦν κόσμος.⁶ It may be added that Plotinus finds this passage of the *Timaeus* not easy to reconcile with his doctrine of an eternal Cosmos.⁷

Albinus in the *Didaskalikos* takes the view that the soul must suffer the affections which proceed from the body as the penalty of incarnation, and emphasizes the Platonic doctrine that God is not responsible for the evil that men do and suffer.⁸ But nowhere does he explicitly identify Matter and evil, nor does he introduce a malevolent cosmic principle on the strength of what Plato says in *Laws* 896 E. Thus he differs from certain other Platonists of his

¹ Euseb. *PE.* 801 D (the phrase Ἕλλην πρὸς Ἕλληνας has the same ring as that in *Enn.* ii, ix, 6: τῆς ἀρχαίας Ἑλληνικῆς—sc. αἱρέσεως—οὐχ ἁπτόμενοι). See also Plut. *An. Pr.* 1014 B, D; *DDG.* 567, 10.

² See Scott, *Hermet.* iii, 196.

³ Phil. *Aet. Mund.* 145, 12, etc.; Procl. *Tim.* i, 289, 7, 11, 95, 29.

⁴ *DDG.* 567, 22.   ⁵ p. 107, *supra.*

⁶ Gaudentius, *De Phil. ap. Rom.* 249, examines this "nodus qui reperitur".   ⁷ Cf. Inge, *Ph. Plot.*³ i, 144 (Dodds, *Procl.* 239, 1).

⁸ *Did.* 72, 8–9. The Basilidian Gnostics held πάθη to belong to the προσφυὴς ψυχή (cf. Dodds, *Procl.* 314).

age. Whatever Plato's own belief may have been,[1] many of those who professed to follow him in the second century associated Matter with evil.[2] So Plutarch, although regarding the World Soul, which exists as a third principle along with God and Matter, as the real cause of evil,[3] yet conceives Matter, or at least the Matter of the sublunar region, to be entirely under its domination. Atticus likewise postulates an evil Soul indwelling in Matter.[4] Harpocration regards incarnation as evil, while Celsus tersely declares that evil does not come from God, but resides in Matter.[5] In an Essay which anticipates the eighth Essay of the first *Ennead* of Plotinus, Maximus raises the question: τοῦ θεοῦ τὰ ἀγαθὰ ποιοῦντος πόθεν τὰ κακά;[6] His answer is that τὰ κακὰ ἐξ αὐτοφυοῦς μοχθηρίας ἀνίσταται. διττὴ καὶ αὕτη, ἡ μὲν ὕλης πάθος, ἡ δὲ ψυχῆς ἐξουσία, and that πάθη ἃς καλοῦμεν κακῶν ἀνθρωπίνων ἐμβολὰς are τῆς τοῦ ὅλου δημιουργίας ὥσπερ τινὰς ἀναγκαίας καὶ ἑπομένας φύσεις.[7] But none of these Platonists endows Matter with that Satanic spirit which Numenius seems to attribute to it.[8] Nor is there any trace in orthodox second-century Platonism of the view that ὁ κόσμος πλήρωμά ἐστι τῆς κακίας which appears in the Hermetic Literature and which is due to the total exclusion of God from the material Universe.[9]

In Cicero's day the School of Plato was ethical rather than religious. The philosophical outlook of Antiochus was in the main anthropocentric. For him πίστις had much epistemological, but no theological, importance. Whatever views may have been entertained on the subject by Posidonius,[10] eschatology seems to have had

[1] Eudemus, says Plutarch, κατειρωνεύεται τοῦ Πλάτωνος ὡς οὐκ εὖ τὴν πολλάκις ὑπ' αὐτοῦ μητέρα καὶ τιθήνην προσαγορευομένην αἰτίαν κακῶν καὶ ἀρχὴν ἀποφαίνοντος (*An. Pr.* 1015 D).

[2] Perhaps after Xenocrates (Baeumker, 205).   [3] *An. Pr.* vi.

[4] Procl. *Tim.* I, 391, 10.   [5] *CC.* IV, 65.   [6] *Diss.* 41.

[7] For evil as a by-product cf. *DDG.* 570; Apul. 95. 17. Scott, *Hermet.* 14, 7 (like rust on metal, or dirt on the body).

[8] Cf. Milton's lines: "Ever to do ill our sole delight,/As being contrary to His high will/Whom we resist."

[9] Lib. VI, 4 a, Scott (and see his introduction, II, 169, where he contrasts *Laws* 906 A and Plot. II, ix).

[10] Gerhäusser holds that his *Protreptikos* is the source followed in *Somnium Scip.* The Posidonian "Himmelfahrt" may have influenced Plotinus in *Enn.* IV, iii (cf. Dodds, *Procl.* 318, 2).

no attraction for Antiochus, who occupied himself, in the manner of the early Stoics, with the problems of this life, knowledge and conduct being the chief of them. Two centuries later Platonism has experienced a transformation. The robust optimism and anthropocentric outlook which Antiochus shared with the Stoics no longer have the same appeal. Man is felt to be a mean and insignificant part of the Universe: ἐν πόστῳ βωλαρίῳ τῆς ὅλης γῆς ἕρπεις; It is true that this is the utterance, not of the Platonist professor, but of the Stoic emperor.[1] Yet Marcus Aurelius here expresses, albeit in an exaggerated form, the view which was accepted at this time by philosophers of every School. That it could be approved by Platonism is clear from the words of Celsus: οὔκουν ἀνθρώπῳ πεποίηται ταῦτα, ὥσπερ οὐδὲ λέοντι οὐδὲ ἀετῷ οὐδὲ δελφῖνι....[2] But the Platonist, or at any rate the orthodox Platonist, could hardly allow himself to despair of the Universe because of the littleness of Man. The Supreme God is remote: θεὸς ἀνθρώπῳ οὐ μίγνυται. But, to the orthodox Platonist, the Universe which God himself has created[3] and which is the best of all possible Worlds[4] is not left without divine protection. God's Sons are entrusted with its management and act in obedience to their Father.[5] Man, despite his lowly rank, is able to enter into communion with these subordinate deities in divination and dreams. The man who loves God awaits his call and knows that, when the divine summons comes at death, then he will behold God himself.[6] To the average Platonist of this period φιλοσοφεῖν signified chiefly what Plato had declared it to be in the *Phaedo*, ἀποθνῄσκειν μελετᾶν.[7]

[1] 12, 32. It should not be forgotten that Marcus Aurelius (cf. also p. 105, n. 3, *supra*) had had not only "Alexander the Platonist" (1, 12) but also Bacchius Paphius, probably Gaius's adopted son (cf. Dittenberger, *Sylloge* 868), as teacher.

[2] *CC*. IV, 99. Cf. 74, 78; Sen. *NQ*. 7, 30: "Neque enim omnia Deus homini fecit"; Plot. III, ii, 8: θαυμάζεται δὲ ἐν ἀνθρώποις ἀδικία, ὅτι ἀνθρώπων ἀξιοῦσιν ἐν τῷ παντὶ τὸ τίμιον εἶναι ὡς οὐδενὸς ὄντος σοφωτέρου. κτα.

[3] *Did*. 71, 18. Plotinus wrote (II, ix) πρὸς τοὺς κακὸν τὸν δημιουργὸν τοῦ κόσμου...λέγοντας. Marcion's conception of the O.T. Jehovah is similar.   4 *Did*. 69, 36.

[5] *Ibid*. 71, 20–21. So Plutarch, Apuleius, Celsus, Maximus.

[6] Cf. M. T. 17, 11 (*Enn*. VI, ix, 10).   7 67 B.

It is therefore true to say that Platonism in the second century, if it had not become a religion,[1] was characterized by its predominantly religious and theocentric world-view. It is a significant fact that one of the most frequently quoted Platonic texts during this period is that which appears in *Didaskalikos* 81, 30–1: ὁ μὲν δὴ θεός, ὥσπερ ὁ παλαιὸς λόγος, ἀρχήν τε καὶ τελευτὴν καὶ μέσα τῶν ὄντων ἁπάντων ἔχων....[2] This age was attracted not so much by Plato the ethical teacher or political reformer, as by Plato the hierophant, Plato who (according to an old legend) had been conceived of Apollo and born of the virgin Perictione.[3] It is true that Albinus in the *Didaskalikos* does not exhibit the religious fervour of Apuleius, Maximus, or Numenius. But even Albinus, although he avoids *Schwärmerei*, holds that the end of human life is ἐνθένδε ἐκεῖσε φεύγειν ὅτι τάχιστα, or ὁμοίωσις θεῷ κατὰ τὸ δυνατόν.[4] Second-century Platonism is theological and otherworldly.[5]

Yet nowhere is there found a coherent system in which the relation between God and the Universe is adequately explained. The doctrine "of an undifferenced ground of all existence, transcending not only Matter but Mind, creative without will or causality, unknowable save in the *unio mystica*, having no character save the character of being a ground"[6]—that is to say the doctrine of the Plotinian One—has not yet been formulated. Outside the sphere of orthodox Platonism, the Neopythagorean Numenius and still more the platonizing Christians belonging to the Alexandrian Catechetical School hold that God, though removed to an infinite distance from the material realm, may yet be mystically apprehended by the human soul even during this present life.[7] But in no religious speculation before the time of Neoplatonism is there any serious attempt to combine transcendence with immanence. Moreover, as

---

[1] Cf. Ascl. 12 b, Scott: "Sola (sc. philosophia) est in cognoscenda divinitate frequens obtutus et sancta religio."

[2] But Plutarch (*Def. Or.* 436 D, and cf. Volkmann, 8–9) argues that Plato harmonized the "philosophy" of the old θεολόγοι καὶ ποιηταί (Ζεὺς ἀρχὴ Ζεὺς μέσσα Διὸς δ' ἐκ πάντα πέλονται) with that of οἱ φυσικοί.

[3] D. L. III, 2; Apul. 82, 7.   [4] 81, 19.

[5] There may have been other sceptical philosophers like Favorinus. But they would have belonged to the minority (cf. also Lucian).

[6] Dodds, *CQ*. XXII, 131.

[7] See *PE*. 543 c; Clem. *Strom*. II, 5, 5.

we may see in *Didaskalikos* x, the orthodox Platonists of the second century, whatever refinements they introduce into their conception of God, are unable to get rid of the belief in his personality. The Good does not yet transcend alike Essence and Intellect,[1] but remains identified with the Demiurge. The Plotinian conception of τὸ ἓν-ἀγαθόν as the First Cause, having νοῦς-δημιουργός as its proximate effect, does not appear in Middle Platonism.[2]

At the beginning of *Didaskalikos* x, Albinus argues for the existence of a Supreme Deity on the ground that where there is a better there must be a best. The inductive method which is here applied is the *via eminentiae* which is dealt with later in the chapter: θεὸν συνεπινοεῖν διὰ τὴν ἐν τῷ τιμίῳ ὑπεροχήν.[3] Better than Soul is Nous, better than Nous in potentiality is Nous in actuality, better than this is its cause, which must therefore be the First God. But, because of erroneous associations, men often fail to apprehend Intelligible Reality clearly. The gods, however, enjoy pure intellection of it, because they are far removed from those objects which human sense perceives (θεοὶ ἀπηλλαγμένοι τῶν αἰσθητῶν εἰλικρινῶς τι καὶ ἀμιγῶς, sc. τὰ νοητὰ νοοῦσι). Men are prone to attribute to God such sensible qualities as magnitude, form and colour (καὶ μέγεθος συνεπινοεῖν καὶ σχῆμα καὶ χρῶμα). Here, as in Celsus's denial that μετέχει σχήματος ὁ θεὸς ἢ χρώματος[4] and in similar passages of the Hermetic Literature,[5] there is an echo of ἡ ἀχρώματός τε καὶ ἀσχημάτιστος οὐσία of *Phaedrus* 247 c. But the theology of this section in its main lines suggests the influence of Aristotle[6] rather than Plato. The best parallel in Middle Platonism is to be

---

[1] Scott on *Herm.* II, 13 holds that the doctrine of a supra-intellectual God was current among Platonists of the Roman empire, but cites only ps.-Archytas (οὐ νόον μόνον εἶμεν δεῖ ἀλλὰ καὶ νόῳ τι κρέσσον, Stob. I, 280). But orthodox Middle Platonists, e.g. Albinus, Atticus, Harpocration (see Procl. *Tim.* I, 304–5), Celsus, and Maximus, regard God only as a superior Nous.

[2] Plut. (*De E.* 393 B) writes ἓν εἶναι δεῖ τὸ ὄν, ὥσπερ ὂν τὸ ἕν. See also Dodds, *CQ.* XXII, 132, 1.

[3] 65, 29. Cf. also Aristotle, fr. 1476 b 22–4.

[4] *CC.* 6, 64.

[5] E.g. Exc. II a, 15.

[6] fr. 1483 a 27 (περὶ εὐχῆς) is of some interest: ὁ θεὸς ἢ νοῦς ἐστιν ἢ ἐπέκεινά τι τοῦ νοῦ.

found in the important Essay of Maximus entitled τί ὁ θεὸς κατὰ Πλάτωνα.

But though Maximus and Albinus arrive at their conception of God by means of the same argument, the former does not use the expressions which appear in the *Didaskalikos*: ἐνεργεῖ ἀκίνητος and ὡς τὸ ὀρεκτὸν κινεῖ τὴν ὄρεξιν ἀκίνητον ὑπάρχον. Their absence, doubtless, has no significance. It is clear from passages in Plutarch[1] that the Aristotelean doctrine of God moving as the object of desire was current among Middle Platonists.[2] In Plutarch, moreover, emphasis is laid on the Aristotelean principle on which Albinus and Maximus alike rely, that νοῦς ψυχῆς ὅσῳ ψυχὴ σώματος ἀμεινόν ἐστι καὶ θειότερον.[3]

In what way Platonism came to adopt the Aristotelean theology it is not easy to determine. By the beginning of the second century it has entered eclectic Platonism, though it finds no favour with the anti-Aristotelean group in the Academy itself. But it cannot have originated with Antiochus. For Antiochus followed Stoicism in regarding God as organic with the Universe, whereas those Middle Platonists who accepted the Aristotelean doctrine of the Unmoved Mover were compelled to deny that the Cosmos or any part of the Cosmos can be the Supreme God. It is curious to observe that Atticus, though on the whole he marks a reaction against the eclecticism which had prevailed among Platonists since the time of Antiochus,[4] and claims to represent a strictly orthodox Platonism, nevertheless in his theology manifests the very same stoicizing tendency as his eclectic predecessor. The transcendent gods of Aristotle he finds to be no better than the gods of Epicurus.[5] There

---

[1] 372 E, 770 A, 944 E.

[2] R. M. Jones (*CP.* XXI, 323) thinks that the doctrine had been accepted by Platonists "long before Alcinous" (*sic*). This appears to be a somewhat hazardous conjecture from the evidence which he brings forward. Nor ought he to have overlooked Antiochus and his eclecticism, in considering Platonism's indebtedness to Aristotle.   [3] 943 A.

[4] Cf. *UPG.* 548 ("*in der Akademie* herrschenden Eklektizismus" is not quite exact).

[5] *PE.* 799 D: τί γὰρ διαφέρει πρὸς ἡμᾶς ἢ τοῦ κόσμου τὸ θεῖον ἐξοικίσασθαι καὶ μηδεμίαν ἡμῖν πρὸς αὐτὸ κοινωνίαν ἀπολιπεῖν (cf. συνδήσαντα καὶ συναρμόσαντα ἑνός τινος ὁμοίου κοινωνίᾳ, *PE.* 814 C) ἢ ἐν κόσμῳ τοὺς θεοὺς καθείρξαντα τῶν ἐπὶ γῆς πραγμάτων ἀποστῆσαι;

must be, he maintains in language suggesting a pantheistic doctrine, a single Force animating and immanent within the Universe, μία τις δύναμις ἔμψυχος διήκουσα διὰ τοῦ παντὸς καὶ πάντα συνδοῦσα καὶ συνέχουσα[1] (cf. *Academica* 28).

If, then, the Aristotelean theology which is so marked a feature in the speculation of such Platonists as Albinus and Maximus cannot be traced back to Antiochus, we may reasonably suppose that it was introduced into Platonism probably soon after, or otherwise slightly before, the beginning of the Christian Era. Since there are so many echoes of Arius Didymus throughout the *Didaskalikos*, it is tempting to suggest that he is the authority followed by Albinus in Chapter x. But there is no evidence that Arius interpreted the Platonic Demiurge in an Aristotelean sense as an Unmoved Mover, or that he ascribed to Plato so exalted a view of God. Arius, moreover, was attached, not to the Academy, but to the Porch.

A more likely suggestion is that the first Platonist to utilize the Aristotelean theology was Eudorus of Alexandria, who perhaps wrote a *Commentary* on the *Metaphysics*[2] and certainly emphasized the transcendence of the Supreme God or τὸ ἕν. But, if we make this assumption, we cannot argue that either Albinus or Maximus is directly indebted to Eudorus, for neither of them refers to God as τὸ ἕν. Instead we must suppose that, after the time of Eudorus, Aristotle's theology, either with or without those Neopythagorean elements which are prominent in Eudorus's system, was generally favoured by Platonists, and had accordingly by the beginning of the second century become part of the tradition of the School. It is then accepted by Albinus and Maximus as the correct view, whereas Atticus rejects it on the very opposite ground.

In order to form a correct appreciation of Albinus's theology, it is necessary to take some account of the Plotinian doctrine of the three Hypostases. Plotinus, in an early Essay, explains why Soul is not to be regarded as the First Cause. Intelligence is different from, and superior to, Soul, and therefore has metaphysical priority.[3]

---

[1] *PE.* 814 B. Cf. *DDG.* 568, 27.

[2] This seems implied in the statement made by Alexander Aphrodisiensis (*in Metaph.* 59, 7) that Eudorus emended *Met.* 988 a 10–11. On the effect of his alteration cf. Dodds, *CQ.* XXII, 139, 3.

[3] *Enn.* V, ix, 4.

Here Plotinus avails himself of the Aristotelean doctrine that actuality is prior to potentiality, in order to controvert the Stoic view that a soul which is potentially intelligent must exist before the faculty of intelligence can be actualized in it.[1] We have already seen that Albinus, following Aristotle, in like manner declares ψυχῆς νοῦς ἄμεινον. Yet, later in the *Didaskalikos*, he tends to adopt the view which Plotinus rejects, ἴσως οὐχ οἵου τε ὄντος νοῦ ἄνευ ψυχῆς ὑποστῆναι. Here Albinus is influenced by *Timaeus* 30 B, to which passage Atticus appeals against the Aristotelean view of a νοῦς χωριστός.[2]

Plotinus in the same Essay insists that νοῦς, when it means an Hypostasis or spiritual force, must receive its proper sense of actual and not potential Intelligence. Only thus will its noetic activity flow from its own nature, or will it have itself as its object and constitute τὰ ὄντα.[3] Plotinus, furthermore, points out that, in describing the Ideas as thoughts of Intelligence, there is a danger that the noumenon may be regarded as being formed or as existing only after Intelligence has conceived it, a doctrine which Plotinus himself rejects: τὸ λέγειν νοήσεις τὰ εἴδη, εἰ οὕτω λέγεται, ὡς, ἐπειδὴ ἐνόησε (sc. νοῦς), τότε ἐγένετο ἢ ἔστι τόδε, οὐκ ὀρθῶς.[4] Now Albinus, in discussing the nature of God, ὁ πρῶτος νοῦς, makes the statement: ἑαυτὸν ἂν οὖν καὶ τὰ ἑαυτοῦ νοήματα ἀεὶ νοοίη, καὶ αὕτη ἡ ἐνέργεια αὐτοῦ ἰδέα ὑπάρχει.[5] Here the Idea is not actually said to be posterior to the Intelligence. Nevertheless, the statement easily lends itself to such an interpretation. Plotinus, in the passage quoted, is doubtless concerned to restate the doctrine of the Ideas as thoughts of Intelligence, in a form in which it would not be liable to such criticisms as might have been brought against the doctrine as expressed by Albinus.[6]

[1] Cf. *SVF.* II, 804. 806 (*Enn.* IV, vii, 11).
[2] *Did.* 70, 2; *PE.* 810 D. Tertullian (*An.* 13) argues at length that the soul is superior to the intellect (e.g. the pilot saves souls, not minds, from shipwreck, the soldier lays down his soul, not his mind, God urges the soul to turn the mind towards him, etc.). Plotinus, *Enn.* IV, viii, 1, understands *Tim.* 30 B to mean that ψυχή was bestowed by the δημιουργός (= νοῦς) πρὸς τὸ ἔννουν τόδε τὸ πᾶν εἶναι,... ἄνευ δὲ ψυχῆς οὐχ οἷόν τε ἦν τοῦτο γενέσθαι.
[3] v, ix, 5.   [4] v, ix, 7.   [5] 64, 26.
[6] This suggestion is made by Theiler, *VN.* 59.

According to the theology of the *Didaskalikos*, ὁ πρῶτος νοῦς, remaining unmoved, moves the Celestial Intelligence. The Prime Mover himself is not in space (ὑπερουράνιος, not ἐπουράνιος, οὐράνιος[1]) and, although he is said to cause movement by being an object of desire and to bring the Celestial Intelligence into harmony with himself and with his intellections,[2] the relation between the two Intelligences is far from clear. It is impossible to assume that the Celestial emanates from the Transcendent. For Albinus denies that the Cosmic Soul (and necessarily, therefore, the Cosmic Intelligence) could have been produced by God (οὐχὶ ποιεῖ ὁ θεὸς ἀλλὰ κατακοσμεῖ).[3] God, however, may (according to Albinus) be said to create them in one sense, since he awakens them from their slumber, with the result that the Cosmic Soul by gazing upon him receives his thoughts. But this amounts to saying that the Cosmic Intelligence did not always exist in actuality. Yet it has previously been described as ὁ κατ' ἐνέργειαν πάντα νοῶν καὶ ἅμα καὶ ἀεί. Moreover, if each of the two Intelligences has the same activity, namely the perfect intellection of all the Forms, it is difficult to see what is gained by the duplication. *Entia non sunt multiplicanda praeter necessitatem.*

Nevertheless, Albinus is not the only philosopher of his time to distinguish between a higher νοῦς which is unmoved, and a lower which moves in response to it. For even Plotinus, when in one of his early Essays he is expounding *Timaeus* 39 E, sees no reason to deny the distinction.[4] Numenius, again, in a somewhat similar way differentiates the First God from the Second or the Demiurge.[5] Neither Albinus nor Numenius, however, posits some more ultimate principle than ὁ πρῶτος νοῦς, whereas for Plotinus νοῦς has as its ground τὸ ἕν. Plotinus, furthermore, when in a later Essay he sets out to contrast as sharply as possible his own system with the theories held by his Gnostic rivals, insists that there can be no

[1] 81, 36; 64, 36.   [2] 64, 36.

[3] 69, 30. It may be noted that in the two oldest MSS. there appears at 71, 18 the scholium: καὶ πῶς πρὸ βραχέος ἐλήρεις τὴν τοῦ κόσμου ψυχὴν οὐχὶ ποιεῖν θεὸν εἰ μὴ κοσμεῖν μόνον;

[4] III, ix, 1. Prof. Dodds (*Proclus* 207) draws attention to this passage and rightly refuses to regard the distinction as more than tentative.

[5] *PE.* 539 B.

dichotomy in the realm of νοῦς. The very concept of a νοῦς ἀκίνητος as distinct from a νοῦς κινούμενος is now flatly rejected. The function which Gnosticism assigns to the latter is quite appropriate to Soul in its intellectual aspect, and there is no need to intercalate a separate hypostasis.[1] In thus condemning the Gnostic view, Plotinus in effect condemns the theory of Albinus and Maximus, that between ψυχή and ὁ πρῶτος νοῦς there exist as intermediate principles[2] a νοῦς ἐν δυνάμει and a νοῦς κατ' ἐνέργειαν.

It is of some historical interest to compare and to contrast the First God of Albinus with the Plotinian One. While Albinus, in accordance with Aristotle, regards God as the object of his own thought, Plotinus declares that the One needs not thought of itself, as being One present to itself. Albinus accepts Aristotle's view that the essence of God is activity. Plotinus describes the One or the Good as ἀνενέργητον and ἐπέκεινα ἐνεργείας.[3] On the other hand, he is able to call it ἐνέργεια ὑπὲρ νοῦν, while yet again he boldly characterizes it as δύναμις τῶν πάντων.[4] Both Albinus and Plotinus agree that the Absolute is ἄρρητος.[5] Already in Plato we find the doctrine of the self-sufficiency of the Good.[6] The doctrine reappears in the *Enneads* as well as in the *Didaskalikos*.[7] Since, however, the One produces Essence and Essence itself is self-sufficing, the One may be said to be ἐπέκεινα αὐταρκείας.[8] The precise meaning which Albinus attaches to the terms θειότης and οὐσιότης cannot be ascertained. Neither is used by Plotinus, who would, moreover, have certainly objected to the description of any of his three Hypostases as συμμετρία.[9] He agrees with

---

[1] II, ix, 1. For the λόγος-ψυχή doctrine see Witt, *CQ.* xxv, 105.

[2] It is true that in *Did.* 69, 32 sqq. νοῦς is not sharply distinguished from ψυχή, and may even appear to be (in the Plotinian phrase) ψυχή νοερά. But the distinction is clearly made in Chapter x (64, 16 sqq.).

[3] v, vi, 6 (Bréhier points out that this Essay is a critical discussion of Arist. *Met.* Λ, ix), I, vii, 1 (cf. Whittaker, *The Neoplatonists* 60).

[4] III, viii, 10, v, viii, 15. Its infinity (ἄπειρον) is marked τῷ ἀπεριλήπτῳ τῆς δυνάμεως (vi, ix, 6). For his dynamic conception of οὐσία see Dodds, *Proclus* 215.   [5] Cf. also M. T. 8, 10 (Hobein, *Diss.* 41).

[6] *Phil.* 20 c. Cf. Arist. *EN.* 97 b 8.

[7] Cf. also Onatas, *FGP.* II, 114; *Hermet.* vi and the late Platonists (influenced perhaps by Xenocrates: cf. Heinze, 122) in Porph. *Abst.* II, 37 (166 N).   [8] v, iii, 17.   [9] Cf. I, vi, 1.

Albinus, however, in making νοῦς the principle of beauty (τὸ καλόν)[1] and truth (ἀλήθεια),[2] but reserves the attribute of goodness (τὸ ἀγαθόν) for the One, which, notwithstanding, because of his anxiety to preserve its transcendence, he is even prepared to call ὑπεράγαθον, i.e. οὐχ ἑαυτῷ τοῖς δ' ἄλλοις ἀγαθόν.[3]

Albinus makes the statement that God has filled all things with himself according to his own will.[4] The meaning of this is, not that the Supreme God is himself immanent in the Universe, but that the latter participates in him, inasmuch as the Cosmic Intelligence has him as the object of thought and of desire.[5] God willed that the Cosmic Soul and Intelligence should awaken and turn towards him, that they should be brought into order or "created", and that the Intelligence should thenceforward preserve the established order throughout the Universe.

The importance of the Divine Will in the cosmogonical speculation of the Platonists of the Empire is not less than that of the Divine Goodness,[6] the Platonic basis on which their doctrines rest being *Timaeus* 29 E–30 A. Thus Pantaenus, the founder of the Christian Catechetical School at Alexandria, declared that God θελήματι τὰ πάντα πεποίηκε, and therefore knows *entia* as what he has willed (ὡς ἴδια θελήματα γινώσκειν τὰ ὄντα).[7] Ammonius is said to have held that Plato δημιουργὸν θεὸν προΰφίστησιν ἐφεστῶτα· πάσης ἐμφανοῦς τε καὶ ἀφανοῦς διακοσμήσεως ἐκ μηδενὸς προϋποκειμένου γεγενημένης· ἀρκεῖ γὰρ τὸ ἐκείνου βούλημα εἰς ὑπόστασιν τῶν ὄντων.[8] In the *Asclepius*, which belongs either to the second or the third century, we read that with God to will is to accomplish.[9]

Plotinus, in discussing how the One may be said to have Freewill (VI, viii), is prepared to declare that the One or the Good, since it cannot be what it happened to be (οὐχ ὅπερ ἔτυχέν ἐστιν), must be characterized by a *will* to be what it is, which is inseparable from

---

[1] I, vi, 9.   [2] V, v, 2.   [3] VI, ix, 6. Cf. VI, ii, 17, VI, vii, 38.

[4] 65, 1. Plutarch (*An. Pr.* 1030 c) uses the verb (of the Soul's operation).   [5] Cf. also Dodds, *Proclus* 211.

[6] On which Albinus insists, *Did.* 67, 11. (For the Plotinian interpretation of this passage cf. Dodds, *Proclus* 213.)

[7] Quoted by Hatch, *Infl. Gk. Ideas* 257. For other references see Witt, *Am. Cor.* 336.

[8] Hier. Phot. *Bibl.* 461 b.   [9] *Hermet.* Scott, I, 300, 9–10.

its *being* what it is.[1] But clearly in his system there is no room for the conception which Albinus adopts of an Absolute, willing that a Cosmos should come into being.[2] Even the νοῦς-δημιουργός is declared, in opposition to Gnostic theories, not to have created the Sensible World by a deliberate act of will, on the ground that *sensibilia* are coeval with the former.[3] From this it is obvious that Plotinus must have disapproved of the expression which is employed by Albinus. His own view of the production of the visible universe by the Intelligible is that it does not result from voluntary choice (since νοῦς does not need the use of discursive reason), but that it is due to the necessity that the self-perfect should reproduce itself.[4]

The doctrine which Albinus holds regarding the Cosmic Intelligence and the Cosmic Soul,[5] that though they are eternal they were "created" by the Demiurge in the sense that they were awakened as out of a deep sleep, is of uncertain origin. Such a view is not found in the works of Plato himself. If, however, we turn to Plutarch, we observe how the conception of a sleeping or, more strictly, a somnolent World Soul may be evolved from the Myth in the *Politicus* (269–70). Plutarch, or the authority whom he follows, elicits from this the doctrine of two alternating cosmic states, the one occurring when the Intelligence of the World Soul is somnolent, the other when it awakens and gazes upon the Archetype to which by God's help it is directed (ἀνέβλεψε πρὸς τὸ παράδειγμα θεοῦ συνεπιστρέφοντος καὶ συναπευθύνοντος).[6]

Probably the theory of the comatose soul—whether the cosmic or the human soul be the subject of discussion—was a common-

---

[1] VI, viii, 13.

[2] Cf. οὐ προσνεύσαντος οὐδὲ βουληθέντος οὐδὲ ὅλως κινηθέντος (sc. τοῦ ἑνός) ὑποστῆναι αὐτό (sc. δεύτερόν τι μετὰ τὸ ἕν), V, i, 6.

[3] V, viii, 12.

[4] On his theory of emanation cf. Dodds, *op. cit.* 212–16.

[5] 69, 30 sqq.

[6] *An. Pr.* 1026 F. Earlier Plutarch has written: ἡ περὶ τοῦτο (sc. τὸ αἰσθητόν) τεταγμένη δύναμις (κινήσεις εἶχε) τὰς πολλὰς ἐνυπνιώδεις (1024C). The *Politicus*-Myth was important for Numenius: βλέποντος μὲν καὶ ἐπεστραμμένου πρὸς ἡμῶν ἕκαστον τοῦ θεοῦ συμβαίνει ζῆν τε καὶ βιώσκεσθαι τότε τὰ σώματα κηδεύοντος τοῦ θεοῦ τοῖς ἀκροβολισμοῖς, μεταστρέφοντος δὲ εἰς τὴν ἑαυτοῦ περιωπὴν τοῦ θεοῦ (272 E–3 A) ταῦτα ἀποσβέννυσθαι (*PE.* 538 B).

place among the Middle Platonists. Maximus of Tyre, in the Essay entitled εἰ αἱ μαθήσεις ἀναμνήσεις, dwells on the theme, to which Plato's Cave Myth had given currency, that for the human soul to be in the body is to be asleep.[1] Yet, continues Maximus, there is another state which resembles a sleep full of vivid dreams and which it should be the aim of the philosopher to enjoy, that is to say the state in which the soul does not suffer from the disturbances of the body and to which the good man may attain as the result of the soul's introversion.[2] The appearance of κάρος and ἐπιστρέφειν[3] in the same Essay suggests that Maximus is here following a source parallel to that on which Albinus relies in the passage quoted above. Both words have a technical ring and doubtless were frequently used by the Middle Platonists in their discussions of the soul.[4]

After emphasizing the completely ineffable nature of the Supreme God, in which connexion the conclusions which Plato reaches on the First Hypothesis of the *Parmenides* are turned to account,[5] Albinus discusses the three ways in which by the use of intelligence[6] God may be apprehended, the way of abstraction or negation, the way of analogy, and the way of gradual ascension (*viae negationis, causalitatis, eminentiae*). The first of these ways can be illustrated from geometry. To reach the conception of the point, it is necessary to abstract first the surface from the body, then the line from the surface, and finally the point from the line. That this illustration was borrowed by the Platonists from the Neopythagoreans is very likely.[7] Perhaps the first to use it was Eudorus. The second way of apprehending God can be connected with what Plato himself declares in *Republic* 508 B. The third way shows the combined influence of the *Symposium* (208 E) and the *Seventh Epistle* (341 C–D). Celsus, it is interesting to observe, closely resembles Albinus. For

---

[1] 16, 1.   [2] 16, 3.   [3] See Dodds, *Proclus* 218.

[4] For the soul asleep or life as a dream cf. Plot. III, vi, 6, IV, viii, 1, v, v, 11, Ph. Al. *Somn.* 165. Plotinus pictures Soul as awakening Heaven, V, i, 2.

[5] For parallels between the *Parmenides* and the *Enneads* cf. Dodds, *CQ.* XXII, 132–3.

[6] The ὡς εἴρηται of 65, 4 seems to refer back to 62, 1.

[7] See Dodds, *Proclus* 312.

he teaches that we may attain some conception of God, despite our inability to describe him in speech: τοῦ ἀκατονομάστου[1] καὶ πρώτου λάβοιμέν τινα ἐπίνοιαν, διαδηλοῦσαν αὐτὸν ἢ τῇ συνθέσει τῇ ἐπὶ τὰ ἄλλα ἢ ἀναλύσει ἀπ' αὐτῶν ἢ ἀναλογίᾳ.[2]

Plotinus, contrasting the mystical apprehension of the Good (ἡ τοῦ ἀγαθοῦ εἴτε γνῶσις εἴτε ἐπαφή) with the method of conceiving it logically (διὰ λογισμῶν), declares that Plato's words (*Republic* 505 A) ἡ τοῦ ἀγαθοῦ ἰδέα μέγιστον μάθημα refer, not to the actual vision (τὸ πρὸς αὐτὸ ἰδεῖν), but to the knowledge about the Good which can be gained before the vision (περὶ αὐτοῦ μαθεῖν τι πρότερον). Such knowledge is acquired as the result of ἀναλογίαι τε καὶ ἀφαιρέσεις καὶ γνώσεις τῶν ἐξ αὐτοῦ καὶ ἀναβασμοί τινες.[3] Here we see clearly the difference between the personal mysticism of Plotinus and the scholastic theology of Albinus. For the latter, God can be known only by dialectical processes. For Plotinus, while the value of these processes is not denied, the One or the Good can be known through an ecstatic experience or *unio mystica*.[4]

It is difficult to see how Chapters X and XII of the *Didaskalikos* are to be brought into agreement. If God is νοῦς ἀκίνητος, it may well be asked: "How can he be also the efficient cause, the Demiurge, of the physical world? How did he *come* or *begin* to create it, if he has been unmoved through all eternity?" We are told in Chapter XII that he took possession of *Matter*, which before the birth of heaven was moving chaotically, and which he reduced to the most excellent order. But the passage, if pressed, cannot be satisfactorily harmonized with the doctrine that order was brought into the Universe by God's willing to arouse and attract to himself the Cosmic *Soul* and *Intelligence*. Neoplatonism, because of its theory of emanation, could hold the Good to be at once the final and the efficient cause of all things.[5] Albinus, however, fails to produce coherence between the two aspects of the Supreme God. His crude and literal interpretation of Plato's cosmogonical account, as for example when he writes of God: ἐξ ἑκάστου τῶν στοιχείων

---

[1] See p. 99, n. 1, *supra*.   [2] *CC*. 7, 42.   [3] VI, vii, 36.
[4] For which see e.g. IV, viii, 1, VI, ix, 11. Cf. Dodds, *CQ*. XXII, 140–1 for the probable relation between the personal experience and the conception of the One. An assimilation to the Supreme God seems quite unthinkable to Albinus (*Did.* 81, 36).   [5] See Dodds, *Proclus* 213, 1.

ἐγέννησε (τὸν κόσμον), διανοηθείς...ἐκ γῆς αὐτὸν καὶ πυρὸς ἐποίησεν,[1] ill accords with the Aristotelean picture of God which has been given in Chapter x. Moreover, the relation of Matter to God is left in complete obscurity. It is not unfair to apply the celebrated question of Origen to the theology of the *Didaskalikos*: "What was God doing before he made the world?" Yet it would seem that Albinus himself was not aware of these difficulties and assumed that the two accounts of God are perfectly compatible.

Such confusion of thought is not uncommon in the Platonism of the first and second centuries and distinguishes it from the coherent system which is finally established in the third century by Plotinus. None of the cosmological subtleties which characterize Neoplatonism can be found in the *Didaskalikos*. Plotinus, as we have seen, in agreement with the second-century Neopythagorean Numenius but in opposition to Middle Platonism, subordinates the Demiurge of the *Timaeus* (identified with νοῦς or ἡ τοῦ ποιοῦντος φύσις of the *Philebus*)[2] to the Good of the *Republic*. Thus he finds himself unable to accept the account of the creation of the Universe by the Demiurge of the *Timaeus* in the purely literal sense which satisfied Albinus. The Intelligence-Demiurge is the product of the One and marks the first stage in the procession which has bare Matter as its last term. For Plotinus, therefore, the question of crucial importance is: How did the One give rise to the Many?[3] As soon as the Neoplatonist has established his laws which account for the existence of the Intelligible World, νοῦς the ἕν-πάντα, in distinction from the One, they may readily be applied to explain every subsequent degradation.

Accordingly, Plotinus concentrates his attention on the first stage rather than on those which come "later" in the process of pluraliza-tion. The First Good is absolute perfection (so Albinus calls his First God παντελής) and the potency of all things. Such a principle can neither grudge giving of its abundance, nor remain impotent.

[1] 67, 18 sqq.
[2] Bréhier, in his *Notice* to *Enn.* v, i, points out that the Demiurge is further identified with the One that Is of the *Parmenides*, the Good being equated with ὁ πάντων βασιλεύς of the *Second Epistle*, and with the One that is One of the *Parmenides*.
[3] v, i, 5. This is τὸ θρυλλούμενον καὶ παρὰ τοῖς πάλαι σοφοῖς.

134

It cannot stay self-contained but must overflow.[1] The process may be exemplified by the emanation of heat from fire, cold from snow, rays from the sun, a stream from its source, sap from the root, and so forth. These illustrations from the physical and biological spheres are not chosen by accident. Plotinus prefers as types ὅσα φύει ἄνευ προαιρέσεως, καὶ τὰ ἄψυχα δὲ μεταδιδόντα ἑαυτῶν καθ' ὅσον δύνανται,[2] for each stage of the process which he seeks to illustrate is reached, not by the exercise of will and reflection, but by a kind of natural necessity.[3] In this respect he differs from Albinus, who— as we have seen—regards creation as depending on God's will and as resulting from his reflection. Albinus, moreover, does not explain how the existence of his second principle, the Celestial Intelligence, is related to the perfection of the first, the transcendent God. The doctrine of Neoplatonism is that νοῦς is inferior to the One, as being its product, but as producing all other things is superior to them all: δεῖ δὴ καὶ τιμιώτατον εἶναι τὸ γεννῶν, τὸ δὲ γεννώμενον καὶ δεύτερον ἐκείνου τῶν ἄλλων ἄμεινον εἶναι.

Plotinus holds that, just as τὸ ἕν is bound by a natural necessity to produce νοῦς, so the latter in its turn is bound to produce the Soul of the Whole, whereby the triad of divine principles is completed.[4] Albinus, on the other hand, although regarding Intelligence as superior to Soul, nowhere expresses the view that Intelligence, whether cosmic or transcendent, gives rise to Soul by emanation.[5] Again, while it is true that he recognizes the existence of three principles,[4] he cannot bring them into a metaphysical system. He fails, because he attempts to combine an Aristotelean theology with a literal interpretation of the *Timaeus*. Plotinus succeeds in con-

---

[1] v, iv, 1 (*Tim.* 29 E).   [2] *Ibid.*

[3] Bréhier, *ad loc.*, well remarks of the life of the One above the level of consciousness, and the life below that level: "C'est cette vie inférieure qui, beaucoup plus que la conscience, nous donne le moyen de concevoir la vie supérieure." Inge[3], I, 144, holds that will is implied in the process.

[4] A triad of divine principles appears in Plut. *Gen. Socr.* 591 B. But, as Prof. Dodds points out (*Proclus* 207), Plotinus first made the triadic doctrine coherent (cf. also Whittaker, *Neopl.* 37).

[5] It may be noted that Plutarch writes: (ἡ ψυχὴ νοῦ μετασχοῦσα) οὐκ ἔργον ἐστὶ τοῦ θεοῦ μόνον, ἀλλὰ καὶ μέρος, οὐδ' ὑπ' αὐτοῦ, ἀλλὰ καὶ ἀπ' αὐτοῦ καὶ ἐξ αὐτοῦ γέγονεν (*Plat. Qu.* 1001 c–d). Here, as Zeller remarks, he is influenced by Stoicism.

structing a coherent system, because he subordinates Aristotle's νοῦς to his own characteristic Absolute, τὸ ἕν, while at the same time he treats the cosmogony of Plato as purely allegorical.

The point may be made clear by comparing the explanation which he offers of *Timaeus* 41 C–D with that which appears in *Didaskalikos* 71, 33 sqq. Albinus is content to say that God assigned the creation of ζῷα θνητά to οἱ ἔκγονοι αὐτοῦ θεοί. It need hardly be pointed out that the young gods of Plato are a somewhat strange progeny, if their parent really is an Aristotelean νοῦς ἀκίνητος. Albinus, moreover, does not raise the question of their relation to the Cosmic Soul and Intelligence, by whom the Ideas are received and imparted to Matter. Plotinus, on the other hand, refuses to take the Platonic text in the literal sense. The "gods" referred to must mean Soul.[1] This is a typical example of the Plotinian method of reading into Plato the doctrine of the Three Hypostases. Had Albinus been capable of constructing a coherent metaphysic, he would doubtless have abandoned the attempt to maintain, along with an Aristotelean theology, a strict adherence to the letter of the *Timaeus*.

But Plotinus does not treat everything in the *Timaeus* metaphorically. One of his favourite texts is: ψυχὴν (sc. θεός) διὰ παντός τε ἔτεινε καὶ ἔτι ἔξωθεν τὸ σῶμα αὐτῇ περιεκάλυψε ταύτῃ (34 B)—on which he bases his well-known paradox that, so far from the Soul being contained within the Body, the Body is in the Soul, as Soul is in Intelligence, which is in the One.[2] By this he means that the lower is at once dependent on the higher and immanent within it. Soul participates not in Body but in Intelligence, and is ubiquitous, being logically prior to the Sensible World over which it presides.[3] Thus Plotinus refuses to allow that the World of Life (ὁ τῆς ζωῆς κόσμος, i.e. Intelligence) and Soul, its emanation, can be extended: οὐκ ἐξετάθη. Accordingly he would have found fault with the expression used by Albinus with reference to the World Soul: ὅλῳ τῷ κόσμῳ αὐτὴν παρεκτεῖναι.[4]

[1] II, i, 5.
[2] V, v, 9. Cf. Dodds, *Proclus* 317. In *Herm.* VIII, 5, we read κόσμος ἐν τῷ θεῷ (and, in a similar way, St Paul writes: τὰ πάντα ἐν αὐτῷ, sc. the Logos-Son, συνέστηκεν).
[3] VI, iv, 1. Strictly this forms part of a disjunctive question. As the alternative is denied by Plotinus, this gives his own view.
[4] *Enn.* VI, iv, 13; *Did.* 70, 5.

His own conception of the relation between the Soul (whether that of the Universe or that of the individual) and the Body, is that Soul is all in all and all in every part: μεριστὴ μέν, ὅτι ἐν πᾶσι μέρεσι τοῦ ἐν ᾧ ἐστιν, ἀμέριστος δέ, ὅτι ὅλη ἐν πᾶσι καὶ ἐν ὁτῳοῦν αὐτοῦ ὅλη.[1] At what date in the history of post-Aristotelean philosophy this conception was first adopted is uncertain. According to Tertullian in the *De Anima*, Strato, Aenesidemus and Heraclitus "unitatem animae tuentur, quae in totum corpus diffusa et ubique ipsa, velut flatus in calamo per cavernas, ita per sensualia variis modis emicet, non tam concisa quam dispensata".[2] Diels has shown that Tertullian's source was the medical writer Soranus.[3] But Soranus can hardly have found any explicit recognition of this doctrine in the three philosophers mentioned. Whoever originated the view of soul-in-body as ὅλη ἐν ὅλῳ, it does not appear in the *Didaskalikos*, and, though outside orthodox Platonism Numenius and Clement adopt somewhat similar positions,[4] the principle does not become of fundamental importance in Platonism before the time of Plotinus.[5]

Iamblichus, in a fragment of which mention has already been made, professes to distinguish the ways in which Plotinus, Empedocles, Heraclitus, the Gnostics and Albinus explain the Soul's entry into Matter and its operating at a lower level than accords with its nature. We are told that Plotinus considers the cause to be Primal Otherness (ἡ πρώτη ἑτερότης), but that the reason given by Albinus is a completely mistaken judgment respecting freedom (ἡ τοῦ αὐτεξουσίου διημαρτημένη κρίσις). Iamblichus is not a very trustworthy authority for the views of earlier philosophers, and in this passage he appears to derive his information mainly from Plotinus (IV, viii, 5; V, i, 1). On what he bases his statement about Albinus is uncertain. His intended contrast is, in any case, without justification. For Plotinus not only brings Empedocles and Heraclitus into agreement with his own doctrine, but besides ἡ πρώτη ἑτερότης gives as reasons why souls have come to forget God their father τόλμα, βουληθῆναι ἑαυτῶν εἶναι, and τῷ αὐτεξουσίῳ ἡσθῆναι.[6]

---

[1] IV, ii, 1. [2] 15. [3] See *DDG.* 210.
[4] Stob. *Ecl. Ph.* I, 41, 32. For Clement cf. Witt, *CQ.* xxv, 200.
[5] Plotinus may have found his Platonic "text" in *Parm.* 131 B. Cf. Dodds, *Proclus* 251. [6] V, i, 1.

Clearly, therefore, even if Iamblichus be citing Albinus at first hand, the explanation offered by the latter is closely akin to that of Plotinus.

When we turn to the *Didaskalikos*, we find the statement made that human souls were "sent down" by God to their earthly habitation: κατέπεμψεν ἐπὶ γῆν τὰς τούτου τοῦ γένους ψυχὰς ὁ τῶν ὅλων δημιουργός.[1] Plato himself describes God as "sowing" the souls (ἔσπειρε, *Timaeus* 42 D). It is, therefore, not impossible that Plotinus echoes Albinus or some other Middle Platonist when, after mentioning ἡ εἰς γένεσιν σπορά, he continues: ὅταν δὲ ταῦτα (sc. τὰ χείρω) πάσχειν καὶ ποιεῖν ᾗ ἀναγκαῖον ἀϊδίῳ φύσεως νόμῳ, τὸ δὲ συμβαῖνον εἰς ἄλλου του χρείαν τῇ προόδῳ[2] ἀπαντᾷ καταβαῖνον ἀπὸ τοῦ ὑπὲρ αὐτό, θεὸν εἴ τις λέγοι καταπέμψαι, οὐκ ἂν ἀσύμφωνος οὔτε τῇ ἀληθείᾳ οὔτε ἑαυτῷ ἂν εἴη.[3]

Plotinus, by treating the sowing of souls mythically, finds that the *Timaeus* and the *Phaedo* are not irreconcilable. Their descent may be said to be due to the necessity of a natural law, and yet they break away from the soul of the whole of their own accord:[4] ἔχει τὸ ἑκούσιον ἡ ἀνάγκη.[5] In the *Didaskalikos* such a reconciliation is not attempted. On the one hand, in Chapter XVI the account which appears in the *Timaeus* is accepted as literally true. The stars are the chariots (ὀχήματα) on which God causes human souls to embark, before sending them down to earth. There he reveals to all of them beforehand the laws of Destiny, and thus is not responsible for the evil which they subsequently do. The end of earthly toil is the soul's return to its appropriate star. It must first, however, rid itself of those θνητὰ πάθη which fasten upon it (τὰ προσφύντα) from the body, a view with which Plotinus is familiar.[6] On the other hand, in Chapter XXIII Albinus takes the view that discarnate human souls possess the same faculties as the souls of the gods: τὸ κριτικόν (γνωστικόν), τὸ ὁρμητικόν (παραστατικόν),

---

[1] 72, 4. Cf. what Celsus holds to be the Christian view: (ὁ θεός) πνεῦμα ἴδιον ἐμβαλὼν εἰς σῶμα ἡμῖν ὅμοιον δεῦρο κατέπεμψεν.

[2] Bréhier prefers προσόδῳ.   [3] IV, viii, 5.

[4] Origen recognized sin as falling away from unity with God: ὁ γὰρ εἷς, ὅτε ἁμαρτάνει πολλοστός ἐστιν, ἀποσχιζόμενος ἀπὸ θεοῦ καὶ μεριζόμενος, καὶ τῆς ἑνότητος ἐκπίπτων (*In Oseam*, 3, 439).

[5] IV, viii, 5.   [6] IV, vii, 19.

τὸ οἰκειωτικόν. Hence, while they remain in that state, they may be assumed to enjoy all the privileges of gods, and their incarnation is the result of self-will. Furthermore, after they have been embodied, they retain their original faculties, τὸ κριτικόν remaining unaltered, but τὸ ὁρμητικόν and τὸ οἰκειωτικόν being transformed into τὸ ἐπιθυμητικόν and τὸ θυμοειδές. Since, then, incarnation does not occasion the birth of anything which was not already present in the discarnate soul, reascent to the divine realm must involve the improvement of the two irrational faculties themselves, rather than the loss of an accretion.[1] In Chapter XVI Albinus considers that the descent of the soul into the body is due to the operation of the law established by the Supreme God. In Chapter XXIII, however, he regards the soul as descending voluntarily—the doctrine which is ascribed to him by Iamblichus.

That the souls of the brute creation are mortal is regarded by Albinus as probably the correct view.[2] But he does not explain how it is to be brought into accord with the doctrine of metensomatosis which he treats as genuinely Platonic, and it is hard to see[3] how a human soul which has once descended into the body of an animal can escape the mortal doom which is experienced by all irrational souls, and (according to Chapters XVI and XXIII) by the irrational parts of the human soul as well.

If we compare Albinus and Plotinus in their psychology, we observe that though even the latter is sometimes in danger of destroying the soul's unity, yet he does not take so crude a view of its connexion with the body as we meet in the *Didaskalikos*, and that he makes better use of the World Soul of the *Timaeus*. Albinus is unaware of the Plotinian principle that neither a part of soul nor its totality is in the body as in a place.[4] Thus he is content to follow the letter of the *Timaeus* in *Didaskalikos* XXIII: θεοὶ δύο αὐτῇ (sc.

[1] Bréhier, on Plotinus IV, viii, 5, points out that Albinus's view in this passage is similar to that which appears in *Enn.* VI, vii.

[2] Speusippus and Xenocrates are said by Olympiodorus to have held irrational souls to be immortal. Perhaps they regarded this as necessarily entailed by the doctrine of metensomatosis. Galen, in his *History of Philosophy*, took the view that the souls of brutes are rational in a special way: νοοῦσι μέν, οὐ δύνανται δὲ φράζειν ἃ νοοῦσι (*DDG.* 645, 11).

[3] The writer of the critical marginalia in Cod. Vind. 314 calls attention to the difficulty. [4] IV, iii, 20.

139

ψυχῇ) προσέθεσαν μέρη θνητά...καὶ αὐτοῖς δὲ τοῖς θνητοῖς αὐτῆς μέρεσιν οἴκησιν ἄλλην ἄλλῳ ἀπένειμαν.[1] The head he regards as the seat of τὸ ἡγεμονικόν.

Plotinus, although he agrees with Albinus in recognizing the brain as the centre of the nervous system, denies that the rational part of the soul is in the head locally. Interpreting the Platonic text (*Timaeus* 69 E sqq.) used by Albinus, he declares that the rational part was assigned this position by "the Ancients" (ἐτέθη τοῖς παλαιοῖς...ἐπὶ τῆς κεφαλῆς) because it is the source from which the faculties which reside in the brain (perception, imagination, and appetition) derive benefit: ἐκεῖ οὖν τὸ λογιζόμενον οὐχ ὡς ἐν τόπῳ, ἀλλ' ὅτι τὸ ἐκεῖ ἀπολαύει αὐτοῦ. The rest of the passage he interprets similarly. The vegetative or nutritive soul (φυτικόν, αὐξητικόν, θρεπτικόν) which actually pervades the whole body affords nourishment to it through the blood. The blood flows in the veins. The veins begin from the liver.[2] The liver, therefore, was made the seat of τὸ ἐπιθυμητικόν. For τὸ ἐπιθυμητικόν is simply an aspect of the vegetative soul.[3] Again, if Plato locates θυμός in the heart, the meaning is that the heart is the fountain of purified blood, which is a fitting instrument for spirited emotion.[4] To suppose, however, that the soul resides there, is a mistake: οὐ γὰρ τὴν ψυχὴν ἐνταῦθα, ἀλλὰ τὴν τοῦ αἵματος τοῦ τοιοῦδε ἐνταῦθα λεγέσθω εἶναι.[5]

Albinus attributes the mortality of the irrational soul to the circumstance that it is created, not like the rational by God the Father, but by the subordinate gods begotten by him. Plotinus, treating these gods symbolically, maintains that all particular souls, whether rational or irrational, whether incarnate or discarnate, are alike present in the Soul of the Whole, and are therefore incapable of being destroyed. In one of his earliest Essays, replying to the possible objection which may be brought against the Platonic doctrine of immortality, that the human soul being of composite nature will at death be subject to dissolution, he affirms that, though that

[1] 76, 9. 15.
[2] IV, iii, 23. Plato himself expressly makes the *heart* the ἀρχὴ τῶν φλεβῶν (*Tim.* 71 A). Cf. *Did.* 74, 18–19.
[3] IV, iii, 23 E.   [4] IV, iv, 28 E.
[5] Cf. *DDG.* 393, 10; Dodds, *Proclus* 306; Scott, *Hermet.* II, 59.

inferior nature which attaches itself at birth to rational souls will be lost by the latter when they quit the body undefiled, yet it will not be lost in the sense of being destroyed. For it is an emanation from the Soul of the Whole, and nothing real can ever perish: ἀφειμένον δὲ τὸ χεῖρον οὐδὲ αὐτὸ ἀπολεῖσθαι, ἕως ἂν ᾖ ὅθεν ἔχει τὴν ἀρχήν. οὐδὲν γὰρ ἐκ τοῦ ὄντος ἀπολεῖται.[1] In another passage Plotinus considers the problem of ψυχὴ ἐν φυτῷ.[2] The root of a tree may be severed or burnt. But there is no destruction of soul. The soul which belonged there still exists in the Soul of the Whole, which, like the Intelligence containing it, is "nowhere and everywhere". In such passages as these Plotinus without much doubt intends to refute those Platonists who, like Albinus and Atticus, relying on *Timaeus* 69 c claimed that the irrational soul must perish.

The purpose of the foregoing inquiry has been to make clear the position occupied by Albinus in the Platonism of the first three centuries after Christ. The transitional character of the philosophy of the *Didaskalikos* has been brought out by comparing it in a number of aspects with the system of Plotinus. It has been shown to be a typical product of eclectic Middle Platonism. Accordingly, we have no reason to regard the views which it contains as simply Albinus's idiosyncrasies. Critics who find fault with Albinus for adding to the doctrines of the Old Academy elements derived from other quarters and for failing to grasp clearly the individuality of the Platonic system,[3] themselves fail to perceive that such criticism really misses the mark. Whatever the Albinus of the *Didaskalikos* may be, he is certainly no innovator. The doctrines which he sets forth are the accepted doctrines of his School.

Nor are those historians of philosophy justified who severely blame the School as a whole on the ground of its failure to keep Plato from contamination and to establish a coherent system.[4] It is true, of course, that in the first two centuries of the Christian Era Platonism, although the prevailing influence, produced no great original thinkers. Yet such men as Plutarch, Albinus and Maximus,

---

[1] IV, vii, 19. Plutarch, in the Myth of *De Fac. Orb.* (Posidonian, according to Reinhardt), speaks of souls being left on the moon, which absorbs them in time. ἀφεθεῖσαι γὰρ ὑπὸ τοῦ νοῦ καὶ πρὸς οὐδὲν ἔτι χρώμεναι τοῖς πάθεσι ἀπομαραίνονται (945 A).   [2] V, ii, 2.
[3] Zeller-Nestle, III, a, 845. Cf. Prantl.   [4] Cf. *UPG.* 528.

because they created no new system, ought not therefore to be regarded as of little historical importance. It is indisputable that Plotinus, as Wilamowitz-Moellendorff observes, is the greatest of all.the Platonists, precisely because he erects on a Platonic foundation a metaphysic of his own.[1] Nevertheless, after making due allowance for philosophical genius, we may still doubt whether Plotinus could have built his edifice, had there been no constructive efforts made during the two preceding centuries.[2] Of the theology of Albinus it has been said: "In his attempt to connect divergent views he foreshadows Plotinus: his complete failure to make anything coherent of them is one measure of Plotinus's greatness."[3] To these incoherences attention has already been drawn. In certain other departments, however, the Middle Platonist's eclectic attempts are more successful, and then he suffers less when compared with his Neoplatonic successor.

Nevertheless, it must be admitted that in general Albinus does not show the same capacity as Plotinus for resolving difficulties. Indeed, he proceeds with his account as though difficulties were almost non-existent. Moreover, although he manifests a certain independence when in the *Prologos* he rejects as useless for his particular purpose the tetralogical classification of the Platonic dialogues which had been made by the Platonists Dercyllides and Thrasyllus,[4] or when in the *Didaskalikos* he transposes the first and second figures of hypothetical syllogism, yet it is evident that in the main he follows tradition without question. Plotinus, on the other hand, is well aware of the difficulties involved in the attempt to extract a coherent system from the Platonic writings and of the existence of particular texts which may be brought forward against certain of his own doctrines. He confesses, for example, that Plato may appear "not always to say the same thing",[5] and recognizes

[1] *Platon*, I, 728. Cf. Dodds, *CQ*. XXII, 140. Whittaker, *Neoplat*. 33, describes him as the greatest thinker between Aristotle and Descartes.

[2] Cf. Geffcken, *Gött. Gel. Anz*. 1932, 244. Ammonius Saccas (who in turn must have experienced the influence of earlier Platonists) first revealed the way for which Plotinus had long been vainly seeking (*Vit*. 3).

[3] Dodds, *loc. cit*. 139.

[4] δοκοῦσι δέ μοι προσώποις καὶ βίων περιστάσεσιν ἠθεληκέναι τάξιν ἐπιθεῖναι· ὅ ἐστι μὲν ἴσως χρήσιμον πρὸς ἄλλο τι, οὐ μὴν πρὸς ὃ ἡμεῖς νῦν βουλόμεθα κτα., 49, 13.　　　　　[5] IV, viii, I.

that stoicizing Platonists may find support for the view that particular souls are parts (ὁμοειδῆ μέρη) of the Soul of the Whole in such passages as *Philebus* 30 A and *Phaedrus* 246–8,[1] and that others again may deny that Plato believed in the earth's divinity, which because of his literal interpretation of *Timaeus* 40 C Plotinus himself defends.[2]

To suggest, therefore, that Plotinus regards Plato as a prophet of the Truth and handles him as Christians handle the Bible,[3] is somewhat misleading. If by this is meant fidelity to the letter of Plato, then such a statement is better made of Albinus than of Plotinus. There can be no doubt that for the writer of the *Didaskalikos* the *Timaeus* has all the importance of a gospel, whereas Plotinus treats the dialogue mainly as a myth. Again, Albinus recommends the reader who would discover Plato's meaning to read him "carefully", but does not go as far on the path of exegetical originality as Plotinus,[4] and though he certainly attributes to Plato views which are typical of Aristotle and Stoicism, yet he does not anticipate Plotinus in first formulating a system of his own and then eliciting the same doctrines from Plato. The *Didaskalikos* is largely a repetition without evaluation of Platonic passages, which Neoplatonism either refuses to take literally or entirely neglects.

Before we conclude this examination of Albinus as a Middle Platonist, some reference may be made to the account of "Alcinous the Platonic philosopher" which is given in the *Encyclopaedia Britannica* and in which this statement appears: "He produced latterly a synthesis of Plato and Aristotle with an admixture of Pythagorean or Oriental mysticism, and is closely allied to the Alexandrian school of thought." This attempt to characterize the philosophy of the *Didaskalikos* is not very successful. We have seen that no trace of personal mysticism is shown by Albinus, despite his acceptance of the Platonic doctrine of being made like God.[5]

---

[1] IV, iii, I. Cf. the ἀπόσπασμα-theory of Stoicism.

[2] IV, iv, 22 (cf. *Did.* 71, 26). Plotinus is not afraid to say: συμβαίνει καὶ τὸ πρᾶγμα ὅπως ἔχει ἐξευρεῖν δύσκολον καὶ μείζω ἀπορίαν ἢ οὐκ ἐλάττω ἐξ ὧν εἴρηκεν ὁ Πλάτων γίνεσθαι.

[3] Wilamowitz, *Platon*, I, 728.

[4] Cf. e.g. V, i, 8. A similar attitude is evinced in III, v *passim*; VI, ii, 1, VI, iv, 16.   [5] *Did.* 81, 16; 82, 23.

So too, when in the *Prologos* he writes that through reading the *Timaeus* we shall behold τὰ θεῖα ἐναργῶς,[1] and that we ought to become spectators (θεαταί) both of our own souls and of those of divine beings and of gods,[2] these words betray no religious emotion.[3] The absence of Pythagorean or Oriental mysticism is easily observed when he is compared with Numenius.[4] Moreover, it is somewhat misleading to say that the author of the *Didaskalikos* is closely connected with the Alexandrian school of thought. That he is in great part dependent for his account of Plato on the Alexandrian Arius Didymus is beyond doubt. But we have still to reckon with Gaius. It is at least possible that Pergamum was an important centre of Platonic study in the second century. Bréhier, discussing the systematization of the Platonic philosophy, is prepared to say that "l'exposé de l'ensemble de Gaius de Pergame, dont nous retrouvons bien des fragments chez Albinus et chez Apulée, a créé le platonisme, en se désintéressant de Platon lui-même".[5] However this may be, it is a mistake to imagine that the writer of the *Didaskalikos* is closely connected with Ammonius Saccas and Plotinus, the best representatives of what is called "the Alexandrian school of thought".[6] The various points of difference between Albinus and Plotinus have already been indicated, and the question of influence of the one on the other hardly arises.[7] More likely is a connexion between Albinus and patristic writers.[8] Thus Tertullian makes explicit reference to him, and probably Geffcken is justified in declaring that the pale Platonism of the Christian apologists "gehört in vielen Fällen unmittelbar an die Seite eines Albinus, Maximus, u. a."[9] Albinus, as we have seen, was known to the later Neoplatonists Iamblichus, Proclus and Priscian, and may have been used by Sallustius and Chalcidius, both of whom were influenced by Middle Platonism.[10] But that he had much importance for Plotinus is unlikely.

[1] 50, 10.   [2] 50, 15. Cf. *Alcib.* I, 133 B.
[3] Cf. Epictetus.   [4] Despite E. Peterson in *Philol.* 1933.
[5] *Rev. Mét. Mor.* 1923, 563.   [6] Cf. Dodds, *CQ.* 1928, 128.
[7] Gaius himself was read in the Plotinian School.
[8] *UPG.* 556.   [9] *GGA.* 1932, 248.
[10] Cf. Sallustius, Nock, xxxix. *UPG.* 649, 2.

LOCI PLATONICI

[References following a colon are, in each case, to the *Didaskalikos*]

Ph. 67 B: 52, 2. 71 C: 77, 30. 72 E: 78, 1. 74 D (*Men.* 81 D): 59, 17; 78, 9.
79 D: 77, 24; 53, 6. 80 B: 77, 21. 81 A: 80, 15. 82 A: 81, 25. 89 E: 83, 29.
101: 57, 34. 105 A: 77, 16–17. 109 A: 71, 28.

Crat. 387 B: 60, 14. 387 C: 60, 16. 387 D: 60, 18. 388 A: 60, 21. 388 B: 60, 23.
388–390: 60, 25–30. 395 D–E and 435 D: 60, 6.

Tht. 176 B: 53, 6–7; 81, 19. 191 C: 55, 11.

Soph. 227 A: 58, 1. 231 D: 89, 10. 253 E–254 A: 89, 14. 254 E: 69, 23. 258 E:
89, 20.

Par. (130 B–C: 63, 10.) 132 D: 63, 12. 134 B: 80, 15. 137 D: 58, 37; 59, 7.
139 B: 65, 12. 145 A: 59, 20.

Phil. 30 C: 70, 2. 35: 85, 34. 40 A: 85, 35. 46 C: 87, 5. 53 C: 87, 4. 64 E: 64,
30 (84, 13). 66 C: 86, 37.

Symp. 186 B: 52, 5. 202 E: 87, 29–32. 210 D, 211 E: 57, 15; 65, 27.

Phdr. 245 C: 57, 25; 78, 17. 246 B–248 B: 80, 18; 81, 33. 246 C: 87, 30.
246 E: 55, 29. 247 A: 61, 5. 247 C: 65, 4–5; 64, 14; 68, 8. 247 D: 53, 5.
249 D: 82, 5–6. 252 E sqq.: 87, 36 sqq. 265 E: 56, 29–30.

Alcib. I, 115 A sqq.: 58, 35.

Alcib. II, 147 A: 81, 13.

Euthyd. 281 D: 81, 4.

Men. 99 E: 84, 33 (cf. *Prot.* 319 B).

Rep. 369 B sqq.: 88, 8. 372 E: *ibid.* 380 D sqq.: 65, 34. 429 B: 89, 14. 429 C:
82, 30. 435: 76, 30; 88, 11. 473 C: 88, 20. 486 A: 52, 16; 88, 17. 493 A:
89, 10. 500 C: 53, 13. 508: 64, 32; 65, 18. 510 B: 57, 13. 514 sqq.: 80,
15 sqq. 515: 80, 34. 521 C: 52, 3. 525 B–C: 61, 16, 18. 527 B: 61, 20.
527 D: 80, 21. 528 E: 61, 23. 532 B: 52, 2. 533 C: 62, 3. 534 E: 62, 19.
540 B: 52, 28. 583 C: 86, 29. (592: 88, 7.) 610 A: 78, 10. 613 A: 81, 29.
617 E: 84, 31 (cf. 72, 8).

Tim. 27 A: 62, 24. 28 A: 56, 5; 63, 15. 28 B: 69, 27; 68, 7; 56, 9. 28 C: 79, 32.
29 A: 67, 6. 29 B: 54, 25. 29 E: 67, 11. 30 A: 67, 13. 30 B: 70, 2. 31 B:
67, 22. 31 C: 67, 26. 32 B: 68, 7. 32 C: 67, 19. 33 A–B: 67, 33 sqq. 33 C:
68, 1 sqq. 34 A: 68, 4. 34 B: 70, 4. 35 A: 69, 20. 36 C–D: 70, 6. 37 A:
69, 20. 37 D: 70, 21. 38 C: 70, 17 sqq. 38 D: 71, 3. 39 B: 70, 20. 40 A:
71, 24. 40 B–C: 71, 25. 40 D: 71, 13. 41 A–B: 71, 19 sqq. 41 C: 71,
36 sqq. 41 D: 72, 6. 41 E: 55, 20; 72, 6. 42 A–C: 72, 9 sqq. 42 B: 72, 7.
42 D: 72, 8. 42 E: 71, 37 sqq. 43 A: 72, 19. 44 B–C: 52, 20 sqq. 44 D:

76, 13. 45 B–46 C: 73, 14–36. 46 D: 66, 29. 47 C: 70, 12. 49 A: 62, 28.
50 C: 62, 32; 66, 4. 50 D sqq.: 62, 34. 51 A: 62, 26. 52 A: 62, 7–8.
52 B: 62, 27. 52 E: 69, 11. 53 A–B: 67, 12–15. 53 C–D: 68, 9. 54 A–B:
68, 22. 54 C: 68, 25. 54 D–E: 68, 27. 55 A–B: 68, 29. 55 B–C: 68, 30.
55 C: 68, 35. 55 E–56 C: 68, 13–19. 56 C: 69, 5. 57 B–C: 69, 6. 58 A: 69,
10. 62 A: 75, 4 sqq. 62 B: 74, 35 sqq. 62 C: 75, 12. 63 E: 75, 3. 64 E:
86, 26. 65 C: 74, 17. 65 D–66 C: 74, 19–32. 66 D–67 A: 74, 6–17. 67 A–C:
73, 37–74, 5. 69 B: 67, 12. 69 C: 76, 7 sqq. 70 A sqq.: 76, 16 sqq. 70 D:
76, 22. 71: 76, 22 sqq. 72 C: 76, 26. 73 B: 72, 23. 73 C: 72, 21. 73 E:
72, 26. 74 A: 72, 30. 74 C: 72, 28. 74 E: 72, 32. 75 C: 73, 7. 77 D: 73, 1.
78 C and 80 D: 72, 35. 79 A sqq.: 75, 20 sqq. 82 A sqq.: 75, 25. 83 C–E:
75, 32. 85 A: 75, 34. 86 A: 76, 2. 89 E: 76, 30.

Crit. 110 D: 88, 32. 111 B: 89, 1. 113 C: 88, 35. 119 A–B: *ibid.*

Laws. 625 D: 88, 37. 631 B: 80, 37. 631 C: 79, 37. 661 A: 80, 8. 704 B:
88, 35. 715 E: 81, 31. 837 (and *Lysis* 214 A): 88, 11 sqq.

(*Epin.* 987 B: 71, 10.)

Epp. 335 A: 85, 15. 341 C: 64, 7.

Did.	Apul. Thom.	Did.	Apul. Thom.	Did.	Apul. Thom.
52, 5	100, 1	70, 33	94, 6	82, 18 sqq.	107–109
52, 9	88, 1	71, 11	94, 20	83, 1	108, 4
52, 14	122, 12	71, 12 sqq.	95, 2 sqq.	83, 11	107, 9
52, 20	122, 10	71, 16	95, 14	83, 14	108, 21
52, 21	122, 17	71, 18	9, 10	83, 16	108, 16
52, 26	126, 16	71, 28	94, 18	83, 18	109, 5
53, 21	6, 1; 85, 1	72, 20	97, 12	83, 19	II, xix
	176, 1	73, 5 sqq.	97	83, 22	108, 20
53, 23	86, 3	73, 37	98, 2	83, 24	107, 16
54, 2	94, 3	74, 7	98, 8	„	108, 14
54, 25, 27	88, 15, 18	75, 28	102, 2	83, 29	105, 12
	92, 20	76, 7 sqq.	97	„	121, 18
55, 31	92, 10	76, 19	99, 20	83, 36	108, 17
56, 37	106, 2	76, 30	102, 4	84, 1	112, 18
58, 4	177, 3	79, 1	96, 15	84, 2	112, 2
58, 9	181, 16	79, 2	95, 17	84, 12	106, 5
58, 12	177, 4	79, 31	86, 17	„	108, 11
58, 17	184, 13–15	79, 37	104, 3	84, 31	113, 25
58, 32	179, 2	80, 4	104, 2	„	119, 20
58, 35	183, 28	80, 10	104, 15	85, 3	114, 6
62, 21 sqq.	86, 8	„	123, 18	85, 15	120, 4
	87, 19	„	127, 3	85, 18	120, 15
63, 7	87, 10, 14	80, 34	116, 1	86, 22	119, 5
63, 11, 32	87, 20, 9	81, 1	104, 11	86, 29 sqq.	115
64, 15	9, 1 sqq.	81, 4	114, 23	87, 2	113, 16
64, 27 sqq.		81, 6	116, 2	„	114, 21
	86, 12 sqq.; 9, 16	81, 14	104, 22	87, 7 sqq.	116
65, 3–4	165, 16	„	113, 19	87, 29	96, 13
65, 28	10, 1	81, 16	126, 4	87, 30	117, 18
66, 35	88, 19	81, 30	127, 8	87, 37	124, 24
67, 12	89, 2	81, 31	126, 12	88, 7	131, 3
67, 19	90, 8	„	175, 2	88, 9	128, 19
67, 27	89, 4	81, 36	96, 3	88, 19	128, 20
67, 35	90, 18	„	95, 8	88, 25	133, 7
68, 3	91, 7	81, 37	126, 20	88, 29	132, 12
68, 7	92, 12	82, 2	23, 10	88, 32	131
68, 12	89, 9	82, 3	108, 24	89, 2	131, 11
69, 27	91, 12	82, 14	107, 19	(89, 11	112, 4)
70, 20	92, 23				

Printed in the United States
By Bookmasters